The Dictionary of
Real Estate Appraisal

The
Dictionary
of
Real Estate
Appraisal

American Institute of Real Estate Appraisers
430 North Michigan Avenue • Chicago, Illinois

Acknowledgments

Director of Publications: Karla L. Heuer
Development Writer: Shiela F. Crowell

Because all copyright acknowledgments cannot be accommodated on this page, they are listed on pages 333–334.

For Educational Purposes Only

The opinions and statements set forth herein do not necessarily reflect the viewpoint of the American Institute of Real Estate Appraisers or its individual members, and neither the Institute nor its editors and staff assume responsibility for such expressions of opinion or statements.

Library of Congress Cataloging in Publication Data

The Dictionary of real estate appraisal.
  Bibliography: p.
  1. Real property—Valuation—Dictionaries.
2. Real estate business—Dictionaries. 3. Real property—Dictionaries. I. American Institute of Real Estate Appraisers.
HD1387.D435 1984   333.33′2′0321   84-16834
ISBN 0-911780-74-2

Contents

Foreword

Since its beginnings in 1932, the Appraisal Institute has devoted itself to being at the forefront of the appraisal profession as it strives to meet the needs of the public it serves. Through constant expansion and refinement of its publications and courses, the Institute has immeasurably aided practitioners, students, and related professionals in the ongoing challenge of keeping abreast of the latest developments in theory and practice.

These continuing efforts have led to the realization that there is a pressing need to recognize and assimilate changes in the vocablulary of the real estate appraisal profession. *The Dictionary of Real Estate Appraisal* has been created in response to the vast array of changes and the expansion of appraisal terminology. A primary objective of those who worked on this greatly needed reference guide was to present concise, clear, and timely definitions of terms that are significant in real estate appraising.

A second major objective was to create a terminology book that reflects the interdependence of appraising and other major professions. Interpretation of the complex modern marketplace can be greatly aided by an appreciation and understanding of tools used by other professionals in their attempts to interpret the same marketplace. In recognition of this reality, it was decided that this reference work should contain terms from the lexicons of such fields as accounting, agriculture, arbitration, architecture, banking, construction, finance, insurance, law, and urban planning. A further addition is the inclusion of pertinent basic terminology from the computer field—an area of expertise that is each day becoming more important in the processing of appraisal data.

Diligent pursuit of these two objectives has resulted in a broad-based work that will be useful to appraisers, students of appraising, and all those who need a complete reference to terms used in analyzing and interpreting market forces that affect the value of real property.

For defining these objectives and carrying them to fruition, the Appraisal Institute recognizes and applauds the long and devoted work of Peter F. Korpacz, MAI, Chairman, Publications Committee, and Richard

Marchitelli, MAI, Chairman, Terminology Subcommittee. The Institute also gratefully acknowledges the contributions of Anthony Reynolds, MAI, and the members of the Terminology Subcommittee: James H. Bulthuis, MAI; David J. Lau, MAI; Thomas M. Rule, MAI; D. Richard Wincott, MAI; Harold Warsawer, MAI. Without their initial work in perceiving and defining the needs to be met and without their dedication to the monumental task they set, *The Dictionary of Real Estate Appraisal* could not have been created.

Finally, on behalf of the Appraisal Institute and the appraisal profession, we gratefully acknowledge the partial funding provided by the Dave Montonna Fund of the Research and Educational Trust Fund of the Appraisal Institute for development and production of this book. The contribution of the Trust has helped the Appraisal Institute to continue to fulfill its founding objective of publishing works that are vital for the real estate appraisal profession and for practicing real estate appraisers everywhere.

Reaves C. Lukens, Jr., MAI
1984 President
American Institute of Real Estate Appraisers

Explanatory Notes

Cross-references

Cross-references in this work are of two types: *See* and *See also* references.

A *See* reference following a word entry indicates that the term is not in current usage. The reader should go to the indicated term for the definition. *See* references are also used after standard abbreviations; the definition is given after the full term.

A *See also* reference following a definition refers the reader to a related term or terms that may provide additional information. *See also* references do *not* indicate synonyms.

Synonyms

An *Also called* reference indicates currently acceptable synonyms for a term. These common synonyms are not entries in the text.

Sources

When a definition is quoted from another copyrighted source, a number indicating that source appears in brackets at the end of the definition. Full copyright information is provided on pages 333–334.

A

AAA tenant. A tenant who has an AAA credit rating according to a recognized rating bureau. *Also called* prime tenant.

abandonment. The relinquishing of all interests in real property and any fixtures thereon with no intention to reclaim or reuse.

abatement
1. An official reduction or invalidation of an assessed valuation after the initial assessment for ad valorem taxation has been completed.
2. The termination of a nuisance.
3. The correction of an unlawful building condition.

ABC roads. A collective term for federally aided primary and secondary roads and urban extensions of federal aid systems.

ABC soil. A soil with a complete soil profile, i.e., well-developed A, B, and C horizons.

abscissa. In the rectangular coordinate system, the horizontal distance from a point to the vertical axis (sometimes called the y-axis); expressed as the first number in an ordered pair, e.g., in (3, 7), the abscissa is 3.

absentee landlord. An owner, lessor, or sublessor of income-producing, rental real estate who does not reside in the area where the real estate is located.

absolute assignment. An outright transfer of title, as opposed to a transfer by way of security. [7]

absolute conveyance. An unqualified, unrestricted, unlimited, or unconditional transfer of property. [7]

absolute owner. One who holds all the real property interests in a parcel of real estate. [7]

absorption rate. The rate at which properties for sale or lease can be successfully marketed in a given area; usually used in forecasting sales or leasing activity. [3]

abstraction. *See* extraction method.

abstract of title. A summary of conveyances, transfers, and any other facts used as evidence of title, together with any other public documents that may impair title. [5]

abut. To touch or border; to share a common boundary with another property.

abutment. The part of a structure that an object borders on or presses; the structural member that receives the pressure of an arch or strut; e.g., the supports at either end of a bridge.

abutter's rights. The right of visibility, i.e., the right to see and be seen from the street and to enjoy the flow of light and air from the street to the property.

accelerated cost recovery system (ACRS). A set of income tax rules established under the Economic Tax Recovery Act of 1981, which covers depreciation deductions and the computation of the tax basis for depreciable property.

accelerated depreciation. In tax accounting, a method of cost write-off in which allowances for depreciation of a wasting asset are greater in early years and decline according to a formula. Technically, the depreciation decelerates over time, but the term *accelerated depreciation*, which has gained acceptance through popular usage, refers to accelerated, or faster, recovery of capital during the early years of an investment. *See also* straight-line recapture.

acceleration clause. A condition in a loan contract or mortgage note that permits the lender to demand immediate repayment of the entire balance if the contract is breached or other conditions for repayment occur, e.g., sale or demolition of the property.

acceleration lane. An additional traffic lane that permits entering traffic to merge with through traffic quickly and safely.

access The path by which a property is approached through a neighborhood; the means of physical entrance into or upon a property.

access connection. *See* acceleration lane.

accessibility. The relative degree of effort, i.e., time and cost, required to reach a site; indicates ease of entrance into or upon a property.

accession. Additional property rights that accrue to an owner when additions or improvements are attached to the property either naturally or by the labor or materials of another. *See also* accretion.

accessory building. A building on the same property as a main building; any outbuilding used in connection with the main building; e.g., garage, pump house, well house.

access rights
1. The right of ingress to and egress from a property that abuts an existing street or highway; an easement in the street that adjoins abutting property; a private right, as distinguished from public rights. *See also* landlocked parcel.
2. The right of a riparian owner to pass to and from the waters on which the premises border.

accommodated room night demand. The number of hotel and motel rooms within a market area that are actually occupied during a 12-month period; calculated by multiplying each competitive property's room count by its annual occupancy and then by 365.

accommodation. An obligation assumed without consideration. [1]

accretion. An increase of dry land created by the gradual accumulation of waterborne solid material over formerly riparian land, i.e., accretion by alluvion. *See also* accession; alluvion.

accrual basis. A method of accounting in which income and expenses are recorded on the books in the fiscal period when they are earned or incurred regardless of when they are actually received or paid. *See also* cash basis. [3]

accruals for depreciation. On accounting statements, the provisions made for anticipated depreciation; usually credits to reserves.

accrued depreciation. The difference between an improvement's reproduction or replacement cost and its market value as of the date of the appraisal.

acknowledgment. A declaration usually made before an official, e.g., a notary public, who attests to the validity of the declarer's signature. [15]

acoustical material. A substance with sound-absorbing qualities that can be applied to walls and ceilings; usually made of mineral fiber or insulated metal materials; e.g., tile, fiber or mineral board, cork, special plaster.

acoustical tile. *See* acoustical material.

acoustic coupler. In computer usage, a telecommunications device that transmits data over telephone lines. The coupler sends and receives information through a standard telephone handset. [16]

acquisition fee. Money paid for arranging for the acquisition of a property, e.g., for a property being syndicated. [1]

acre. A land measure equal to 43,560 square feet.

acreage. Acres collectively; e.g., farm acreage, industrial acreage, residential acreage.

acreage controls. Limits set by the federal government on the number of acres that can be planted with price-supported crops.

acre-foot
1. A volume of water equal to the amount required to cover one acre of land to a depth of one foot; equal to 27,154 gallons or 43,560 cubic feet of water.
2. A measurement of coal in place; equal to a one-acre horizontal bed of coal that is one foot thick.

acre-inch. A volume of water equal to the amount required to cover one acre of land to a depth of one inch.

across the fence method. A means of estimating the price or value of land adjacent to or "across the fence" from a railroad, pipeline, highway, or other corridor real estate; as distinguished from valuing the right-of-way as a separate entity. *See also* value for other use.

ACRS. *See* accelerated cost recovery system.

action in rem. A legal action taken to effect a legal judgment against property to determine its status; e.g., an action to foreclose a mortgage. [1]

actual age. The number of years that have elapsed since construction was completed. *Also called* chronological age.

addition. Part of a building that has been added to the original structure.

additional commitment. The amount, if any, that each investor in a real estate syndication must pay in addition to the initial subscription. [1]

adjacent. Usually used to designate property that is in the neighborhood of another property but does not actually touch it. [2]

adjoining. Touching or contiguous, as distinguished from lying near or adjacent. *See also* abut.

adjustable rate mortgage (ARM). A mortgage loan in which the interest rate is adjusted periodically based on a specified index or formula.

adjusted basis. In accounting, the original cost of a property plus allowable additions, e.g., capital improvements, certain carrying costs, assessments, minus depreciation taken and partial sales. *See also* book value.

adjusted internal rate of return (*AIRR*) procedure. An internal rate of return analysis in which the reinvestment rates for both positive and negative cash flows have been adjusted. The adjusted internal rate applies a safe rate to all negative cash flows, discounts them to time period zero, and adds them to the initial investment. A market rate is applied to all positive cash flows, which are carried forward to the end of the investment holding period.

adjusted sale price. The figure produced when the transaction price of a comparable sale is adjusted for elements of comparison.

adjustments
1. Mathematical changes made to basic data to allow for better comparison or understanding of the data; e.g., dollar adjustments, the identification of individual differences between comparables and the subject property in terms of plus or minus dollar amounts; percentage adjustments, the identification of individual differences between comparables and the subject property in terms of plus or minus percentage differentials; and cumulative percentage adjustments, the identification of individual differences between comparables and the subject property in terms of plus or minus percentage differentials, cumulated by multiplication or division. The process assumes a causal relationship among the various factors for which adjustments are made.
2. Items that should be prorated or apportioned between the purchaser and the seller in a real estate transaction; e.g., taxes, rents, fuel. [2]

administrative expenses. Expenses incurred in directing or conducting a business as distinguished from expenses of manufacturing, selling, etc. The items in this category depend on the nature of the business, but usually include the salaries of officers, rent of offices, office and general expenses, and costs for noncustodial personnel and services needed to operate the property.

ADT. *See* average daily traffic.

administrator. A person appointed by the court to manage and settle the estate of a deceased person; a representative of limited authority who collects the assets of an estate, pays its debts, and distributes the residue to those entitled. An administrator provides security for the due administration of the estate by entering into a bond with sureties, called an *administration bond. See also* executor.

administrator's deed. A deed conveyed by an administrator, i.e., a person lawfully appointed to manage and settle the estate of a deceased person who has left no executor.

adobe. A heavy-textured soil that cracks deeply when dry and breaks into irregular, cubical blocks.

adobe construction. Building method featuring exterior walls built of blocks made from adobe soil mixed with straw and hardened in the sun.

ad valorem. According to value.

ad valorem tax. A real estate tax based on property value.

adverse possession. The actual, exclusive, open, notorious, hostile, and continuous possession and occupation of real property under an evident claim of right or title. The time required to obtain title legally by adverse possession varies from state to state.

aeloian soil. Soil developed from material transported and deposited by wind.

aeration zone. The upper ground water zone that retains water for plant use and permits excess water to seep into the saturation zone.

aerial photograph. A photograph of the earth's surface taken from the air.

affidavit. A sworn or affirmed statement or declaration in written form.

affiliation agreement. A contract, such as that entered into by a local broadcasting company and a major network, that provides valuable advantages to both. [12]

affirmative easement. The right to perform a specific action on a property owned by another. *Also called* the dominant estate. *See also* negative easement.

AFLM. Accredited Farm and Land Member. *See also* Farm and Land Institute (FLI).

after-completion costs. Costs incurred after regular construction has been completed.

after-tax cash flow (*ATCF*). Income remaining from net operating income after debt service and ordinary income tax on operations are deducted.

after-tax equity yield rate. The annualized rate of return on equity after payment of income taxes, including those that are or will be incurred upon disposition of the investment; the internal rate of return after taxes. *See also* internal rate of return (*IRR*).

after-tax income. In accounting, the income that remains after deducting income tax liability from taxable income.

after-tax net cash proceeds of resale. The after-tax reversion to equity; the estimated resale price of the property less commissions and other expenses of sale, outstanding debt, and tax claims on the ownership interest.

age-life method. *See* economic age-life method; modified economic age-life method; physical age-life method.

agency. A fiduciary relationship in which one party, the agent, acts as a representative of the other, the principal, in matters specified in a contract between them. [15]

agent. A person who has been given the authority to act for another. *See also* agency.

agents in production. The elements of labor, capital, coordination, and land, which together create wealth, income, or services.

aggregate
1.   Materials used in the manufacture of concrete or plaster, except water and the bonding agents; e.g., cement, lime, plaster, sand, gravel, cinders, rock, slag. *See also* soil aggregate.
2.   In statistics, the sum of all the variates within a population; e.g., the aggregate sale price of all the houses sold in a given community.

agreement of sale. A written contract of sale between a buyer and a seller, drawn up before the actual transfer of title or assumption of ownership, which states the conditions necessary for the transfer of ownership.

agricultural districting. The designation of certain geographic areas for long-term agricultural use.

agricultural property. Improved or unimproved land that is devoted to or available for the production of crops and other products of the soil, e.g., fruits, timber, and for the raising of livestock.

agricultural use value. An estimate of value based solely on the property's agricultural productivity; used by taxing authorities to provide preferential assessment or decrease estate taxes of land devoted to farming.

A horizon. Upper horizon, surface soil from which material is removed by percolating water. *See also* B horizon; C horizon; D horizon.

air conditioning. A system designed to control room temperature and humidity through ventilation, air circulation, air cleaning, and air cooling.

AIREA. *See* American Institute of Real Estate Appraisers.

airport zoning. A system that limits the height of structures and natural growth and controls land uses around an airport to eliminate hazards to aircraft, e.g., smoke, electronic interference, structural interference.

Air Quality Control Region. An area designated by the federal government that encompasses two or more communities that share a common air-pollution problem. [3]

Air Quality Maintenance Area. A geographical area designated by the Environmental Protection Agency for the administration of air quality standards; may include several municipalities and more than one state. [3]

Air Quality Standard. The prescribed level of air pollutants that cannot be lawfully exceeded during a specified time in a specified geographical area. [3]

air rights. The property rights associated with the use, control, and regulation of air space over a parcel of real estate. *See also* transferable development right (TDR).

Akerson format. The mortgage-equity procedure that substitutes an arithmetic format for the algebraic equation in the Ellwood formula.

alcove. A recessed area connected to a room or hallway.

ALGOL. Algorithmic language; an international programming language for problem solutions that can be expressed algebraically.

alienation. A transfer of title from one person to another. [1]

alkali. Describes certain soluble salts that are toxic to plant growth when abnormal concentrations are present in soils.

alkaline soil. Any soil that has a pH above seven.

alley. A relatively narrow public or private way that serves as a secondary means of access and affords light and air to abutting properties.

alley influence. The effect of a side or rear alley on the value of abutting property, especially commercial property.

all-inclusive deed of trust. A junior deed of trust in which the beneficiary (lender or seller) agrees to pay one or more senior lienholders and the trustor (borrower or buyer) makes one payment to the beneficiary rather than separate payments to the junior and senior lienholders. *See also* deed of trust. [1]

all-inclusive mortgage. A junior mortgage in which the mortgagee agrees to pay one or more senior lienholders and the mortgagor makes one payment to the mortgagee, rather than separate payments to the junior and senior lienholders. *See also* mortgage.

allocation. A method used to estimate land value in which an appraiser analyzes sales of improved properties to establish a typical ratio of site value to total property value and applies this ratio to a property being appraised or comparable sale being analyzed.

allotment
1. A tract of land that has been divided into smaller parts; a subdivision.
2. An allowance established by the United States Department of Agriculture designating the specific amount of crops that may be produced or the acreage that can be devoted to the production of a specific crop.
3. Funds allocated by an institutional investor to purchase mortgages for its portfolio within a designated period.

alluvial. Deposits made by flowing water.

alluvial fan. A sloping, fan-shaped deposit of boulders, gravel, and sand left by a stream or river where it spreads out into a level plain or meets a slower stream or river.

alluvial soil. An azonal, unstable soil formed from materials transported by flowing water.

alluvion. The addition made to dry land by the washing of a sea, a navigable river, or another body of water; a gradual increase that cannot be perceived at any one moment of time. *See also* accretion.

alluvium. A fine material, e.g., sand, mud, carried by water and deposited on land.

alternative mortgage instrument (AMI). A mortgage form that differs from the standard fixed-rate, level-payment mortgage instrument. *See also* Flexible Loan Insurance Plan (FLIP); graduated-payment mortgage

(GPM); reverse annuity mortgage (RAM); variable-rate mortgage (VRM).

amenity
1. A pleasant quality.
2. A tangible or intangible benefit of real property that enhances its attractiveness or increases the satisfaction of the user, but is not essential to its use. Natural amenities may include a pleasant location near water or a scenic view of the surrounding area; man-made amenities include swimming pools, tennis courts, community buildings, and other recreational facilities. [3]

American bond. A masonry process in which every fifth, sixth, or seventh course of bricks is laid with the length perpendicular to the wall as a header course.

American Institute of Real Estate Appraisers (AIREA). The organization dedicated to the development of excellence in the real estate appraisal profession. The Appraisal Institute has been a pioneer in appraisal education and is the foremost publisher of appraisal literature. The Institute confers the MAI designation on individuals who demonstrate the knowledge, experience, and judgment necessary to appraise all types of real property and the RM designation on those who demonstrate the ability to value one- to four-family residences.

American Society of Real Estate Counselors (ASREC). The organization of professionals qualified to provide real estate advice and guidance on a fee basis. The Society confers the CRE designation.

American standard. A system for measuring office areas in buildings which was established by the American National Standards Institute.

AMI. *See* alternative mortgage instrument.

AMO®. ACCREDITED MANAGEMENT ORGANIZATION®. *See also* Institute of Real Estate Management (IREM).

amortization. The process of retiring a debt or recovering a capital investment through scheduled, systematic repayment of principal; a program of periodic contributions to a sinking fund or debt retirement fund.

amortization rate. The ratio of the periodic amortization payment to the total principal amount to be amortized; corresponds to a sinking fund factor or rate; the difference between the mortgage (annual) constant (R_M) and the nominal rate of interest (I).

amortization schedule. A schedule of debt repayment specifying the timing and amount of payments; a program of retiring debt through the scheduled, systematic repayment of principal.

amortizing mortgage. A mortgage requiring periodic payments that include both a partial repayment of the debt and interest on the outstanding balance. *See also* fully amortizing mortgage loan.

amount of \$1 (S^n). The compound interest factor that indicates the amount to which \$1 will grow with compound interest at a specified rate for a specified number of periods.

amount of \$1 per period ($S_{\overline{n|}}$). The compound interest factor that indicates the amount to which \$1 per period will grow with compound interest at a specified rate for a specified number of periods. *Also called* sinking fund accumulation factor. *See also* annuity.

anchor bolt. A bolt used to secure a structural member to a masonry support to prevent upward and lateral movements of the superstructure; e.g., a bolt set into a concrete foundation, extended up through the sill, and secured with a nut at the top.

anchor tenant. The major store within a shopping center that attracts or generates traffic for the facility; e.g. a supermarket in a neighborhood shopping center, a major chain or department store in a regional shopping center.

animal unit (AU). A unit of measure equivalent to an animal weighing 1,000 pounds; e.g., a 500-pound weaner calf represents one-half animal unit. The term is subject to some local variation.

animal unit month (AUM). The quantity of feed that one animal unit needs for one month to sustain life and achieve good growth.

annualizer (*a*). An element in yield and change formulas that converts the total change in capital value over the projection period to an annual percentage; varies with the pattern of the income stream.

annual percentage rate. The effective annual interest rate. Truth in lending legislation requires that loan instruments and advertising show the interest cost to the borrower in the form of an annual rate.

annuals. A type of range vegetation in which annual forbs or annual grasses constitute the dominant vegetation.

annuity. Annual income; a program or contract requiring regular payments of stipulated amounts. *See also* annuity certain; annuity payable in advance; constant dollar change per period annuity; constant ratio change per period annuity; decreasing annuity; deferred annuity; increasing annuity; Inwood annuity; level annuity; life annuity; ordinary annuity; reverse annuity mortgage (RAM); step-down annuity; step-up annuity; variable annuity.

annuity capitalization. *See* yield capitalization.

annuity certain. An annuity that is assured for a specified period of time, as distinguished from a life annuity, which terminates with the death of an individual.

annuity due. *See* annuity payable in advance.

annuity payable in advance. A type of level annuity in which payments are received at the beginning of each period.

anodized aluminum. Aluminum that is covered with a hard, corrosion-resistant, oxide film using an electrochemical process.

anticipated use procedure. *See* development procedure.

anticipation. The perception that value is created by the expectation of benefits to be derived in the future.

antilogarithm. The natural number corresponding to a logarithm.

apartment. A dwelling unit of one or more rooms designed to provide complete living facilities for one or more occupants.

apartment building. A structure containing four or more dwelling units with common areas and facilities, e.g., entrances, lobby, elevators or stairs, mechanical space, walks, grounds. *See also* condominium; cooperative apartment; flat; high-rise apartment building; tenement.

apartment hotel. A furnished apartment building with more or less permanent tenants that offers hotel facilities, e.g., reception desk, telephone switchboard, maid service, utilities.

applications software. In computer usage, programs designed to solve specific problems or perform specified functions; e.g., a cost-analysis program, a discounted cash flow analysis program. [16]

appraisal. An unbiased estimate of the nature, quality, value, or utility of an interest in, or aspect of, identified real estate and related personalty. *See also* evaluation; valuation.

Appraisal Institute. *See* American Institute of Real Estate Appraisers (AIREA).

appraisal process. *See* evaluation process; valuation process.

appraisal report. A report of the results of an appraisal which begins with the definition of an appraisal problem and leads to a specific conclusion using reasoning and relevant descriptive data.

appraised value. *See* estimate.

appraiser. One who performs an appraisal.

appreciation (*app*). An increase in property value.

approaches to value. Systematic procedures used to derive value indications in real property appraisal. *See also* cost approach; income capitalization approach; sales comparison approach.

approach nose. An area of land between highways that faces approaching traffic, which may pass to either or both sides of this land.

approach zone. The designated path or corridor that represents the air space through which aircraft can legally descend to or take off from an airport.

appropriation
1. The taking of a public thing for private use; e.g., the appropriation of water from a natural stream for a beneficial use.
2. The dedication of land for a particular use, e.g., a public park, a school.

appurtenance. Something that has been added or appended to a property and has become an inherent part of the property; usually passes with the property when title is transferred.

apron
1. A hard-surfaced entrance to a loading dock or portion of a building.
2. A portion of a private driveway or roadway that connects with a public street or road.
3. A portion of a wharf or pier lying between the waterfront edge and the buildings.
4. A wooden barrier along a sea wall or the face of a dam.
5. The inside wood finish piece of a window underneath the sill.

aqueduct. An artificial channel to convey water from place to place; a major conduit that may be open or covered.

arable. Describes land suitable for cultivation; tillable.

arbitrator. A person who decides a dispute to avoid a court determination.

arcade
1. A series of arches on the same plane that are either open or closed.
2. A walkway or passageway with an arched roof, which frequently has shops along one or both sides.
3. A passageway open on the street side that is usually colonnaded.

arch. A convexly curved vertical span of steel, concrete, stone, or wood; a structural section with end base supports designed to support itself, the superstructure, and the attached or suspended structure.

architect's approval. An architect's written or imprinted acknowledgment that the materials, equipment, and methods of construction are acceptable for use in the work, or a statement that a contractor's request or claim is valid. [1]

architect's punch list. A list of items to be completed that is prepared by the architect during final inspection of the structure. [1]

architectural concrete construction. Concrete with little or no reinforcement, poured against a form that bears a design to produce a decorative treatment simulating stone masonry.

architectural style. The character of a building's form and ornamentation.

architecture. The art or science of building design and construction; the style, appearance, and character of buildings.

architrave. The molding above and on both sides of a door or other rectangular opening.

area. The surface extent of a building, a site, a neighborhood, a section of a city, a tract, or a region, measured in square units.

area controls. A zoning provision limiting use densities.

area sample. A limited number of observations selected from an entire aggregate of phenomena on the basis of geographical location.

areaway. An uncovered space next to a building which provides for light, air, or access. *See also* light well.

arithmetic mean. The sum of a series of values divided by the number of values in the group. It is the simplest, most commonly used average, but its value may be distorted by extreme figures.

ARM. *See* adjustable rate mortgage.

arm's-length transaction. A transaction arrived at in the open market by unrelated parties under no duress.

array. The listing of a set of observations in a specific order, e.g., alphabetical, alphanumeric, chronological, order of magnitude.

arroyo. A dry gully that can become flooded without warning.

Art Deco. A decorative style popular in the 1920s and 1930s that is based on geometric forms and patterns, some derived from nature; promoted the use of ornament for its own sake; used in architecture, furnishings, textiles, and decorative arts.

arterial highway. A major highway usually on a continuous or through route; describes the character of use not the character of the improvement.

Art Nouveau. A decorative style popular in the late 19th and early 20th centuries; characterized by assymetric, curvilinear forms inspired by nature; used in all the arts and crafts of the period, including architecture and interior design.

asbestos. A nonflammable, natural mineral fiber currently being investigated for potential health-threatening properties.

ASCII. American Standard Code for Information Interchange; in computer usage, a widely used standard for character representation which aids communication among different brands of computers. [16]

ashlar. Squared stone carefully laid in a wall with uniform joint thickness; further defined according to the coursing, as range, broken range, or random. Stone more than 12 inches thick is rough ashlar.

aspect
1. Position facing, fronting, or regarding a particular direction; e.g., a house with a southern aspect; the part so fronting. *Also called* exposure.
3. In forestry, the direction toward which a slope faces according to the main points of the compass.

asphaltic concrete. Asphalt binder combined with stone or another aggregate and used to produce a hard surface for streets, airstrips, and other paved areas.

asphalt tile. A resilient floor covering laid in mastic.

ASREC. *See* American Society of Real Estate Counselors.

assart rent. Rent paid for land that has been deforested.

assemblage. The combining of two or more parcels, usually but not necessarily contiguous, into one ownership or use. *See also* plottage.

assess
1. To estimate property value as a basis for taxation.
2. To fix or determine, e.g., by a court or commission, the compensation due a property owner for the taking of real property.

assessable improvement. An improvement that increases the value of a property and should, in the absence of a contrary law, increase the assessment.

assessed valuation. *See* assessed value.

assessed value. In ad valorem taxation, the value of a property according to the tax rolls.

assessment
1. The identification of property to be valued for ad valorem taxation.
2. The official valuation of property for ad valorem taxation.
3. A single charge levied against a parcel of real estate to defray the cost of a public improvement that presumably will benefit only the properties it serves; e.g., assessment for the installation of sidewalks, curbs, sewer or water lines. *See also* special assessment.
4. An official determination of the amount to be paid by or to the owners of real estate to defray the cost of a public improvement that is presumed to benefit the properties it serves in an amount at least equal to the cost of the improvement; e.g., assessment of benefits and damages for public sewer or water lines.

5. An official determination of the amount to be paid a property owner for the taking of all or part of a property for an improvement designed to benefit the general public; e.g., assessment of benefits and damages in property takings for highway or school construction.

assessment base. *See* property tax base.

assessment district. A jurisdiction, e.g., a county, under the authority of an assessor; may be a single tax district or may encompass several districts.

assessment period. The period during which all property in the assessment district must be reassessed. *Also called* assessment cycle or assessment frequency.

assessment process. The discovery, listing, and valuation of property for taxation.

assessment ratio. The relationship between assessed value and market value.

assessment roll. An official list that reflects the allocation of property tax among property owners in a jurisdiction; usually lists an identifier for each taxable parcel in the jurisdiction, the name of the owner of record, the address of the parcel or the owner, the assessed value of the land, the assessed value of the improvements, any application exemption codes, and the total assessed value.

assessment/sales ratio. The number derived by dividing the assessed value by the selling price; used as a measure of the relationship between an assessment and market value.

assessor. One who discovers, lists, and values real property for ad valorem taxation.

assessor's manual. A manual that lists specific requirements for property assessment; used as a guide to ensure uniform treatment of similar properties.

asset. Any owned property that has value; may be financial, e.g., cash, bonds; or physical, e.g., real and personal property. *See also* capital assets; cash assets; current assets; diminishing assets; fixed assets; intangible assets; liquid assets; working assets.

assignee. A person or corporation to whom a contract is assigned.

assignment. A written transfer of right, title, or interest. [1]

assignor. A person or corporation from whom a contract is assigned.

assisted housing. Housing for which the government provides assistance in occupancy, construction, or financing. [1]

assumable mortgage. A mortgage in which the existing debt may be transferred to a third party without the approval of the lender.

assumed mortgage. An existing mortgage for which a new owner becomes liable when the property is purchased and transferred.

atrium. A central area in a structure with a ceiling of translucent material that admits sunlight.

atrium house. A dwelling with an open interior court onto which rooms open; may be of two or more stories, freestanding or joined in rows, groups, or clusters. A variation of the patio house.

attachment. Seizure of property by court order. [1]

attic. Accessible space between roof rafters and ceiling joists.

attic ventilators. Openings in a roof or in gables that allow for air circulation. [8]

attorney-in-fact. One who is authorized to perform certain acts for another under a power of attorney; power may be general or limited to certain acts. [15]

AU. *See* animal unit.

AUM. *See* animal unit month.

authority. A government agency, usually independent, that is established for a specific purpose, e.g., to construct and operate housing projects, toll roads, turnpikes, ports, public transportation.

auxiliary lane. A portion of pavement adjoining the traveled way, which is designed for parking, acceleration, deceleration, or another use facilitating traffic flow.

average absolute deviation. In statistics, the sum of the absolute (sign ignored) differences between the individual observations and the average of all the observations, divided by the number of observations. [10]

average daily traffic (ADT). The average, one-day traffic volume measured at a selected highway location; the sum of all traffic recorded for a given period of time divided by the number of days in that period.

average deviation. In statistics, the number obtained by subtracting the arithmetic mean of all the items from each item, adding up these differences without regard to sign, and dividing this sum by the number of items.

average household income. Estimated average income, or salaried income, per household. [17]

avigation easement. The right, granted by the owner of land adjacent to an airport, to the use of the air space above a specific height for the flight of aircraft; may prohibit the property owner from using the land for structures, trees, signs, or stacks higher than the altitude specified; the degree of the restriction is dictated by the glide angle necessary for the safe use of the airfield's runway.

avulsion. The sudden removal of land from the property of one owner to that of another, e.g. by inundation or a change in the course of a river. The land so removed remains in the original ownership.

awning. A roof-like shelter extending over an area, e.g., the deck of a ship, a doorway, a window, a porch, that provides protection from the sun or rain.

awning window. A type of window having a sash with hinges at the top, which permit the window to open horizontally, forming an awning over the opening.

axial growth. Urban growth that takes the form of finger-like extensions moving out along main transportation routes. [15]

axial theory. A theory of land use development that postulates that land uses tend to develop in relation to the time-cost functions of transportation axes that radiate out from the central business district. [3]

azimuth. The angle between an object and true north or true south. In surveying, it is measured clockwise from true north.

azonal soil. A soil without horizons, insufficiently developed, and lacking a definite soil profile.

B

back band casing. A common butt casing with a molded and/or mitered trim piece around its outer edge.

backfill
1. To replace earth removed during excavation.
2. The subsurface material placed against structures, foundations, or footings.

backup
1. The cheaper material in a masonry wall that is covered by more expensive, ornamental material, e.g., face brick, stone, marble, metal panels.

2. In computer usage, an extra copy of a program or data file stored in a safe place, usually on a diskette or magnetic tape, to be used in case the original is damaged. [16]

backwater valve. An automatic valve set in the sewer lateral to prevent sewage from backing up during flood periods.

balance. The principle that holds that real property value is created and sustained when contrasting, opposing, or interacting elements are in a state of equilibrium.

balanced operation
1. An enterprise in which the gross income either equals or exceeds the cost of production.
2. In ranching, a livestock enterprise that provides sufficient feed and forage resources in each season to sustain its livestock and game throughout the year.

balance outstanding (B). The unpaid portion of a mortgage loan at a specific date.

balance sheet. An itemized listing of the total assets, total liabilities, and net worth of an entity.

balcony
1. A balustrade or railed platform that projects from the face of a building above the ground level; it has an entrance from the building interior, and is usually cantilevered or supported by columns.
2. In a theater or auditorium, a partial upper floor furnished with seats.

balloon frame. In construction, a type of framing in which the studs extend from the sill to the roof; the second floor is supported by a horizontal ribbon or ledger board and joists that are nailed to the studs.

balloon mortgage. A mortgage that is not fully amortized at maturity, and thus requires a lump sum, or balloon, payment of the outstanding balance.

balloon payment. The outstanding balance due at the maturity of a balloon mortgage.

baluster. A short pillar or post that supports a rail, usually circular and tapered at the top; the uprights supporting the handrail of a staircase.

balustrade. A row of balusters surmounted by a rail, coping, or cornice.

band of investment. A technique in which the weighted-average rates attributable to the components of a capital investment are combined to derive a weighted-average rate attributable to the total investment.

band sill. In the construction of pier and beam foundations, the two horizontal members that connect the pier to the floor joist. The boards are joined to create a right angle, and the joist is placed perpendicular to the upright board to give the foundation rigidity. *Also called* box sill. [8]

banker's acceptance. A bank's obligation or promise to pay; a marketable, short-term obligation similar to commercial paper.

bar chart. A graphic method of presenting data in which bars of uniform width and varying height are used to indicate differences in the size of two or more variables.

barn. A building specifically designed to house farm animals and store hay and grain. This use is becoming obsolete due to current farm operation, and the buildings are often converted to equipment storage and other uses.

barren. A tract of land that has little or no natural vegetation; e.g., intermittent lake beds, saline flats, active sand dunes, shale, rock slides, lava flows.

basal area. In forestry, the breast-height cross-sectional area of a single tree or of all trees in a stand, expressed in square feet.

base
1. In compound interest tables, one plus the periodic rate; denoted by the symbol S in mortgage-equity formulas.

2. In building construction, the lowest part of a wall, pier, pedestal, or column.

baseboard. A piece of finishing material placed at the bottom of interior walls to conceal the area where the base of the wall meets the floor.

baseboard heating. A system of perimeter heating with radiators, convectors, or air outlets located at the base of the wall where the baseboard would be; may be hot water, forced air, or electric. *Also called* base panel heating.

base line
1. In the government survey system, a line running due east and west through the initial point of a principal meridian from which township lines are established.
2. A topographic center line of a survey such as one used for the route of a highway.
3. In construction, an established line from which measurements are taken when laying out building plans or other working plans. [3]

base map. A map with enough points of reference, e.g., state, county, or township lines, and other physical features to allow the plotting of other data.

basement. The lowest story of a building, which may be partially or wholly below ground level; as distinguished from a cellar.

base mold. A decorative strip of molded material laid along the top of a baseboard.

base periods. Time intervals or reference points used for business and economic data. In the formulation of index numbers, the figures for a base period are usually averaged and the average is adopted as 100.

base plate. The horizontal member at the bottom of a column or post that transmits the column loads to its foundation. *See also* anchor bolt.

base property. The private holdings of a stock raiser, i.e., fee-owned land, water sources, or private leased property, used as the base required for the issuance of a grazing permit on public domain under the Taylor Grazing Act.

base rent. The minimum rent stipulated in a lease.

base sale. In paired data set analysis, the sale against which other sales are compared.

BASIC. Beginner's all-purpose symbolic instruction code; a popular, English-like, high-level computer language. [16]

basic activities. In economic base analysis, activities that produce goods intended for export to other areas.

basic crops. Staple commodities, e.g., corn, wheat, cotton, tobacco, rice, peanuts, that are often subject to price supports.

basic multiplier. The ratio of an area's total economic activity, e.g., total employment, to basic activities, e.g., basic employment.

basic rate (r). The portion of the overall capitalization rate that provides for all of the income requirements except depreciation or appreciation.

basis. In income taxation, the portion of total property value most likely to be affected by depreciation or capital improvement.

basis point. One one-hundredth of one percentage point.

bathroom. A room containing a toilet, a lavatory, and a bathtub or shower.

batten. A narrow strip of wood used to cover a joint between boards or to simulate a covered joint for architectural purposes.

batter. The slope of a wall, terrace, pier, or bank from the perpendicular; the vertical incline is generally expressed in inches horizontal to inches vertical.

batture land. Land situated between the water's edge at low tide, or low water stage, and the river bank or levee; generally held in the same ownership as the abutting land, but it can be sold separately from the adjoining land.

Bauhaus. A school of design founded in Germany in 1919 by Walter Gropius to synthesize the fine and applied arts by incorporating architecture, painting, sculpture, and industrial arts into one curriculum; developed a style based on using current technology, meeting utilitarian requirements, and creating unity between design and materials.

bay
1. An opening in a wall.
2. The space between columns or piers.
3. A division of a barn or another building, e.g., industrial building, warehouse, service station.

bay depth. In floor area measurement, the distance from the tenant side of the corridor wall to the exterior wall.

Bayesian analysis. A statistical technique in which probabilities, called *prior probabilities*, are assigned to a set of mutually exclusive and exhaustive events on the basis of whatever evidence or information is currently available; if additional evidence is subsequently obtained, the initial prior probabilities are revised using Bayes' Theorem. The probabilities resulting from the revision process are called *posterior probabilities. See also* posterior distribution.

Bayesian decision rule. A rule that states that one should choose the action that is expected to produce the best gain; to optimize the expected gain and minimize the expected loss, where gains and losses are defined in terms of utility or cash.

Bayes' theorem. A formula central to the Bayesian approach to statistical estimation which is used to incorporate sample information about a particular situation into the total amount of information available; the formula used in the revision of probabilities.

bay window. A window that forms a bay in a room and projects outwardly from the wall; it is supported by its own foundation, as distinguised from an oriel or box bay window, which lacks foundation support.

beam
1. A principal load-supporting member of a building; may be made of wood, steel, or concrete.
2. The lumber in a rectangular cross section of a building, five or more inches thick and eight or more inches wide. *See also* bond beam; cantilever beam; constrained beam; grade beam.

beamed ceiling. A ceiling with exposed beams. A false beamed ceiling has ornamental boards or timbers that are not load-bearing.

bearing
1. The position or horizontal direction of one point or object with respect to another, or to the points of the compass.
2. The portion of any building member that rests on its supports.

bearing partition. *See* bearing wall.

bearing value of soil. The ability of the soil and other underlying material to support a load, e.g., foundations and a building.

bearing wall. A wall that supports part of a building, usually a floor or roof above it. *See also* wall-bearing construction.

bed-a-tree. To prepare the path where a tree is to fall so that it will not shatter.

bedrock. The solid rock underlying soils and other surface formations.

bedroom community. A suburban community where a large number of residents work in a major city. [2]

before-and-after rule. In eminent domain valuation, a procedure in which just compensation is measured as the difference between the value of the entire property before the taking and the value of the remainder after the taking.

before-tax cash flow. *See* pre-tax cash flow (*PTCF*).

belt. A horizontal course of distinctive masonry around an exposed wall or walls of a masonry building; usually, but not necessarily, of decorative natural or cast stone.

belt highway. An arterial highway that carries traffic partially or entirely around an urban area and is connected with the city by principal streets or highways.

bench mark. Identification symbols inscribed on stone, metal, or other durable objects permanently fixed in the ground from which differences of elevation are measured for tidal observations or topographical surveys.

benchmark. The standard or base from which estimates are made.

beneficial interests
1. Benefits, profits, or advantages resulting from a trust contract.
2. The equitable title in a property, as distinguished from the legal title.

beneficial use
1. The right to the enjoyment of property when legal title is held by one person and the right to use the property is held by another.
2. In water rights, the doctrine that holds that the water resources of the state must be put to their most beneficial use. In some states, this doctrine supersedes the doctrine of riparian rights. *See also* riparian rights.

beneficiary of trust deed. The lender, who is one of three parties in a trust deed agreement. The borrower, or trustor, gives the title to a third party, the trustee, who holds the title in trust for the benefit of the borrower and the lender. [10]

benefits. In eminent domain valuation, the advantageous factors that arise from a public improvement for which private property has been taken in condemnation. *See also* general benefits; set-off rule; special benefits.

bent
1. A transverse frame designed to support horizontal or vertical loads, e.g., elevated railroad tracks.

2. A section of a tobacco shed.

BEPS. *See* Building Energy Performance Standard.

berm
1. A horizontal ledge or bench part way up a slope.
2. A mound of earth, sometimes paved, that is used to divert or control the flow of surface drainage, mark property boundaries, or alter topography.
3. The earthen or paved extension of a roadway; the shoulder along a highway.

betterment. Substantial improvements to real property, i.e., more than mere repairs. [1]

beveled siding. Clapboard.

B horizon. The subsoil; a layer of deposit to which materials are added by percolating water; the horizon lying beneath the A horizon. *See also* A horizon; C horizon; D horizon.

bidirectional. In computer usage, the ability of a printhead to print right to left, as well as left to right, which enables the printer to operate quickly. [16]

bikeways. A continuous path designated for the use of bicycles and other vehicles propelled by human power.

bilevel. A house built on two levels; a split-level house.

binary. In computer usage, a numbering system that uses combinations of only two numerals, 0 and 1; this numeric structure is employed by all computers. *Also called* the base two system. [16]

binomial distribution. In statistics, a discrete distribution that characterizes situations in which samples are taken from a population of attributes with only two values, e.g., yes or no, success or failure.

birth rate. The number of births per 1,000 persons per year.

bit. In computer usage, a shortened term for binary digit; an electrical signal that represents either 0 or 1 in the binary system. Depending on the internal specifications of the computer, a group of eight, 16, 32, or even 64 bits may form one byte. [16]

blacktop. Bituminous or asphaltic material used in hard surface paving.

blanket mortgage. A mortgage that covers more than one property; common in subdivision development and in situations where the equity in one property is insufficient to satisfy loan policy. Usually individual properties are released from the blanket mortgage as they are sold.

blight
1. Decay caused by the failure to maintain the quality of real estate and public services.
2. Describes plant diseases that cause withering and death of part or all of a plant.

blighted area. An area or district subject to detrimental influences, e.g., adverse land use mixture, that are severe enough to affect desirability adversely, causing a decline in property values.

blind fund. *See* open-end fund.

blind pool. *See* open-end fund.

block
1. A segment of a city; usually a square area lying between intersecting streets or other physical boundaries; the length of one side of such a square.
2. A preformed structural component made of concrete and used in construction. *See also* concrete block.

blowdown. A tree or an area of trees blown down by the wind. *Also called* windslash.

blueprint. A working plan used by workers on a construction job; an architectural drawing that is transferred to chemically treated paper using a strong light, which turns the paper blue and reproduces the drawing in white.

blue sky. The process of qualifying an issue, e.g., a real estate syndication, under a state securities act. [1]

blue sky law. A state law that regulates the solicitation and sale of securities to protect investors. [1]

board and batten. A type of siding, typically vertical, composed of wide boards and narrow battens. The boards are nailed to the sheathing with a half of a space between them and the battens are nailed over these spaces.

board foot. A unit of lumber measurement that is one foot long, one foot wide, and one inch thick, i.e., one square foot, one inch thick (144 cubic inches). A board foot differs from a square foot in that it has depth and its dimensions are nominal, not actual, i.e., board measurements are quoted as full before dressing or planing.

board measure
1. A system for measuring lumber. Quantities of lumber are designated and priced in terms of board feet. *See also* board foot.
2. The volume of logs, trees, or stands in terms of the estimated amount of lumber they will yield according to various log rules. Usually abbreviated B.M.; larger quantities stated in thousands are abbreviated M.B.M. or M. *See also* log rules.

boards. Yard lumber eight or more inches wide, and less than two inches thick.

boatel. An adjunct to a marina that provides guests traveling by boat with accommodations and services comparable to those of a motel.

bog soil. An intrazonal group of marshy or swampy soils underlying peat; common to humid or subhumid climates.

bole. The trunk of a tree.

bolster. In construction, a horizontal timber on a post used to lessen the free span of a beam.

bolt
1. Any of several types of strong fastening rods, pins, or screws, usually threaded to receive a nut.
2. A movable bar or rod that fastens a door or gate when slid into a socket.

BOMA standard. The first standard method of floor measurement for office buildings.

bona fide sale. A sale made in good faith that represents an agreement between the buyer and the seller at the current market price. *See also* arm's-length transaction.

bond
1. A capital market instrument issued with a fixed interest rate for a term of one year or more.
2. In construction, the arrangement of individual masonry units in an overlapping pattern to give the finished structure greater strength and bind the individual elements into a cohesive, integrated unit. *See also* brick masonry.

bond beam. A continuous beam placed in masonry walls to tie them together, add lateral stability, and distribute concentrated vertical loads along the wall; usually made of reinforced concrete, but sometimes of reinforced brick or concrete block.

bond for deed. An executory contract for the sale of property that provides that the title remain with the grantor until the purchase price is paid; ordinarily binding on both parties.

book cost. The cost of acquisition as shown in the general ledger of an individual, a partnership, or a corporation; generally includes direct and indirect financing and all development costs, except preliminary operating losses.

book depreciation. The amount of capital recapture written off an owner's books.

book value. The capital amount at which property is shown on the account books; usually equals the original cost less reserves for depreciation plus additions to capital. *See also* basis.

boom
1.   A period of rapid economic growth characterized by the expansion of business facilities and activities.
2.   In construction, a heavy crane or lift arm. *See also* log boom.

boot
1.   Any asset or liability transferred as part of an exchange of realty; typical forms include cash and debt existing prior to the exchange, purchase-money mortgages created within the exchange, and debt instruments transferred in lieu of cash.
2.   In computing, to execute the boot strap program.

boot strap program. A program used to start a computer; usually includes clearing the memory, initializing peripheral devices, and loading the operating system.

boring test. A study of the load-bearing qualities of a subterranean surface performed by analyzing bore or drilling residue, called *core samples.*

borrow. Suitable soil material brought from outside the construction project and used for regrading or backfilling.

borrow bank. The source from which borrow is obtained.

borrowed light. Glazing in an interior partition that allows outside light to enter interior areas.

borrow pit. In the construction of highways and railroads, land that is excavated to obtain dirt for making fills. Often land is condemned to make a borrow pit. [7]

bottom rail. A horizontal member that forms the bottom of a window or paneled door. *Also called* bottom stile.

boulevard. A broad street or promenade that is often planted with rows of trees along its border or on a median strip.

boundaries
1. The perimeters of land parcels.
2. The lines demarcating the physical area that exerts relevant influences on a subject property's value; may coincide with changes in prevailing land use, occupant characteristics, or physical characteristics.

bounded description. The earliest form of land description in which property boundaries were described in terms of impermanent features, e.g., items of terrain, fences, ownership of adjacent property. [10]

bowstring truss. A steel or wooden truss with a top member that resembles a bow or an arch.

box construction. A construction system using horizontal framing members to which vertical siding is attached; frequently used for farm buildings.

box girder. A girder with a hollow cross section similar to a rectangular box.

brace. A structural member that reinforces a frame or truss.

braced framing. A type of heavy timber framing in which posts, girts, and braces are used to reinforce the frame, forming a more rigid structure than balloon framing.

bracket. A horizontal projecting support that bears an overhanging weight; e.g., a cornice, eaves.

Bradley fountain. A large, circular basin featuring a central column equipped with faucets or spray heads to provide washing facilities for several persons at one time; frequently found in industrial buildings.

branch store. A secondary or outlying store owned, supplied, and operated by a larger, more centrally located store.

breakdown method. A method of estimating accrued depreciation in which the total loss in property value is estimated by analyzing and measuring each cause of depreciation separately.

break-even point
1. In real estate analysis, the point at which a property's effective gross income equals the sum of its normal operating expenses and debt service.
2. In financial analysis, the point at which total cost equals total revenue.

breast-height. In forestry, a height 4½ feet above the average ground level, or above the root collar; the height at which the diameter of a standing tree is ordinarily measured. *See also* diameter-breast-high (DBH).

breather roof. A roof on a storage tank that rises and falls with the level of the stored material, which is usually liquid; it prevents loss through rapid vaporization or the mingling of gases with the outside air.

breeding herd. In ranch operations, the livestock retained to provide for the perpetuation of the herd.

brick cavity wall. A wall with a space between the inner and outer tiers of brick; the space may be filled with insulation.

brick masonry. The arrangement or overlapping of bricks, blocks, or stones to tie a masonry wall together and add to its strength. *See also* header; stretcher.

brick veneer. A single tier of brick used as decorative facing on a wall of another material.

bridge financing. Short-term financing between 1) the termination of one loan and the commencement of another, 2) the acquisition of a property and the improvement or rehabilitation that will make it eligible for a permanent mortgage, or 3) the maturity of a construction loan and the negotiation of permanent financing. [3]

bridging. Small wood or metal structural members inserted between joists or studs to give them lateral rigidity.

broad-leaved trees. A type of range vegetation including all deciduous trees; e.g., aspen, cottonwood, birch, alder.

broker. A person who acts as an intermediary, bringing together two or more participants in a market transaction. [11]

brooder house. A heated building for raising young fowl.

browse-shrub. A type of range vegetation that includes foothills or mountain ranges where browse, but not sagebrush, is predominant; characteristically located in the transition zone of lower foothills or mountain slopes.

Btu. British thermal unit; a standard unit for measuring heat equal to the amount required to raise the temperature of one pound of water by one degree Fahrenheit. In the United States, the rated capacity of furnaces and boilers is expressed in terms of Btus emitted per hour. All heat sources, e.g., fuel oil, natural gas, electricity, are measured in Btus.

buck
1. Wood framework for a door opening in a masonry wall to which jambs and casings are attached.
2. Fabricated steel frame prefitted for doors in a masonry wall; sometimes includes the entire assembly, except the door. *Also called* door buck, meaning the entire assembly.

budget motels. Motels that can offer substantially lower rates due to high volume, lower initial investment costs, and efficient operations.

buffer. In computer usage, a block of memory where data or characters are stored until the computer or peripheral is ready to process them. [16]

buffer strip. A parcel of land, usually unimproved except for landscaping and screening, that separates parcels with different uses; ensures that incompatible or inharmonious uses, e.g., industrial sites and residences, are not adjacent.

bug. In computer usage, a problem in a program that has not yet been fixed; typically causes erratic results in a piece of software. [16]

builder-seller sponsor. A sponsor of a project that is undertaken specifically to be sold, immediately upon completion, to a private, nonprofit organization at the certified cost of construction. [1]

building. A structure, usually roofed and walled, that is erected for permanent use.

building capitalization rate (R_B). The rate that reflects the relationship between building income and building value; used to convert building income into an indication of building value in certain residual techniques.

building code. A local or state ordinance or regulation that controls the design, construction, alteration, repair, quality of materials, use, and occupancy of any building in its jurisdiction; enforced by police power in the interest of public health, safety, and welfare.

Building Energy Performance Standard (BEPS). A standard requiring that a building be designed to meet a specified level of energy use per year.

building line. A line established by ordinance or statute; between this line and the street line no structure is permitted.

building orientation. The direction that a building faces. [8]

building paper. A heavy, waterproof paper used as sheathing in wall or roof construction. [2]

building permit. Authorization by a local government for the erection, alteration, or remodeling of improvements within its jurisdiction. [2]

building residual technique. A capitalization technique in which the net operating income attributable to improvements is isolated and capitalized to indicate the improvements' contribution to total property value.

building restrictions. Limitations imposed on a building by codes, easements, deed restrictions, or statute.

building service systems. The systems and components that provide plumbing, sewerage, heating, ventilating, air conditioning, lighting, power, vertical transport, fire protection, and special services, e.g., public address, oxygen, to a building.

building site. A parcel of land on which a building may be erected, including all surrounding land allocated to the improvement. [6]

building standards. Specific construction elements that the owner or developer chooses to use throughout a building. [8]

built-ins. Items that are permanently attached to the building structure and cannot be removed without leaving evidence of removal; e.g., cabinets, counters, desks, benches, shelving, equipment. *See also* fixture; trade fixture.

built-up method. A method of identifying the basic elements of compensable contribution in the development of a discount rate or capitalization rate. There are four basic components of a discount or capitalization rate: the pure or riskless rate, management, nonliquidity, and risk.

built-up rate. An overall capitalization rate or a discount rate that represents the combination of a safe, or risk-free, rate and rates that reflect other factors, e.g., nonliquidity, management, risk.

built-up roofing. Roofing that is applied by laying felt paper with the seams overlapping and sealing with hot asphalt or roofing compound. The final coat may be asphalt or asphalt covered with small gravel.

bulb tee. A rolled steel shape with a cross section resembling a bulbous T; often used as a purlin.

bulkhead
   1. A retaining wall that is backed with solid fill and erected along the water to extend the upland out to the bulkhead line; serves as protection against tidal or watercourse erosion of land.
   2. The wall beneath a store display window.

bulkhead line. A line in navigable waters, established by the federal government through the Army Corps of Engineers, beyond which no solid filling is permitted. It is inshore from the structure limit line or the two are coincident.

bulk regulations. Zoning laws or other regulations that control the height, mass, density, and location of buildings, setting a maximum limit on the intensity of development to ensure proper light, air, and open space. *See also* zoning. [6]

bullet loan. Gap financing for leased-up properties used when the construction loan has expired and acceptable permanent financing has not been found; typically an interest-only loan for two to ten years that cannot be prepaid. [3]

bumper strips. Timbers placed along the outer edge of a loading dock to protect it from damage during the loading and unloading of trucks.

bundle of rights theory. The concept that compares property ownership to a bundle of sticks with each stick representing a distinct and separate right of the property owner, e.g., the right to use real estate, to sell it, to lease it, to give it away, or to choose to exercise all or none of these rights.

Bureau of Public Roads. A unit of the Department of Transportation of the Federal Highway Administration that administers federal grants-in-aid to states for the construction and maintenance of major highways; cooperates with the Department of Agriculture and the Department of the Interior in the construction of roads in national forests, national parks, and elsewhere.

Bureau of Reclamation. A major bureau of the U.S. Department of the Interior that is engaged in irrigation projects and related activities, e.g., the construction of dams, reservoirs, power plants, transmission lines, canals, tunnels, and aqueducts; supplies water to arid sections of 17 western states. Major projects of the bureau include the Colorado-Big Thompson, the Missouri Basin, the Central Valley, and the Columbia River projects.

burn off. Amortization of prepaid interest and other similar prepayments. [1]

business cycle. A recurring cycle of economic activity that moves through prosperity, recession, depression, recovery, and back to prosperity.

business valuation. An appraisal of a business, usually performed to determine the present and future monetary rewards of complete or partial ownership rights in the business.

butt. A door hinge.

butt casing. A very plain casing formed by installing a piece across the top of an opening and bringing up two side pieces to butt against it from beneath.

butterfly roof. An inverted gable roof with two sides that slope downward and inward, forming an inverted ridge in the center. The two gables resemble the wings of a butterfly.

butt joint. A joint formed when two timbers or members are joined by butting, or meeting end to end.

butt log. The log in a tree that is closest to the stump.

buttress. An external structure, usually of brick, stone, or concrete, that supports a wall or building by receiving lateral pressure acting at a particular point and in a single direction.

buydown. A lump-sum payment to the lender that reduces the interest payments of the borrower. The buydown period, during which the interest rate is reduced, may range from one year to the entire term of the mortgage. The cost of the buydown is usually reflected in the price paid.

buyer's extras. Improvements not included in original plans or cost, but requested by the buyer. [1]

buyer's market. The condition that exists when market prices are relatively low and buyers have an advantage; an oversupply that causes prices to decline.

BX. Electrical cable consisting of two or more wires in a flexible metal covering.

bypass. *See* belt highway.

byte. In computer usage, the smallest identifiable unit of information in a computer; consists of a group of at least eight bits; equivalent to one alphanumeric or graphic character, or to a single control code. [16]

C

cabinet work. Any interior finish, usually in hardwoods, that involves the skills of cabinetmakers rather than carpenters; built-in fixtures; e.g., kitchen cupboards, counters.

caisson. A large, strong, watertight box or casing in which work is done below water level, usually under artificial air pressure; also used as a retaining structure in an open excavation to prevent cave-ins; used as a supporting member of a structure when sunk to a high bearing stratum and filled with concrete.

caisson foundation. A foundation system in which holes are drilled into the earth down to bearing strata and then filled with concrete.

calcareous soil. A soil containing carbonate of calcium, or limestone.

calf crop. The number of calves produced by a given number of cows, usually expressed as a percentage of calves weaned of cows bred.

California ranch architecture. A modern residential style that originated in California; characterized by a sprawling, one-story design that is easily adapted to floor plan variations.

call provision. A clause in a mortgage or deed of trust that gives the mortgagee or beneficiary the right to accelerate payment of the debt if the mortgage security is sold or transferred. [1]

camber
  1. In construction, slight, convex arching of a load-bearing beam, girder, or timber to compensate for, and thus eliminate, sagging or concavity due to superimposed weight.
  2. The slight arching of a structure, e.g., a road, the deck of a ship.

campanile. A bell tower; usually a tall tower built apart from a church.

canal
1. An artificial, open watercourse that joins rivers, lakes, or seas for inland navigation.
2. A channel used in irrigation.

candle. A measure of light intensity approximately equal to the light from a 78-inch sperm candle burning at the rate of 120 grains per hour.

candle power. The luminous intensity of a light expressed in candles.

cantilever
1. The part of a structural member that extends beyond its support and is rigid enough to support loads and resist lateral pressure.
2. Either of two structural members that project from a pier and are joined directly or by a suspended span to form the span of a cantilever bridge.

cantilever beam. A beam with one end that projects beyond the point of support and is free to move under the influence of vertical loads placed between the support and the free end.

cantilever construction. A building technique in which a portion of the structure is supported by one or more cantilever beams.

cap
1. A ceiling, or limit, on monetary charges, e.g., rent, interest, escalation income.
2. The top part of a structural member, e.g., column, door, molding; a cornice or lintel.
3. A threaded plumber's fitting used to close a pipe end.

Cape Cod house. A residential architectural style, popular from the 1920s to the 1950s, that is a development of the one-story cottage; characterized by the main cornice line at the second-story level, a sloping roof, and dormer windows.

capital
1. Accumulated wealth; a sum of money available for investment.

2. In building construction, the uppermost part of a column which is usually ornamented.

capital assets
1. Any asset of a permanent nature used to produce income; e.g., land, buildings, machinery, equipment. [2]
2. In accounting, the liquid or readily convertible assets of a corporation as of a certain date; e.g., cash, accounts receivable, merchandise inventories. *See also* current assets.

capital expenditure. Investments of cash or the creation of liability to acquire an asset, e.g., land, buildings, building additions, site improvements, machinery, equipment; as distinguished from cash outflows for expense items that are normally considered part of the current period's operations.

capital expense. The amount required to satisfy the interest on and amortization of an investment. *Also called* capital charge.

capital gain. The amount by which the net proceeds from the resale of an asset exceed the adjusted cost, or book value, of the item; used primarily in income tax computations; may be short or long term. *See also* capital loss.

capital grant. A cash contribution to the cost of a project, usually supplied by government.

capital improvement plan. A schedule of capital improvement projects that the local government intends to complete over a specified period of time; includes project descriptions, a schedule of priorities, cost estimates, and methods of finance. [9]

capitalism. An economic system based on the principles of private property ownership and personal rights. [2]

capitalization. The conversion of income into value. *See also* direct capitalization; yield capitalization.

capitalization in perpetuity. Capitalization at a rate that provides for a return *on* the investment, but no return *of* the investment.

capitalization of ground rental. A procedure used to estimate the value of a leased fee estate.

capitalization rate (*R*). Any rate used to capitalize income.

capital loss. The amount by which the net proceeds from the resale of an asset fall short of the adjusted cost, or book value, of the item; used primarily in income tax computations; may be short or long term. *See also* capital gain.

capital market. The interaction of buyers and sellers trading long- or intermediate-term money instruments.

capital recovery. The return of equity in an investment; as distinguished from a return on equity.

capital recovery method. One of several alternative methods that provide for the recovery of capital; each method can be expressed in the form of a sinking fund. *Also called* capital recapture method.

capital recovery payments. Annual amounts to cover the anticipated decline from initial investment to reversion. *Also called* capital recapture payments.

capital recovery period. The period over which invested sums are returned to the investor.

capital recovery rate. The return of invested capital, expressed as an annual rate; often applied in a physical sense to wasting assets having a finite economic life. Used interchangeably with amortization rate to express investors' desire to recover their equity investment over a specified time period. *Also called* capital recapture rate.

capital requirements. The total monetary investment needed to establish and operate an enterprise; usually the appraised investment in plant facilities and normal working capital; may or may not include the appraised cost of business rights, e.g., patents, contracts.

capital stock. The permanently invested capital of a corporation contributed by the owners at the time the corporation is organized or afterwards. Capital stock is divided into shares, with each share representing a proportionate ownership in the corporation; shares are issued as stock certificates that usually can be transferred only by endorsement.

capture rate. The estimated percentage of the total potential market for a type of property, e.g., office space, retail sales, single-family homes, that is currently absorbed by existing facilities or is forecast to be absorbed by proposed facilities.

car float bridge. A landing place where railroad cars are transferred between shore tracks and tracks on floats; a movable section of a lighterage pier that accommodates itself to the change in water elevation and is used for the same purpose.

carport. A roofed auto shelter without walls.

carrying capacity. The maximum number of animals that can be grazed without damaging the forage production, quality, or soil of the range; expressed in AUs, AUMs, or CYLs.

carrying charges. Expenses incurred while holding idle property or property under construction; e.g., taxes, insurance premiums, standby water and sewer rents, security or protective service.

case. The framework of a structure; the external facing of a building that is made of material superior to the backing.

casement window. A type of window with a sash and side hinges.

cash. Money, especially ready money; money on deposit or due on demand.

cash assets. Cash on hand and working funds immediately available to satisfy the current needs of a business.

cash basis. A method of accounting in which income and expenses are recognized at the actual time they are received or paid out. For income tax purposes, taxpayers use either a cash basis or an accrual basis and recognize and report their income accordingly. *See also* accrual basis. [3]

cash crop. Farm crops grown for direct sale, as distinguished from those fed to farm animals.

cash equivalency analysis. The procedure in which the sale prices of comparable properties sold with atypical financing terms are adjusted to reflect typical market terms.

cash equivalent. A price expressed in terms of cash, as distinguished from a price expressed totally or partly in terms of the face amounts of notes or other securities that cannot be sold at their face amounts.

cash flow. The periodic income attributable to interests in real property. *See also* after-tax cash flow (*ATCF*); pre-tax cash flow (*PTCF*).

cash on cash. The ratio of annual equity income to the equity investment. *Also called* equity dividend rate.

cash rent
1. The amount of rent paid in money, not including services rendered in lieu of cash.
2. A fixed, negotiated money rent for a farm, usually in dollars per acre per year.

casing. A piece of trim material used around the sides and top of doors, windows, and other wall openings. *See also* back band casing; butt casing.

casualty loss appraisal. An appraisal to estimate the decrease in property value due to fire, storm, or some other casualty; usually performed for income tax or insurance claim purposes.

catena. A group of soils within one zonal region that developed from similar parent material but differ in solum characteristics due to differences in relief or drainage. *See also* solum.

cattle guard. An opening in a fence that is closed, not by a gate, but by a ground grill that cattle will not cross.

cattle squeeze. A mechanism in a corral chute that closes on the animal and immobilizes it so that various treatments, e.g., branding, dehorning, can be performed.

catwalk. In construction, a narrow footing on a bridge or along a girder of a large building; a walkway strung from one girder to another or placed over uncovered attic joists.

caulking. A flexible material, e.g., sealant, putty, glazing compound, used to fill gaps at fixed joints in a building to reduce the passage of air and moisture; to apply such material.

causeway. A raised roadway on fill material or a bridge-like structure over a low area, e.g., a swamp, a lake, a bay.

caveat. A formal notice, filed by an interested party with a court or officer, requesting that a proceeding be postponed until he or she is heard.

caveat emptor. Let the buyer beware; a maxim of the common law stating that the buyer purchases at his or her own risk. [7]

cavity wall. A wall, usually of masonry, that consists of two vertical components with air space between.

CBD. *See* central business district.

CCIM. Certified Commercial Investment Member. *See also* REALTORS NATIONAL MARKETING INSTITUTE® (RNMI).

CD. *See* certificate of deposit.

ceiling joists. The horizontal structural members to which the ceiling is fastened; may support a floor above.

ceiling loan. A part of a total loan that will be disbursed when special requirements are met, e.g., rent roll achievement. *See also* floor loan.

cellar
1. A storage space, usually but not necessarily below ground.
2. An underground chamber.

cellular concrete. A lightweight, insulating concrete.

cellular steel deck. A structural floor system consisting of two layers of sheet metal shaped to form cells and welded together; the cells serve as electrical raceways.

cement blocks. Blocks composed principally of cement and gravel formed into shape under pressure; typically used for walls.

census tracts. Relatively uniform areas of about 4,000 residents into which large cities and adjacent areas are divided by the U.S. Census Bureau. [17]

center line profile map. A type of right-of-way map that shows a center line elevation profile of a proposed roadway.

center to center. The measurement between the centers of two adjoining, parallel structural members. *See also* on center (O.C.).

central assessment. An assessment of property, e.g., railroads, public utilities, commercial and industrial property, held under a single ownership, but located in more than one assessment district.

central business district (CBD). The core, or downtown area, of a city where the major retail, financial, governmental, professional, recreational, and service activities of the community are concentrated.

central city. The primary city in a standard metropolitan area, from which the name of the area is usually taken. *See also* Metropolitan Statistical Area (MSA); Standard Metropolitan Statistical Area (SMSA).

central limit theorem. In statistics, a principle that identifies the tendency of the arithmetic mean to be normally distributed in a given number of size increases, almost without regard to the shape of the distribution of the original population.

central place theory. The theory that cities arise in response to the service needs of surrounding rural areas and that the location of urban settlements can be understood in terms of the functions they perform for these outlying areas. [6]

central tendency. In statistics, the tendency of samples to cluster around a central point, or representative value, in a frequency distribution. The measures of central tendency are the mean, the median, and the mode. [10]

certificate. An instrument that formally assures the existence of a fact or set of facts; used as evidence of a right or obligation.

certificate of beneficial interest. A document that identifies an owner's interest in the assets and earnings of a business enterprise; may be issued to stockholders when the stock of a corporation is surrendered to a trustee or trustees.

certificate of deposit (CD). A financial instrument that represents a time deposit with a banking organization.

certificate of limited partnership. A summary of the major provisions of a limited partnership agreement, which is filed in the county recorder's office in the county where the partnership operates its business. [1]

certificate of occupancy (C of O). Written authorization that allows a structure to be inhabited. [1]

certificate of reasonable value. A document required for a federally insured or guaranteed loan that states the value on which the loan amount may be granted. [1]

certificate of title. A document, usually given to a home buyer with the deed, that states an opinion that the title to the property is clear; usually prepared by an attorney or another qualified person who has examined the abstract of title for the property.

certiorari
1. A writ from a superior to an inferior court officer, board, or tribunal directing that a certified record of its proceedings in a designated case be reviewed.
2. A remedy calling for judicial review of an alleged illegal or erroneous tax assessment of real estate.

cesspool. An underground catch basin for household sewage or other liquid waste. *See also* septic tank.

chain of title. A historical record of all conveyances and encumbrances affecting a property title from the time the original patent was granted. *See also* abstract of title. [1]

chain store. One of a number of retail stores or shops under the same ownership and management, selling uniform merchandise and following a uniform policy.

chamfer. To bevel or round off a right-angle corner.

change. The result of the relationship between cause and effect that affects real property value.

change order. A change in the original plan of construction due to the upgrading of material or the inclusion of additions. [1]

channel
1. The bed of a stream of water; the deeper part of a river, harbor, strait, or bay where the main current flows; a ship's passageway.
2. A long gutter, groove, or furrow.
3. A closed course or conduit through which something flows or passes, e.g., a duct.

channelization. The direction of traffic flow into definite paths, accomplished with traffic markings, islands, or other means.

characteristic. In decimal arithmetic, the number(s) to the left of the decimal point in a logarithm; as distinguished from the mantissa, the numbers to the right of the decimal point. *See also* mantissa.

chattel. In law, any property other than a freehold or fee estate in land; treated as personal property, although divisible into chattels real and chattels personal.

chattel mortgage. A lien on chattels.

chattels personal. Tangible, movable property items; e.g., furniture, refrigerators.

chattels real. An intangible personal property right; historically, personal property has involved ownership rights in real estate for a fixed number of years; e.g., leasehold estates, interests in real estate other than the freehold or fee estate.

check rail. The horizontal members, or rails, that form the top of the lower sash and the bottom of the upper sash in a double-hung window; two rails in combination.

check row. A type of planting in which the plants are grown at the intersections of lines on a field resembling a checkerboard; frequently used for corn, melons, and tomatoes.

check valve. A plumbing valve that closes automatically, preventing the backflow of water or other liquids.

chernozem. A zonal group of soils with a deep, nearly black surface horizon, rich in organic matter, that grades into lighter-colored soils and finally into a layer of lime accumulation; developed under tall and mixed grasses in a temperate to cool, subhumid climate.

Chicago school. A school of architecture popular from 1875 to 1900 and noted for the development of the multistory commercial building with elevators, made possible by the new technique of riveted steel framing. The building exteriors were characterized by large areas of glass in indented bands of windows, terra-cotta facing, and elaborate projecting cornices. Among the leading exponents of the Chicago school were William Le Baron Jenney, Louis Sullivan, Daniel H. Burnham, and John Wellborn Root; the architects designed not only the new skyscrapers but also residences, factories, railroad stations, theaters, museums, and churches.

chimney. A stack of brick or other masonry that extends above the surface of the roof and carries the smoke outside. [8]

chimney back. The rear wall of a furnace or fireplace.

chimney cap. Ornamental stone or concrete edging at the top of the chimney stack that protects the masonry from the elements and improves the draft in the chimney. [8]

chimney flashing. A strip of material, usually metal, placed where the chimney meets the roof to make the joint watertight; used wherever the slope is interrupted by a vertical structure. [8]

chimney pot. A fire clay or terra-cotta pipe projecting from the top of the chimney stack; is decorative and increases the draft of the chimney. [8]

C horizon. Soil layer of relatively unweathered material that lies below the B horizon; parent material; the substratum. *See also* A horizon; B horizon; D horizon.

cinder block. A concrete block made using cinders as the coarse aggregate to achieve a lighter weight.

cinder fill. In construction, a layer of cinder placed between the ground and the basement floor or between the ground and foundation walls to enhance water drainage. [8]

circlehead window. A small, half-oval window often used as decoration over a door; resembles an open fan, with the ribs represented by the sash bars.

circuit breaker
1. In property taxation, a method of providing property tax relief for the elderly and poor by rebating, through income tax credits or cash payments, that portion of the taxpayer's payment that exceeds a certain percentage of his or her income; usually limited to residential property taxes paid by homeowners or renters.
2. A permanent, electrical safety device that substitutes for a fuse by automatically turning off an electric circuit that is overloaded.

circulating capital. *See* current assets.

circulation pattern. The traffic pattern established in moving from one place to another on foot or by car; e.g., from home to business, to or past a specific location.

circulation system. A network of transportation modes that provides for the safe, efficient, and convenient movement of people and goods within a city or region.

circumferential highway. *See* belt highway.

cistern. An artificial reservoir or tank, often underground, that stores rainwater.

city. In the United States, a municipal corporation that occupies a definite area and is subject to the laws of the state in which it is located. In Canada, a municipality of the highest class.

city planning. A discipline concerned with the orderly development, growth, arrangement, and change of urban environments. *Also called* urban planning. [6]

civic center. A building or place where a city's principal public buildings and cultural institutions are concentrated. [6]

civil law. The body of private law developed from Roman law and used in Louisiana and in many countries outside the English-speaking world. *See also* common law.

clapboard. An exterior wood siding with one edge thicker than the other, which is laid so the thick edge of one board overlaps the thin edge of the board below.

classified basal area. In forestry, the grouping of the total land area tallied per sample point into diameter classes to record and describe forest growing stock.

classified property tax. A method of ad valorem taxation in which the effective tax rate varies with the classification of property, e.g., residential, commercial, agricultural. Different classes may be assessed at different percentages of market value and taxed at uniform rates, or they may be assessed uniformly and taxed at different rates.

class of construction. The classification of buildings according to the fire-resistant materials from which they are constructed, e.g., structural steel, reinforced concrete, masonry, frame.

clay. Small mineral soil grains, less than 0.005 millimeter in diameter; plastic when moist, but hard when baked or fired.

clay loam. A soil that contains a moderate amount of fine material mixed with coarser soil grains.

claypan. A dense, heavy soil horizon under the upper part of the soil that interferes with water movement and root development.

clearance. A type of urban renewal project in which the predominant activities are land acquisition, demolition and removal of structures, relocation of residents and businesses, and preparation of land for redevelopment.

clearance easement. A type of avigation easement that governs structure height so that aircraft have an unobstructed view and a safety margin for descent.

clear cutting. A timber harvesting technique in which all growing stock is removed from the land.

clear headway. In construction, the vertical measurement from the floor to the lowest overhead framing member.

clear lumber. Lumber practically devoid of defects, e.g., knots.

clear span. A portion of a structure built without internal supporting columns.

clear title. A title free of any encumbrances or defects. [2]

clerestory window. A window or series of windows placed at the top of a building that provide additional light and ventilation for the interior; usually found in churches and similar structures, but also used in modern residences.

climatic zone. A section of the country where residents experience similar climatic conditions as established by the number of heating and cooling degree days.

clock thermostat. A device designed to reduce energy consumption by regulating the demand on the heating or cooling system of a building. *See also* thermostat.

closed-end trust. A trust with a fixed number of shares that are traded on the open market like stocks and bonds, not sold and redeemed by the trust.

closing. A meeting of the parties to a real estate transaction held to execute and deliver mortgage or property title documents. [5]

closing costs. The costs of the settlement in the transfer of property ownership; e.g., recording fees, attorney fees, title insurance premiums. [2]

closing statement. A listing of the debits and credits of the buyer and seller in the final financial settlement of the real estate transaction. [2]

cloud on title. An encumbrance that may affect the fee holder's ownership and the marketability of the title.

cloverleaf. A grade-separated intersection designed to eliminate all left-turn and cross-traffic conflicts and to accommodate turning movements from four directions; loops are used for left turns and outer connections facilitate right turns, or two-way ramps are provided for turning. A full cloverleaf has two ramps for turning movements in each quadrant.

cluster sampling. In statistics, a two-stage sampling procedure in which a population is divided into several groups or clusters; some of these clusters are drawn into the sample, and then a subsample of elements is selected from each of the specified clusters.

cluster zoning. A type of residential zoning designed to preserve open space by permitting houses to be built in groups or clusters on less land than would normally be permitted under the zoning ordinance. [9]

CMSA. *See* Consolidated Metropolitan Statistical Area.

coarse-textured soil. A soil that contains a preponderance of grains larger than 0.25 millimeter; e.g., sandy loams, gravelly sandy loams, loamy sands.

Coastal Zone Management Act. A nationwide land planning measure that provides for federal control over virtually any large-scale development along the shores of 30 coastal and Great Lakes states. [9]

coat. A single layer of paint, plaster, or other material.

COBOL. Common business-oriented language; a computer programming language used extensively in business and science. [16]

coefficient
1. A dimensionless statistic, useful as a measure of change or relationship; e.g., coefficient of multiple regression, coefficient of determination.
2. A number, a letter, a group of letters, or a combination of numbers and letters that precedes another variable by which it is to be multiplied; e.g., 2 is the coefficient of X in the expression, $2X$.

coefficient of correlation (r). In statistics, a measure of the degree of relationship between variables and the way in which they change together. The correlation coefficient can range in value from -1 (perfect negative correlation) to 0 (independence) to $+1$ (perfect positive correlation).

coefficient of determination (r^2). In statistics, the proportion of the total variance in the dependent variable that is explained by the independent variable; the proportion of total variance explained by the regression; in business and economics, preferred to the term *coefficient of correlation* because it states the proportion of the variance in the dependent variable more clearly.

coefficient of dispersion
1. In statistics, the ratio of a measure of absolute dispersion to an appropriate average, usually expressed as a percentage, computed from either the quartile or the mean deviation, but usually

expressed as a ratio of the standard deviation to the mean; a measure of relative dispersion.

2. In assessment administration, the ratio of a measure of absolute dispersion to the median. *Also called* index of assessment inequality or Russell Index. *See also* coefficient of variation.

coefficient of multiple correlation (R). In statistics, the square root of the coefficient of multiple determination.

coefficient of multiple determination (R^2). In statistics, indication of the proportion of total variance in the dependent variable explained by all independent variables in the regression equation; the ratio of explained variance to total variance.

coefficient of partial determination. In statistics, indication of the increase in explained variance, relative to prior unexplained variance, caused by adding a given variable to the regression equation.

coefficient of performance. A measure of operating efficiency, expressed as a ratio of useful energy output to input. In percentage terms, indicates the portion of the fuel input that is converted to useful heating or cooling.

coefficient of skewness. In statistics, a measure expressed in standard deviation units that is used to compare distributions that differ in the unit of measurement or in average size; of limited practical use because skewness is ordinarily described not measured.

coefficient of variation. In statistics, the standard error of the estimate divided by the mean value of the dependent variable; a measure of the relative chance for error in a forecast or estimate of the dependent variable. *See also* coefficient of dispersion.

cofferdam. A temporary, watertight enclosure from which water is pumped to expose underwater land so that work can be done there; a caisson. A similar structure on the side of a ship used in making repairs below waterline.

C of O. *See* certificate of occupancy.

coignes. In architecture, stone or contrasting material used at the corner of a masonry wall, normally of alternating size and larger units than the remainder of the wall.

coinsurance. The amount of insurance an insurer requires a property owner to carry; equal to a specified percentage of the property's value.

cold storage. Refrigerated storage of perishable commodities.

colinearity. In statistics, the relationship between independent variables in a multiple regression which may affect the reliability of the net regression coefficients; affects the reliability of individual variables in a regression, but may not alter the predictive power of the total regression equation.

collar tie. *See* tie beam.

collateral. Security offered as a guarantee for the fulfillment of a financial obligation. [10]

colluvial soil. Soil material that has been transported by gravity or water; usually found at the base of a steep hill or slope.

Colonial architecture. A residential style characteristic of New England colonial homes; usually of two stories and characterized by balanced openings along the main facade, windows subdivided into small panes, shutters and dormer windows, small scale, and painstaking attention to detail.

colonnade. A group of columns at regular intervals, usually supporting an architrave.

column. A vertical structural member that supports horizontal members, e.g., beams, girders; designed to transmit a load to bearing material at its base.

column footings. Reinforced concrete footings that support load-bearing columns.

column lots. Small sections of land acquired with air rights for the placement of the columns, piers, and caissons needed in the construction of a foundation.

column steel. A vertical bar of reinforcing steel in a concrete column; an H-shaped, structural steel member used as a column.

combination door. An outer door frame with an inside removable section into which a screen panel is inserted in warm weather and a glass panel in winter.

combination sewer. A sewer that carries both sewage and surface or rainwater.

combination windows. An outer window frame with an inside removable section into which a screen is inserted in warm weather and a glass storm panel in winter.

commensurability. The measure of a rancher's ability to take care of his livestock without using public land; the property so used is commensurate property. *See also* base property.

commercial bank. An institution that offers businesses and individuals a variety of financial services; may be state or federally chartered and is subject to government regulation; managed by a board of directors who are selected by stockholders.

commercial paper. A corporation's promissory notes used to borrow short-term funds for current operations; enables organizations with excess cash to lend to those in need of money.

commercial property. Real estate used for business purposes; e.g., office buildings, stores, banks, restaurants, service outlets.

commission. An agent's compensation for the performance of his or her duties; in real estate, a percentage of the selling price of property or a percentage of rentals which is received by the salesperson. [2]

commitment. For a mortgage, a promise or statement by the lender of the terms and conditions under which the loan will be made. [15]

commitment fee. A fee paid by a borrower to a lender who agrees to make funds available at a future date; frequently expressed as a percentage of the expected loan. [5]

committee deed. A deed by a committee or commission appointed by a court to sell a property.

common area. The total area within a property that is not designed for sale or rental, but is available for common use by all owners, tenants, or their invitees; e.g., parking and its appurtenances, malls, sidewalks, landscaped areas, recreation areas, public toilets, truck and service facilities. [14]

common area charges. Income collected from owners or tenants for the operation and maintenance of common areas. [14]

common base. In construction, a single-member base, usually from four to six inches high.

common costs. Costs for items that benefit more than one portion of a project or more than one project within a development, e.g., hallways and elevators in a condominium, streets, parking areas, amenities. [5]

common law
1. The body of customs, usages, and practices developed by the Anglo-Saxons; English law as distinguished from Roman law, canon law, and other legal systems.
2. An ancient, unwritten body of law founded on customs and precedents, as distinguished from statute law.
3. A system of elementary rules and judicial principles that are continually expanded, adapting themselves to changes in trade, commerce, arts, inventions, and the needs of society.

common property. Land in general or a tract of land that is considered public property, in which all persons enjoy equal rights; property not owned by individuals or government, but by groups, tribes, or formal villages. In law, the incorporeal, heritable right of one person in the land of another, e.g., of estovers, of pasture, of piscary.

common stock. A share of ownership and usually a voting interest in a corporation.

common wall. A single wall used by two buildings or two sections of a single building. *See also* party wall.

communications software. In computer usage, programs that enable a microcomputer equipped with a modem to communicate over standard phone lines; instructs the microcomputer to perform as a terminal. [16]

community associations. Organizations formed for the ownership, maintenance, and operation of commonly owned facilities in open space communities. [13]

community facilities
1. Facilities used in common by a number of people and often owned by the general public; e.g., streets, schools, parks, playgrounds. [6]
2. Facilities owned and operated by nonprofit private agencies; e.g., churches, settlement houses, recreation and neighborhood centers. [6]

community property. Property acquired by either spouse during their marriage, excluding gifts or inheritances, which belongs to them as a unit, and not individually; the death of either person results in full ownership for the other.

community shopping center. A shopping center of 100,000 to 300,000 square feet that provides a wider range of facilities and merchandise than a neighborhood shopping center. It usually has a junior department store, a variety store or discount department store, a supermarket, and specialty stores.

comparables. A shortened term for competitive property sales, rentals, or operating expenses used for comparison in the valuation process. *Also called* comps.

comparative-unit method. A method used to derive a cost estimate in dollars per square foot or cubic foot of area, based on known costs of similar structures adjusted for time and physical differences.

comparison goods. Merchandise offered by department, apparel, furniture, and other stores in sufficient variety to permit a wide range of choice between the merchandise offered by each store. [17]

comparison method. *See* sales comparison approach.

compatibility. The concept that a building is in harmony with its use and environment.

compensable damages. Damages for which a condemnor is legally required to compensate the owner or tenant of the property that is being wholly or partially condemned. In most jurisdictions, physical invasion of the property by a condemning authority or the taking of some property right must occur before damages are considered compensable. *See also* consequential damages; inverse condemnation.

compensable interest. A property right for which the owner would receive just compensation if it were acquired for public purposes.

compensation. *See* just compensation.

competition. The active demand for real estate in short supply by two or more market participants.

compiler. In computer usage, a language translator that converts programs, commands, and statements expressed in high-level, English-like languages into machine language for execution. [16]

completed contract method. In accounting, a method of revenue recognition used in long-term construction contracts when the date of completion cannot be estimated; revenue and related costs are recognized when the project is completed. [5]

component. Construction elements, e.g., complete exterior walls, framing, floor and roof construction, interior finish, building service systems, that are considered individually.

component construction. *See* prefabrication.

component depreciation. The allocation of the cost of a building to its various structural components and the computation of depreciation for each component based on its separate useful life. [1]

component panel. A wall unit ready for installation, consisting of a panel with finished inner and outer surfaces, or skins, framing, insulation, etc.; either solid or with door and window framing.

composition siding. A manufactured exterior wall covering often finished to resemble brick.

compound interest. The continuous and systematic additions to a principal sum over a series of successive time periods.

compound slope. A slope made up of two or more slopes with different gradients.

comprehensive plan. An official document adopted by a local government which sets forth its general policies regarding the long-term, physical development of a city or other area. [6]

computer-assisted mass appraisal program. The application of computer technology and statistical techniques to the solution of appraisal problems; used in assessment administration to derive value indications in the cost and sales comparison approaches and to perform other functions, e.g., assessment ratio analysis.

computer program. *See* software.

concealed heating. *See* radiant heating.

concentrates. In agriculture, milled and blended high-protein feed used to supplement farm-grown forage.

concentric zone theory. A theory of urban growth, developed by Ernest W. Burgess in the 1920s, that holds that predominant land uses tend to be arranged in a series of concentric, circular zones around a city's central business district. [6]

concession
1. A franchise for the right to conduct a business, granted by a governmental body or other authority.
2. The floor space used to conduct a business on the property of another; may be a right under a lease.

concrete. A hard, stone-like material formed by mixing sand, an aggregate, e.g., crushed stone, gravel, and cement with water and allowing the mixture to harden. *See also* poststressed concrete; prestressed concrete.

concrete block. Concrete compressed into a block, hardened, and used as a masonry unit.

concrete construction. *See* architectural concrete construction; reinforced concrete construction.

concretion. Local concentrations of certain chemical compounds, e.g., calcium carbonate, compounds of iron, that form hard grains or nodules of mixed composition in various sizes, shapes, and colors.

condemnation. The act or process of enforcing the right of eminent domain.

condemnee. The owner of the property right taken in eminent domain.

condemnor. The taking agency, e.g., federal, state, county, or municipal government, other public authority or utility, vested with the right of eminent domain.

conditional probability. The probability of one event, given the occurrence of another.

conditional sale. *See* contract sale.

condominium
1. A form of fee ownership of separate units or portions of multiunit buildings that provides for formal filing and recording of a divided interest in real property, where the division is vertical as well as horizontal; fee ownership of units in a multiunit property with joint ownership of common areas.

2. A multiunit structure or property in which persons hold fee simple title to individual units and an undivided interest in common areas. [5]

condominium conversion. Conversion of rental properties, e.g., residential, commercial, office, or industrial buildings, into condominium ownership.

conduction. Transmission through a conductor; in heating, the transfer of heat from one object to another, as distinguished from convection or radiation.

conductor
1. A substance or body capable of transmitting heat, electricity, etc.
2. A wire or cable through which electricity flows.
3. A rod used to carry lightning to the ground; a lightning rod.
4. A pipe that carries rainwater from the roof gutter to the drain pipe; a downspout.

conduit
1. An artificial or natural channel for the conveyance of water or other fluid; e.g., pipe, canal, aqueduct, flume.
2. A pipe or tube used to convey and protect electric wires or cables.
3. The conveyance of income from one entity to another so that the final recipient incurs tax liability.

conduit system. An electrical wiring system with conductors encased in metal tubing.

confidence interval. In statistics, the specification of a zone, based on a sample mean and its standard error, within which one may be confident the true population mean lies.

conformity. The concept that the form, manner, and character of structures are in harmony with one another.

conifer. Trees or shrubs that bear cones. As range vegetation, includes all rangeland dominated by coniferous timber with supporting grasses, forbs, or browse.

connection. A part that fastens, joins, links, or unites; e.g., bolted connections that unite structural steel columns, girders, and trusses in a building.

consequential damages. A damage to property caused by taking or construction on other lands; compensability varies from state to state. *See also* inverse condemnation.

conservation
1. As applied to real estate, the protection of neighborhoods and structures from blight or other influences that might affect desirability or value adversely.
2. As applied to natural resources, the care and preservation of limited resources to prolong their use and effectiveness.

conservation easement. A restriction that limits the future use of a property to preservation, conservation, or wildlife habitat. [6]

consideration
1. The price or subject matter that initiates a contract; may involve money, commodity exchange, or a transfer of personal effort.
2. In appraising, the actual price for which property is transferred.

consistent use. The concept that land cannot be valued on the basis of one use while improvements to the land are valued on the basis of another.

Consolidated Metropolitan Statistical Area (CMSA). A large geographic area that consists of two or more Primary Metropolitan Statistical Areas (PMSAs); designated under standards set in 1980 by the Federal Committee on MSAs. *See also* Metropolitan Statistical Area (MSA); Primary Metropolitan Statistical Area (PMSA).

consolidation. The combining of two or more corporations into one, which implies the dissolution of one or more individual corporations. *See also* merger.

constant dollar change per period annuity. A type of increasing or decreasing annuity that increases or decreases by a fixed dollar amount.

constant dollars. Dollars that account for real growth only, not for inflation.

constant-payment mortgage. A mortgage that has an unvarying debt service, although the amortization and interest payments of which it is composed vary. If the debt service fully liquidates the loan at maturity, the constant-payment loan is self-liquidating. *See also* variable-payment mortgage (VPM).

constant ratio change per period annuity. A type of increasing or decreasing annuity that increases or decreases at a constant ratio, thus compounding the increases or decreases. *Also called* exponential annuity.

constrained beam. A beam that is rigidly fixed at one or both points of support.

construction cost. The cost to build, particularly an improvement, usually including direct costs of labor and material plus contractor's overhead and profit. *See also* development cost; direct costs.

construction loan. Financing arranged for the construction of real estate, which is generally short-term and repaid with the proceeds from permanent financing. Construction loans with a permanent financing commitment are designated as loans "with a takeout commitment" and those that do not have permanent financing are loans "without a takeout commitment." [5]

constructive notice. Notice assumed by the existence of public records. The law presumes that an individual has the same knowledge of all instruments properly recorded as if he or she were actually acquainted with them.

consumer good. A durable or nondurable economic good that satisfies human want.

contemporary. A type of modern architecture designed to promote a close relationship with the outdoors, to incorporate new construction methods and materials, and to create new uses for old materials. It is characterized by large windows, open planning, horizontal lines, and simple details.

contingent fees. Remuneration that is based or conditioned on future occurrences or conclusions or on the results of services to be performed.

contingent interest. Interest that may be added to a loan's fixed interest rate. Commitment calls for an additional fixed interest rate, which is a percentage of the annual gross or net project income that exceeds a base amount to be paid to the lender. [1]

continuous distribution. In statistics, a distribution in which the random variable can take on any value within the interval, rather than a restricted set of values, e.g., only integers.

continuous growth. Growth as it occurs in nature, as distinguished from periodic growth, as in finance, when interest is compounded at regular intervals; growth at compound interest with instantaneous compounding or compounding at infinitely short time intervals.

continuous windows. Windows designed for sawtooth roofs or roof monitors of industrial buildings; usually top hinged and opened mechanically.

contour furrows. Furrows plowed at right angles to the direction of the slope, at a constant level and usually at comparatively close intervals. The furrows and the ridges they produce intercept and retain runoff water, thereby facilitating erosion control, moisture distribution, penetration, and retention.

contour leveling. Land leveling in an area with little change in elevation, resulting in terraced land.

contour line. An outline of a figure, body, or mass; lines representing an outline such as the edge of a lake; e.g., on a topographic map or chart, a line connecting the points on a land surface that have the same elevation.

contour map. A map that shows the configuration of a surface with contour lines that represent regular intervals of elevation.

contract. An agreement between two or more persons that represents their consideration to do or not to do a particular thing; where real property is concerned, a dated, written, signed statement between two or more competent parties who agree to perform or not to perform a legal act, for legal consideration, within a specified time.

contractor's overhead. The general costs, other than the direct costs of material and labor, which are assumed by a contractor on any construction work. *See also* contractor's profit.

contractor's profit. The amount by which the price received by a contractor for work performed exceeds the total direct costs of materials and labor, plus overhead. *See also* contractor's overhead.

contract rent. The actual rental income specified in a lease.

contract sale. A sale in which the title to the property or goods remains with the seller until the buyer has fulfilled the terms of the contract, which usually call for payment in full. *See also* land contract.

contribution. The concept that the value of a particular component is measured in terms of its contribution to the value of the whole property, or as the amount that its absence would detract from the value of the whole.

controlled-access highway. A highway specially designed for through traffic; owners or occupants of abutting land may have 1) no easement rights over, from, or to the highway, or 2) only controlled easement rights of access, light, air, or view.

control program for microcomputers. *See* CP/M.

convection. Motion within a fluid or gas that results in a difference in density and gravity. In heat transmission, this includes both natural motion and forced circulation.

convector. A radiator designed to furnish a maximum amount of heat by convection; equipped with many fins or plates closely fitted on pipes that carry hot water or steam and heat the circulating air.

convenience goods. Commodities purchased frequently and without extensive comparison of style, price, or quality.

convenience shopping center. A planned development in which most retailers sell daily necessities. [17]

conventional home. A home that is constructed totally on site, as distinguished from a factory-built or mobile home. [2]

conventional loan. A mortgage that is neither insured nor guaranteed by an agency of the federal government, although it may be privately insured.

conversion factor. In forestry, a factor that is multiplied by the tree count or volume for a given size class to yield the number of trees or volume per acre for that size class.

conversion period. The interval of time used in the computation of compound interest.

convertible debentures. Debentures that can be converted into stock in the issuing corporation, either directly or through the use of warrants or options attached to the debentures. [11]

convertible mortgage. A mortgage in which the lender may choose to increase its equity interest in the real estate in lieu of cash amortization payments by the borrower. Thus, the mortgage interests of the lender may be converted into equity ownership over the life of the mortgage. [3]

conveyance. A written instrument that passes an interest in real property from one person to another; e.g., a deed, mortgage, lease, but not a will.

conveyor belt. A belt used to move items continually in production or to convey materials from their source to a place of transport or usage.

cooling tower. A tower designed to cool water by evaporation.

coop. Housing for chickens or other fowl.

cooperative apartment. An apartment in a building owned by a corporation or trust, in which each owner purchases stock representing the value of a single apartment unit and receives a proprietary lease as evidence of title.

cooperative conversion. Conversion of rental properties, e.g., apartments, into cooperative ownership.

cooperative interest. The ownership interest of the shares attributable to the cooperative unit, exclusive of the pro rata share of the blanket mortgage(s).

cooperative ownership. A form of ownership in which each owner of stock in a cooperative apartment building or housing corporation pays a proportionate share of operating expenses and debt service on the underlying mortgage, which is paid by the corporation. This proportionate share is based on the proportion of the total stock owned. *See also* cooperative apartment.

coordinates. In graphic analysis, any of a number of magnitudes that determine position; e.g., points, planes, lines.

coping. The covering course of a wall or roof, usually sloping on its upper surface to permit water runoff.

corbel. A beam or bracket that projects from a wall and supports another object or structural part of the building; may be decorative rather than structural.

cord. A cubic measure, especially of wood; the quantity of wood in such a measure; equal to a pile of cut wood eight feet long, four feet high, and four feet wide, totaling 128 cubic feet.

cordage. In forestry, a forest product measured in cords.

corn crib. A farm building designed to store harvested, unshelled, undried corn.

corner
1. The point or place where two converging lines or planes meet; e.g., where two streets intersect.
2. In surveying, a point marked by a monument.

corner influence. The effect on value produced by a property's location at or near the intersection of two streets; the increment of value resulting from this location or proximity.

corner lot. A lot abutting two intersecting streets.

cornice
1. A horizontal projection, usually molded, that finishes or crowns an interior or exterior wall.
2. The enclosure at the roof eaves or at the rake of a roof, crown mold, fascia, soffit, or frieze.

corn suitability rating. A system of estimating a soil's capacity to produce primary crops that is used mostly in the Midwest. Various types of soil on a property are rated on the basis of their potential for crop production; these ratings are converted into a single index, and this index is used to compare or rate farms.

corporation. In law, an organization that acts as a single legal entity in performing certain activities, usually business for profit; also includes charitable, educational, and religious organizations.

corporeal. Pertaining to a visible and tangible right or group of rights.

corporeal property. Tangible property.

corral. A small enclosure for handling livestock in close quarters.

correction lines. In the government survey system, east and west lines inserted at intervals to take care of convergence caused by the shape of the earth. *See also* standard parallels.

correlation. In statistics, an estimation of the degree, or closeness, with which two or more variables are associated.

correlation analysis. A statistical technique that relates a dependent variable to one or more independent variables to determine the extent and direction of any change in the dependent variable associated with change in the independent variable(s). Simple correlation involves one independent variable; multiple correlation involves more than one independent variable.

correlation coefficient. *See* coefficient of correlation (*r*).

correlation matrix. A table of numbers used to display the correlation coefficients for each pair of variables when three or more variables are thought to be correlated.

correspondent. *See* mortgage correspondent.

corridor
1. A passageway or hall that connects parts of a building.
2. A strip of land between two destinations where traffic, topography, environment, land uses, and other characteristics are evaluated for transportation purposes.

corrugated siding. Siding made of sheet metal or asbestos cement composition board used on industrial facilities and other inexpensive buildings. Corrugation increases the structural strength of the material.

corrugated wall tie. A piece of thin sheet metal about six inches long and one inch wide that is folded repeatedly and laid in the mortar courses between the bricks to bind a wall where a brick bond cannot be used.

cost. *See* construction cost; development cost; direct costs; indirect costs.

cost approach. A set of procedures in which an appraiser derives a value indication by estimating the current cost to reproduce or replace the existing structure, deducting for all accrued depreciation in the property, and adding the estimated land value.

cost/benefit ratio. The relationship between the benefits generated by an improvement and the cost of that improvement; must exceed 1:00 for the improvement to be considered desirable. *Also called* benefit/cost ratio.

cost/benefit study. Analysis of all the benefits that a proposed investment will create, including nonpecuniary benefits, weighted against the cost of creating the improvement; generally used by public agencies in making decisions pertaining to the construction of capital improvements.

cost effectiveness. The comparison of alternative courses of action in terms of their dollar costs and their relative effectiveness in achieving a particular goal.

cost estimating
1. In appraising, the estimation of the reproduction or replacement cost of an improvement by one or more methods. *See also* comparative-unit method; quantity survey method; unit-in-place method.
2. In construction, the cost to build a structure based on the costs of all materials and labor to be employed and other essential expenses incurred in the process.

cost index. A multiplier used to translate a known historical cost into a current cost estimate.

cost of remodeling. Expenditures made or required for alterations to change the plan, form, or style of a structure or its potential for use.

cost of repairs. Expenditures made or required to mend or restore deterioration caused by decay, wear and tear, or partial destruction.

cost of replacement. *See* replacement cost.

cost of reproduction. *See* reproduction cost.

cost-plus contract. A contract in which the contractor's profit is a fixed percentage of the actual direct costs of labor and materials or a flat amount above these costs.

cost to cure. The cost to restore an item of deferred maintenance to new or reasonably new condition.

co-tenancy. A tenancy in common; a joint ownership or common unity of possession.

coterminous. Having the same boundaries.

cottage. A small, single-family house; a small resort, or summer, house. [6]

counseling. *See* real estate counseling.

count plots. In forestry, sampling points at which tallied trees are counted by species to determine the average basal or stem area per unit of area.

county. The largest division of local government in all states except Louisiana and Alaska, where the comparable units are parish and borough, respectively.

county highway. A road under the jurisdiction of a county; in many states, includes all rural public roads outside the state highway system.

course
1. A continuous, horizontal layer of bricks or masonry; one of a series of layers of material in construction.
2. The natural direction or path of a stream; a natural channel for water.

court
1. An uncovered area bounded wholly or in part by buildings or walls.
2. An open space; e.g., a short street.
3. In law, the place where justice is administered; the persons duly assembled under the authority of law to administer justice; a tribunal established for the administration of justice; a session of a judicial assembly.

court award. Any decision resulting from a contested trial or hearing before a jury, commission, judge, or other legal entity with the authority to establish compensation for a taking under the right of eminent domain.

cove. A concave molding; the edge of a ceiling that is curved or arched where it meets the side walls.

covenant. A promise between two or more parties, incorporated in a trust indenture or other formal instrument, to perform certain acts or to refrain from performing certain acts. *See also* restrictive covenant.

cover. In the restaurant business, one meal sold to one person; a unit of demand representing one patron dining at one mealtime.

coverage. The proportion of the net or gross land area of a site that is occupied by a building or buildings. [6]

cover crop. A crop planted principally to control wind or water erosion during the dormant season; usually plowed under, not harvested.

cow unit. *See* animal unit (AU).

cow year long (CYL). The total number of stock that can be nourished properly for a full year on a given piece of land without harming the natural adult vegetative cover divided by the number of cows in that total that can produce calves. *See also* animal unit (AU); animal unit month (AUM).

CPM®. CERTIFIED PROPERTY MANAGER®. *See also* Institute of Real Estate Management (IREM).

CP/M. In computer usage, a system for operating personal computers developed by Digital Research, Inc.; modeled after commercial mini-computer operating systems and widely used for systems with 8080 and Z80 chips.

cps. In computer usage, characters per second; the amount specified is the rate at which a printer can imprint characters on paper; e.g., a 20-cps printer can operate at about 1,200 characters per minute. [16]

CPU. Central processing unit; the intelligent component of a computer system that executes the machine-language instructions.

cradle. A bed where large trees are felled to prevent breakage; the ground surface is prepared by excavating, filling, or both.

crane. A device for lifting and moving heavy weights; e.g., overhead crane, gantry crane, one-leg gantry crane, jib crane.

craneway. Column and girder supports of steel or concrete and rails on which a crane travels.

crawl space. An unfinished, accessible space below the first floor that is usually less than full story height.

CRB. Certified Real Estate Brokerage Manager. *See also* REALTORS NATIONAL MARKETING INSTITUTE® (RNMI).

CRE®. Counselor of Real Estate. *See also* American Society of Real Estate Counselors (ASREC).

credit report. A report on the credit standing of a prospective borrower, which is sent to a prospective lender. [1]

creosote bush. A type of range vegetation that includes areas where creosote (*covillea*) constitutes the predominant vegetation.

crop. The harvest or yield of a single field or a single variety that is gathered in one season or a part of a season.

crop acres. *See* cropland.

crop allotment. The acreage allotted to farms under the federal government's Crop Production Program. *See also* acreage controls.

crop insurance. Programs designed to compensate farmers when they cannot plant or when yields are drastically reduced due to drought, flood, natural disaster, or other conditions beyond their control.

cropland. A portion of farm acreage normally used for the production of annual crops, summer fallow, or rotation pasture, as distinguished from wood lots, marshes, etc.

crop rotation. The practice of alternating field crops, e.g., corn, wheat, with legumes, on an annual basis to maintain or improve the structure and productivity of the soil.

crop share rent. A rent set at a percentage of the crops grown by the tenant, which may vary depending on local custom and the landowner's contribution of seeds, fertilizer, harvesting costs, irrigation, water supply, etc.

cross-bridging. Cross-bracing between floor joists that provides rigidity, permits the transfer of an isolated, heavy-bearing weight to a broader supporting area, and prevents warping.

cross-connecting road. A connecting roadway between two nearby, generally parallel roads.

cross-easements. Reciprocal easements created by contract; an easement is granted in favor of the premises of one party in return for a grant by that party in favor of the premises of the other party.

cross fence. An interior fence on a farm or ranch that divides the property into fields or pastures. *See also* division fence.

crossover point. The point in the life of a real estate investment when a tax benefit is replaced by a tax burden. [3]

cross section. A transverse section at a right angle to the longitudinal axis of a piece of wood, a drawing, or another piece of work.

cross tie. A lightweight structural member that is attached to rafters to brace them on opposite roof slopes.

CRS®. Certified Residential Specialist. *See also* REALTORS NATIONAL MARKETING INSTITUTE® (RNMI).

cruise. A survey of land performed to locate standing timber and estimate its quantity by species, products, size, quality, or other characteristics; the estimate obtained in such a survey.

cubic content. The cubic volume of a building, usually measured from the outer surfaces of the exterior walls and roof to the level of the lowest floor or six inches below the finished surface of the lowest floor.

cubic foot cost. The cost of a building divided by its cubic content.

cubic foot method. *See* comparative-unit method; quantity survey method; unit-in-place method.

cubic foot per second. A flow of water equal to a stream with a width and depth of one foot, or one square foot, that flows at the rate of one foot per second.

cubic yard. A measure of volume three feet wide, three feet high, and three feet deep; 27 cubic feet.

cul-de-sac. A street with one open end and an enlarged turnaround at the closed end.

culvert. A generally small structure that provides drainage under a traveled way, parking lot, or other area.

cupola. A small structure built on top of a roof.

curable depreciation. Items of physical deterioration and functional obsolescence that are economically feasible to cure. *See also* curable functional obsolescence; curable physical deterioration.

curable functional obsolescence. An element of accrued depreciation; a curable defect caused by a flaw in the structure, material, or design.

curable physical deterioration. An element of accrued depreciation; a curable defect caused by deferred maintenance.

curb. The stone or concrete edge of a sidewalk or paved street; the raised edge of a floor or well opening.

curb line. The line that divides the roadway itself from the areas on either side of the roadway reserved for the use of pedestrians.

current assets. Assets that will, most probably, be realized in cash, sold, or consumed during the normal operation of a business.

current dollars. Dollars that account for real growth and inflation.

current liability. A liability that will be paid in the normal operation of business; a short-term debt.

current value. In accounting, synonymous with market value.

current yield. In finance, income return on investment.

cursor. In computer usage, a flashing bar, square, triangle, or other symbol that indicates where the next character on a video screen will be displayed. [16]

curtain wall. An exterior wall that encloses, but does not support, the structural frame of a building. *See also* panel wall.

curtesy. In common law, the estate to which a husband is entitled in the lands of his deceased wife, which varies with statutory provisions.

curtilage. Fenced-in ground surrounding a building.

curvilinear. Consisting of, or bounded by, curved lines; e.g., curvilinear streets.

custom-built house. A house sold before construction and built to the owner's specifications. [2]

cut
1. The output of a sawmill over a given period of time; a season's output of logs.
2. Removal of earth to change the terrain.

cutover land. An area from which all or most of the salable timber has been removed by logging.

cuts. In highway construction, excavations to establish the grade of the right-of-way through lands of higher elevation.

cyclical fluctuation. Variations around a trend in activity that recur from time to time; remains after trend and seasonal factors have been removed. [15]

cyclical movement. *See* business cycle.

CYL. *See* cow year long.

D

dam. A barrier across a watercourse that restricts or confines the flow of water; e.g., a simple earthen bank or masonry wall across a minor stream, a large engineering structure across a river for a hydroelectric plant.

damper. A hinged plate in the flue of a furnace or fireplace that functions as an air valve to regulate the draft; a device to deaden vibration.

dampproofing. To coat a surface to prevent the passage of moisture.

dark store clause. A clause in a lease that states that the tenant must do business at the site throughout the full term of the lease and cannot open a competitive store within six months prior to the expiration of the lease, which could put the subject property in a very poor re-leasing position; vital in a straight percentage lease involving a major tenant.

data. In statistics, information or facts, usually in numerical form, that can be classified by qualitative characteristics in ratios, by size in frequency distributions, or by time in time series or regression analysis.

database
1. All data collected and stored. [10]
2. In computer usage, a set of related records structured so that various programs can gain access to the information contained in them, although each record is entered only once; in communications, an information utility, e.g., The Source or CompuServe, although the utility actually contains many separate databases. [16]

data mode. In computer usage, the modem setting that permits information to be transmitted in digital form to other computers; distinguished from talk, voice, or conversation mode, which is the normal operating mode of a telephone. Typically, a user establishes contact in the talk mode, then switches to the data mode to exchange computer information. [16]

datum. In city planning, the horizontal baseline from which heights and depths are measured. The datum level adopted as a base or starting point for the grades or levels of the municipality is typically recorded in the codes that control building standards.

daylight factor. An indicator of the level of natural, interior lighting established by British town and country planning authorities based on a ratio between the daylight available inside a building and the total light available outdoors on a clear day. [6]

DBH. *See* diameter-breast-high.

DCF. *See* discounted cash flow analysis.

dead-end street. A street that is open at one end and does not have any special turning provisions at the closed end.

dead load. The permanent, inert weight of a structure itself plus any fixed loads, e.g., boilers, heavy machinery, equipment; does not include variable, live loads, e.g., furniture, merchandise, people.

dead rent. A fixed, annual sum paid for the use of a mine or quarry in addition to the payment of royalties, which vary with the yield.

dead storage. The storage of items not in use, as distinguished from live storage of items in active or daily use.

death loss. The reduction in the number of animals through loss of life from natural causes, e.g., plant poisoning, accident, disease; as distinguished from reduction by other causes, e.g., straying, theft, sales.

death rate. The number of deaths per 1,000 persons annually. *Also called* crude death rate.

debenture. An obligation that is not secured by a specific lien on a property; e.g., an unsecured corporation note.

debt. Money borrowed, usually for a specified period of time; may be secured or unsecured.

debt coverage. The ability of a property to meet its debt service out of net operating income.

debt coverage ratio (*DCR*). The ratio of net operating income to annual debt service.

debt/equity ratio. The ratio between an enterprise's loan capital and its equity capital, i.e., the ratio between the amount owed to lenders and the capital account of shareholders or partners. [3]

debt financing. Paying for all or part of a capital investment with borrowed funds; in real estate, the property itself may serve as security for the debt.

debt service. The periodic payment that covers interest on and retirement of the outstanding principal of the mortgage loan.

decentralization
1. Dispersion from a center; movement of people, industry, and business away from the city and to suburbs, rural-urban fringe areas, or smaller cities.
2. In business, the construction of plants outside large cities and at some distance from one another; dividing an existing business into smaller units or expanding a business by establishing separate business units.

deciduous. Trees that shed their leaves annually.

decision trees. In statistics or decision theory, a method of analyzing problems that involve a sequence of decisions; alternative actions are represented as branches of the tree.

deck. An open, second-story porch, usually on the roof of a ground floor porch or wing; in modern architecture, may be supported by piers or cantilevers.

decking. The surfacing material applied to the rafters or floor joists before the roof cover or floor cover material is applied.

deck roof. A nearly flat roof constructed without a fire wall.

declination. In surveying, the angle formed by the compass' magnetic needle and a geographical meridian.

declining-balance depreciation. In accounting, a method of depreciating an asset by applying a fixed percentage rate to the successive balances remaining after previously computed amounts of depreciation have been deducted.

decomposition. The breaking down of complex chemical compounds into simpler ones; the breaking down of soil minerals by solution and chemical change.

decreasing annuity. An income stream consisting of evenly spaced periodic payments that decrease in a systematic pattern. *Also called* declining annuity.

dedicated. Property in public use, e.g., a roadway, that was originally obtained from the fee owner; also describes land acquired and dedicated to burial purposes.

dedication. A voluntary gift by the owner of private property for some public use; e.g., the dedication of land for streets and schools in a development.

deed. A written, legal instrument that conveys an estate or interest in real property when it is executed and delivered. *See also* administrator's deed; bond for deed; committee deed; executor's deed; mortgage deed; quitclaim deed; trust deed; warranty deed.

deed description. A recitation of the legal boundaries of a parcel of land as contained in a deed of conveyance.

deed in fee. Sufficient conveyance of a fee simple, free of all encumbrances with the usual covenants of the vendor.

deed in lieu. A deed given by an owner, or debtor, in lieu of foreclosure by the lender, or mortgagee. *See also* foreclosure. [1]

deed of release. A legal instrument, subscribed and acknowledged by the mortgagee, by which the mortgaged property is absolved from the lien of the mortgage.

deed of trust. A legal instrument similar to a mortgage that, when duly executed and delivered, conveys or transfers property to a trustee; usually, but not necessarily, used to secure real property.

deed restriction. A limitation that passes with the land regardless of the owner; usually limits the real estate's type of use or intensity of use. *See also* restrictive covenant.

default. The failure to fulfill a contractual agreement. [5]

default ratio. The occupancy level at which the effective gross income from an income-producing property is insufficient to pay operating expenses and debt service, thus creating the risk of default; calculated by dividing effective gross income into operating expenses plus debt service. [3]

defeasance. A legal instrument that defeats the force or operation of another deed or estate.

defeasible title. A title that can be annulled or made void, but not one that is already void or in absolute nullity.

deferred annuity. An income stream that begins at some time in the future.

deferred liability. Liability from transferred real property interests that does not become an obligation to the transferee until some time after the transfer.

deferred maintenance. Curable, physical deterioration that should be corrected immediately, although work has not commenced; denotes the desirability of immediate expenditures, but does not necessarily suggest inadequate maintenance in the past.

deferred payment sale. A sale in which the proceeds are to be received in more than one installment. The Internal Revenue Code provides for several methods of reporting the gain.

deficiency. An inadequacy in a structure or one of its components.

deficiency judgment. Judgment granted in a suit initiated to recover the difference between a legally imposed indebtedness and the dollars received from a foreclosure sale of the debtor's assets.

deficit. An insufficiency of funds; e.g., a deficit in an expense fund; the amount by which the total assets of a business fall short of its total liabilities plus invested capital.

deflation. A decrease in the general price level; a period when the purchasing power of money is rising.

degree day. A unit of fuel consumption equal to the number of degrees deviation from 65° F, usually totaled over a number of days, e.g., annually or for a heating season; used to project annual heating or cooling costs.

degrees of freedom. In statistics, the difference between the size of a sample and the number of variables used in arriving at an unbiased estimate or equation; as this number decreases, the related variance and standard deviation increase.

delta (Δ). In yield and change formulas, the variable that represents the expected percentage change in value over the projection period; usually relative change in value or income of overall property or components, e.g., land, building, mortgage, equity, leased fee estate, leasehold estate.

demand
1. The desire and ability to purchase or lease goods and services.
2. In real estate, the amount of real property that is desired at a specific price or rent at a specified time.

demand deposits. Any deposit that is payable on demand and may be withdrawn by check, draft, negotiable order of withdrawal (from a NOW account), or another similar instrument for payment to third parties. Money market accounts are excluded because they are considered acquisitions of shares.

demand unit. An economic unit that is or may be eligible to express demand for a product.

demise. A conveyance in fee for life or for a number of years; strictly, denotes only a posthumous grant.

demography. The study of population and population change. [6]

density. The number of units present per unit of area; e.g., dwellings per acre or persons per square mile. *See also* forage density; height density; traffic density; use density; vegetative density. [2]

density zoning. A system of land use control in which residential occupancy is limited by the number of families per unit of land area, e.g., an acre, rather than the number of families per building.

Department of Housing and Urban Development (HUD). The department of the federal government responsible for major housing and urban development programs, e.g., urban renewal, low-rent public housing, mortgage insurance, metropolitan planning; the twelfth department in the President's Cabinet, created in 1965 to replace the Housing and Home Finance Agency.

Department of Justice. A major administrative unit of the federal government, headed by the attorney general, that has supervisory powers over federal prosecuting agencies and provides representation in court cases involving the federal government.

Department of the Interior. A major administrative unit of the federal government that controls many subsidiary agencies including the U.S. Fish and Wildlife Service, the Bureau of Mines, the Reclamation Bureau, and the Bonneville Power Administration.

department store-type merchandise. General merchandise, apparel, furniture, and other merchandise so defined by the Department of Commerce's *Census of Retail Trade. Also called* GAFO or DSTM. [17]

depletion. A reduction in the value of an asset due to the removal of exhaustible material assets or resources; e.g., the removal of trees from a forest, the taking of minerals from a mine, the pumping of oil from a well.

depletion rate. The periodic rate or percentage at which a quantity, usually a natural resource, is exhausted; calculated as the amount of commercially recoverable reserves divided by the volume of production contemplated; may be expressed in monetary units.

depreciation
1. In appraising, a loss in property value from any cause; in yield and change formulas, anticipated property loss; designated by the symbol *dep*.
2. In regard to improvements, deterioration and obsolescence.
3. In accounting, an allowance made against the loss in value of an asset for a defined purpose and computed using a specified method.

depreciation allowance. In accounting, the amount charged against earnings to write off the cost of an asset; used more properly in accounting for income tax purposes than in appraising.

depreciation recapture. The difference between capital gain and ordinary gain when capital gain treatment is disallowed and the gain is taxed at ordinary rates.

depreciation reserve. In accounting, the account on a business' books where accruals for depreciation are accumulated.

depression. A severe economic crisis in which business activity is down over a long period, purchasing power is declining, and unemployment is high.

depth curve. A graph of depth factors that shows the estimated percentage relationships between the front foot values of lots of various depths and the front foot value of a lot of standard depth.

depth factor. A factor, or percentage, that represents the relative value of a lot of a given depth as compared to the value of a lot of standard depth. *See also* depth table.

depth influence. The effect of depth on the value of a lot or parcel with a given frontage; the increase or decrease in value arising from a depth that is greater or less than the standard.

depth table. A table of depth factors showing the estimated percentage relationship between the front foot value of a lot of a given depth and the front foot value of a lot of standard depth. *See also* depth factor.

descent. A transfer of property when the owner dies without leaving a will; transfer by inheritance.

descriptive statistics. A branch of statistics concerned only with characterizing, or describing, a set of numbers; the measures used to characterize a set of data, e.g., average, maximum, coefficient of dispersion.

desert shrub. A type of range vegetation that includes areas where desert shrubs of unspecified type dominate but pure types of each are too limited to characterize a separate type; includes blackbush (*coleogyne*), coffee berry (*simmondsia*), cat's claw (*acacia* and *mimosa*), gray molly (*kochia*), hopsage (*grayia*), horse brush (*tetradymia*), and little rabbit brush (*crysothamnus stenophyllus*).

desert soil. A zonal group of soils with a light-colored surface soil usually covering calcareous material and possibly hardpan; nurtures extremely scant shrub vegetation in dry, moderate climates.

design. An architectural drawing or draft of the plan, elevation, and sections of a structure.

destination resort. A year-round vacation facility that caters to visitors who usually arrive by air from a wide geographical area.

deterioration. Impairment of condition; a cause of depreciation that reflects the loss in value due to wear and tear, disintegration, use in service, and the action of the elements. *See also* curable physical deterioration; depreciation; incurable physical deterioration.

developer's profit. *See* entrepreneurial profit.

development cost. The cost to create a property and bring it to an efficient operating state, as distinguished from the cost to construct the improvements.

development fund. A syndication formed for the sole purpose of developing real estate projects. [1]

development procedure. A procedure for valuing undeveloped acreage that involves discounting the cost of development and the probable proceeds from the sale of developed sites.

development right. The right to build on or beneath a property, subject to local zoning, building codes, etc. *See also* transferable development right (TDR).

deviation. In statistics, the difference between one number in a set of numbers and the mean of the set. *See also* average deviation; coefficient of dispersion; standard deviation.

devise. A gift or transfer of real property by the owner's last will and testament; an estate so transferred.

D horizon. Calcareous material beneath the C horizon that shows some oxidation. *See also* A horizon; B horizon; C horizon.

diagram rules. Full-sized circles of all diameters drawn to represent the top ends of logs. On these cross sections, the boards that could be sawed from each log are drawn, leaving between each board a space equal to the width of the saw kerf.

diameter-breast-high (DBH). The diameter of a tree at breast height, 4½ feet above the average ground level. The abbreviations, o.b. and i.b., indicate whether the diameter is measured outside or inside the bark. *See also* breast-height.

differential assessments. Assessments in a system of law that requires that different classes of property be assessed with different assessment ratios; usually used where the classes are easily divisible, e.g., classified property tax systems, use value farmland assessment systems. A similar effect is achieved by partial homestead exemptions and temporary exemptions to encourage rehabilitation.

dike. An embankment that restrains the waters of a sea or river; a levee; a causeway.

diluvion. The gradual washing away of soil along the banks of streams. *See also* alluvion.

dimension lumber. Lumber as it comes from the saw; all yard lumber, except timbers, strip, and board, of two to five inches in depth, and of any width.

dimension shingles. Shingles cut to a uniform size.

diminishing assets. Assets that are periodically reduced by exhaustion, lapse of time, etc., so that their value must also be reduced; include mineral deposits, copyrights, franchises for limited terms, and similar wasting properties in which value loss cannot be arrested by expenditures, e.g., maintenance of tangible fixed property.

diminishing returns. *See* increasing and decreasing returns.

diminishing utility. The concept that the consumption of each succeeding unit of an economic good yields less satisfaction than the preceding unit. Thus, total utility increases at a decreasing rate.

direct capitalization. The capitalization method used to convert an estimate of a single year's income expectancy or an annual average of several years' income expectancies into an indication of value in one step, either by dividing the income estimate by an appropriate rate or by multiplying the income estimate by an appropriate factor.

direct compensation. *See* just compensation.

direct costs. Expenditures for the labor and materials necessary to construct a new improvement, including contractor's overhead and profit. *Also called* hard costs. *See also* indirect costs.

direct labor. Labor costs that are directly connected with a specific product or project, as distinguished from indirect labor, e.g., overhead, management.

direct reduction mortgage. A loan that is repaid in periodic, usually equal, installments that include a repayment of part of the principal and interest due on the unpaid balance; an amortizing loan.

direct sales comparison approach. *See* sales comparison approach.

direct steam system. A heating system in which steam or vapor is delivered from the boiler to room radiators through piping; e.g., a one-pipe gravity system for smaller installations, a two-pipe system for larger installations.

dirt tank. A small reservoir with an earth-filled dam that collects natural runoff to provide water for livestock.

discount
1. Money paid at the beginning of a time period for the use of capital during that period; commonly deducted from the principal when the funds are advanced.
2. Conversion of future payments to present value.

discounted cash flow (DCF) analysis. A set of procedures in which an appraiser specifies the quantity, variability, timing, and duration of periodic income, as well as the quantity and timing of reversions, and discounts each to its present value at a specified yield rate.

discounted rate of return. *See* internal rate of return (*IRR*).

discount house. A retail store that can offer merchandise at a price below the usual or advertised price through self-service shopping and other low-overhead methods.

discounting. The procedure used to convert periodic income and reversions into present value; based on the assumption that benefits received in the future are worth less than the same benefits received now.

discount point. *See* point.

discount rate. A rate of return on capital used to convert future payments or receipts into present value.

discovery
1. The process in which an assessor identifies all taxable property in a jurisdiction and ensures that it is included on the assessment roll.
2. In law, the process in which lawyers prepare their cases for trial by requiring, with court authority, that witnesses from the opposing side answer a number of written questions.

disintermediation. The transfer of money from one type of interest-bearing account to another that yields a higher rate; usually disrupts the flow of funds for real estate mortgages. [15]

dispersion. In statistics, the degree of scatter of a set of terms or observations, usually measured from a central value, e.g., the mean, the median. [16]

disposable income. The personal income remaining after deducting income taxes and all other payments to the government.

disposal field. An area where waste, or effluent, from a septic tank is dispersed, draining into the ground through a tile and gravel leaching field.

distemper. A composition of pigments mixed with size, glue, egg whites, or egg yolks that is used for painting walls and murals.

distributed cash flow. Revenue from any source that is or can be distributed to the investor. [1]

distributed load. Weight that is evenly spread over an entire surface or along the length of a girder or beam; measured in pounds or tons per square or lineal foot.

distribution box
1. A fuse box; a metal box containing fuses and circuit breakers that permits access to connecting branch circuits.
2. An underground box that receives waste from a septic tank and distributes it to the laterals of a disposal field.

distribution panel. An insulated board from which electrical connections are made between the main feed circuit and branch distribution circuits.

distribution tile. Concrete or clay tile laterals leading from a septic tank distribution box; laid with open joints through which effluent drains and seeps into the soil. *See also* leaching trenches.

district
1. A type of neighborhood that presents a common use characteristic, e.g., multifamily, commercial, industrial.
2. A unit of local government with the authority to levy taxes and issue bonds to finance schools, parks, sewers, etc.

district mutation. A phenomenon observed frequently in rapidly growing cities in which the centers of various types of districts, e.g., retail districts, financial districts, move in the direction of city growth.

ditch. A man-made or natural small surface drain; a narrow, open excavation.

diversified farming. Farming in which there are several sources of farm income.

divided interest. An interest in part of a whole property; e.g., a lessee's interest.

division fence. A cross fence used to divide a ranch into various pastures. *See also* drift fence; line fence; snow fence.

division wall. An interior, load-bearing wall that divides a structure into rooms; a load-bearing or self-sustaining masonry wall that separates two abutting buildings.

dock
1. An elevated floor or platform used to facilitate the transfer of goods to or from a vehicle.
2. A structure extending from the shore into the water that permits the mooring of vessels; a wharf.

3. A slip or waterway that extends between two piers for the reception of ships; such a waterway, closed or open, and any surrounding piers and wharves.

documentation. In computer usage, written information describing the specifications and proper operation of a piece of hardware or software. [16]

dog. A metal gripping or fastening implement used to bind timbers or other materials.

dolphin. A post or pile cluster that is used to moor a boat; also, a bumper that protects the dock or wharf from vessels or floating objects.

dome. A hemispherical roof or ceiling constructed to exert equal, oblique thrust in all directions.

domicile. The locality where a person or corporation has legal residency.

door stop. A trim piece placed around the inside face of side and top door jambs to prevent damage from the door swinging too far.

dormer. A window set upright in a sloping or pitched roof; also, the roofed structure in which this window is set.

double-declining balance method of depreciation. A depreciation method in which the initial cost of a capital asset is spread over time by deducting, in each period, twice the percentage recognized by the straight-line method, and applying that double percentage to the undepreciated balance at the start of each period. *Also called* 200% declining balance.

double floor. Wood construction using a subfloor and a finished floor.

double framing. A building technique using double joists, trimmers, and other structural members where reinforcement is needed.

double-gabled roof. *See* butterfly roof; M roof.

double glazing. A double-glass pane hermetically sealed with an air space between the two panes to provide insulation.

double-hung window. A window with two movable sashes that slide vertically.

double pitch. Sloping in two directions.

double-pitch roof. A roof that slopes in two directions. *See also* butterfly roof.

double plate. In construction, two horizontal boards that cover and connect the studs; serves as a foundation for the rafters. [8]

double window header. Two boards laid on edge to form the upper portion of a door or window. [8]

dovetail. An interlocking joint commonly used in carpentry, e.g., in drawers, cases.

dowel. A wooden or metal pin used to hold or reinforce the juncture of two timbers.

dower. The portion of, or interest in, a deceased husband's real estate that the law gives to his widow for life; varies with statutory provisions.

downspout. A pipe that carries rainwater from roof gutters to the ground or the storm sewer system. *See also* leader.

downzoning. A public action in which the local government reduces the allowable density for subsequent development, e.g., fewer housing units, fewer stores, or changes the allowable use from a high use to a low use, e.g., multifamily to single-family. [2]

drainage. A system of drains, e.g., tiles, pipes, conduits, designed to remove surface or subsurface water or waste water and sewage.

drainage district. A unit of local government set up to construct and operate a drainage system for the area, usually to achieve a higher and better use of the land.

drainage ditch. An open watercourse other than a gutter.

drainage easement. *See* drainage right-of-way.

drainage right-of-way. The right to drain surface water from one owner's land over the land of one or more adjacent owners.

drain field. An area with a system of underground lateral pipes to drain septic systems of other types of liquid overflow.

drain tile. A specially designed pipe used in a drainage system.

draw. A natural path of drainage on land, usually not of great depth.

draw request. Schedule prepared by the borrower requesting construction funds from the lender at specific points in the construction process; based on the percentage of work completed. [1]

dress. The planing and finishing of a wood surface; to cut, trim, and smooth a material.

dressed and matched boards. Boards that are finished on one or two sides with tongue and groove edges.

dressed lumber. Lumber machined and surfaced on all four sides at a mill.

drift. Material moved from one place and deposited in another; glacial drift includes glacial deposits and unstratified till as well as stratified glacial outwash materials.

drift fence. A partial fence, open at both ends to keep stock from grazing in an area. *See also* division fence; fence; line fence; snow fence.

drill track. A rail track serving industrial property from which individual industry tracks branch off to plant sites; track kept open for the movement of locomotives in sorting cars or moving them to and from yards; a track on which a locomotive works, not one on which cars stand. *Also called* lead track.

drip

1. A projecting structural member that throws off rainwater and protects structural parts below; a channel cut underneath a sill.
2. Describes the part of a piping system that conveys condensation from the steam pipes to the water or return pipes.
3. Describes an easement or servitude derived from civil law that grants permission for the falling or dripping of water from the roof of one property owner onto the estate of a neighbor.

drop panel. In reinforced concrete slab construction, an area around a column head or mushroom column where the slab is deeper.

drop siding. A type of tongue and groove weatherboard applied to the exterior of frame structures. *See also* lap siding.

drought. Lack of rain; a relatively long period without rainfall, causing crop damage and the depletion of moisture in the soil.

droughty soil. A loose-textured soil with poor water-holding capacity due to the presence of sand or gravel subsoil.

drumlin. A long, narrow hill or ridge of unstratified glacial drift, normally compact, positioned with its length parallel to the movement of ice responsible for its deposition; because parallel ridges give the land poor drainage, drumlins are surrounded by swampy terrain.

dry dock. An artificial basin for the reception of vessels from which water can be removed; used to repair ships below waterline.

dryer. A facility used to dry or dehydrate farm crops prior to storage or milling.

dry farming. Land use under semiarid conditions, facilitated by irrigation and other methods that conserve moisture, e.g., allowing moisture to accumulate one season for use during the next.

dry rot. A decay of seasoned wood caused by a fungus.

drywall. Any finish material applied to an interior wall in a dry state, as distinguised from plaster; e.g., gypsum wallboard, plywood, fiberboard.

drywall construction. A type of interior wall construction using wood paneling, plywood, plasterboard, or any other type of wallboard instead of plaster as the finish material.

dry well. A drainage pit lined or filled with stone so that roof runoff, liquid effluent, or other sanitary wastes will leach or percolate into the surrounding soil.

ducts
1. In construction, pipes used to transmit and distribute warm or cooled air from a central unit to the rooms.
2. The space in an underground conduit that contains electrical cables or conductors.

due diligence. Used in connection with the public sale of securities in real estate syndicates or corporations to refer to the duty of the underwriting, or selling, group to ensure that the offering statement or prospectus does not misstate or omit material information. [3]

due-on-sale clause. A clause in mortgage contracts that provides that the outstanding loan balance is due when the mortgaged property is sold or transferred; precludes loan assumption by a new buyer.

duplex. A house containing two separate dwelling units, side by side or one above the other; also describes apartments that occupy two levels or a portion of two floors.

durable capital goods. Goods that can be used repeatedly; e.g., machinery, as distinguished from raw material.

durable goods. Consumer goods that can be used repeatedly; e.g., a refrigerator, as distinguished from short-lived goods, e.g., bread.

Dutch Colonial architecture. A residential style of architecture characterized by gambrel roofs, exterior walls of masonry or wood, and side porches.

Dutch door. A door divided horizontally in the middle so that the bottom half can remain closed while the top is open.

dwelling. A structure designed or occupied as the living quarters of one or more households; usually equipped with cooking, bathing, toilet, and heating facilities, where necessary. [6]

E

earnest money. A part of the purchase price given to bind a bargain. [1]

earning power. The capacity to generate income.

earnings. *See* income.

earnings approach. *See* income capitalization approach.

easement. An interest in real property that conveys use, but not ownership, of a portion of an owner's property.

easement appurtenant. An easement that is attached to, benefits, and passes with the conveyance of the dominant estate; runs with the land for the benefit of the dominant estate and continues to burden the servient estate, although such estates may be conveyed to new owners. [2]

easement by prescription. A right to use another's land which is established by exercising this right over a period of time; although not specifically granted, it is understood. *Also called* prescriptive easement. [7]

easement in gross. An easement that is not attached or appurtenant to any particular estate; does not run with the land nor is it transferred through the conveyance of title. [2]

eaves. The lower or outer edge of a roof that projects over the side walls of a structure.

ecology. The pattern of relations between living things and their environments.

economic age-life method. A method of estimating accrued depreciation in which the ratio of effective age to total economic life is applied to the current cost of the improvements to obtain a lump-sum deduction.

economic approach. *See* income capitalization approach.

economic base. The economic activity of a community that enables it to attract income from outside its borders.

economic base analysis. A technique that uses the relationship between basic and nonbasic employment to predict population, income, or other variables that affect real estate values or land utilization.

economic feasibility. The ability of a project or an enterprise to meet defined investment objectives; an investment's ability to produce sufficient revenue to pay all expenses and charges and to provide a reasonable return on and recapture of the money invested.

economic impact statement. A statement of a major real estate project's potential impact on the local economy, which may include estimates of the project's market value, potential gross sales, and its business, occupational, and tax impact on the community.

economic life. The period over which improvements to real property contribute to property value.

economic obsolescence. *See* external obsolescence.

economic rent
1. In appraisal, *see* market rent.
2. In economics, the surplus payment in excess of the amount necessary to justify the development of a property or to attract any factor of production into an enterprise.

economics. A social science concerned with the description and analysis of the production, distribution, and consumption of goods and services.

economic system. The nature of proposed or actual economic life as a whole with particular emphasis on the ownership and use of property and the extent of government regulation and controls; e.g., capitalism, socialism, communism.

effective age. The age indicated by the condition and utility of a structure.

effective demand. The desire to buy coupled with the ability to pay; when *demand* is used in economics or real estate analysis, effective demand is usually presumed.

effective gross income (*EGI*). The anticipated income from all operations of real property adjusted for vacancy and credit losses.

effective gross income multiplier (*EGIM*). The ratio of sale price or value to effective gross income; used to convert a single year's effective gross income expectancy or an annual average of several years' gross income expectancies into an indication of property value.

effective interest rate (*i*). Interest per dollar per period; the nominal annual interest rate divided by the number of conversion periods per year; also, the lender's internal rate of return. [15] *Also called* effective rate. *See also* nominal interest rate (*I*).

effective tax rate. The ratio between a property's annual property tax and its market value; the tax rate times the assessed value divided by the market value; the official tax rate times the assessment ratio.

efficiency ratio
1. In appraising, the ratio between a building's net rentable area, i.e., the space used and occupied exclusively by tenants, and its gross area, which includes the building's core.
2. In economics, the ratio between the ends produced, or output, and the means used, or input.
3. In land utilization, the ratio between the value of the product flowing from the site and the expense of the labor and capital that produced it; refers to the average amount of net product, e.g., rent, returned per unit of labor and capital applied.

efflorescence. A white powder on brick or stone that forms as a result of a chemical action and can be washed off without damage; deposits of soluble salts on the surface of masonry.

effluent. Liquid sewage that has passed through any stage of purification.

egress. A way out; an exit or outlet. [2]

EIS. *See* environmental impact study.

elastic. In economics, describes the responsiveness of prices to changes in the supply or demand for a good.

electrical outlet. A point on the wiring system where current can be taken to activate equipment.

electric heating. Any of several methods that convert electric energy into usable heat.

eleemosynary. Of or pertaining to charity; a charitable institution.

elements of comparison. The characteristics of properties and transactions that cause prices to vary: financing terms, conditions of sale, market conditions (time), location, and physical characteristics.

elevation
1. A geometric projection of a vertical plane perpendicular to the horizon, e.g., of the external, upright parts of a building from a front, side, or rear view.
2. Altitude; the height of a place or point above mean sea level.

elevator
1. A raising and lowering mechanism that moves on tracks up and down a shaft between the floors of a building and is equipped with a car or platform to transport passengers and freight.
2. A farm storage building in which a commodity, e.g., wheat, is stored.

Ellwood formula. A mathematical formula used to calculate an overall capitalization rate.

eminent domain. The right of government to take private property for public use upon the payment of just compensation.

employment base. The number of gainfully employed persons in a community or city.

employment density. The ratio between the number of employees actually working in the largest, normal daily shift at a plant site and the land area of the site. [11]

enclosure. Land enclosed with a visible or tangible obstruction, e.g., a fence, a hedge, a ditch, to protect the premises from encroachment by animals.

encroachment
1. Trespassing on the domain of another.
2. Partial or gradual displacement of an existing use by another use; e.g., locating commercial or industrial improvements in a residential district.

encumbrance. An interest or right in real property that may decrease or increase the value of the fee but does not prevent its conveyance by the owner. Mortgages, taxes, and judgments are encumbrances called *liens*; restrictions, easements, and reservations are encumbrances, but not liens.

energy audit. An inventory of the physical characteristics of a building that affect thermal efficiency; conducted to identify appropriate energy conservation measures, estimate the cost of installing these measures, and calculate the savings they are likely to produce.

energy efficiency. The ability of an appliance or a building's energy system to produce a given effect with minimum effort, expense, and waste; quantitatively, the ratio between an output and the energy expended to achieve that output. *See also* energy efficiency ratio (EER).

energy efficiency ratio (EER). A measure of the efficiency of an electric heat pump, air conditioner, or vapor compressor heating or cooling device; the ratio between output, expressed in Btus per hour, and energy input, expressed in watts.

engineering breakdown method. *See* breakdown method.

English architecture. A residential architectural style incorporating the features of Elizabethan, Tudor, Cotswold, and other English architectural styles; characterized by large, stone houses with slate shingles on gable roofs, mullioned casement windows, wainscoted interiors, and sometimes exposed timbers. *See also* English Cotswold architecture; English half-timbered architecture; English Tudor architecture.

English Cotswold architecture. A residential architectural style patterned after English country houses and characterized by sills, mullions, porches, stone chimneys, heavy details, and a roof of irregularly shaped variegated slates.

English half-timbered architecture. A rustic, informal, residential architectural style characterized by exterior ornamentation of half-timber and plaster, carved wood, stone, and brick and steep roof slopes that end in barges rather than cornices. *Also called* Elizabethan architecture.

English Tudor architecture. A formal, residential architectural style characterized by exterior walls of stone or brick laid in a formal pattern, window and door trim of dressed or cut stone, casement-type windows, and roofs of slate spaced to resemble stone.

ensilage. Green fodder that is chopped or shredded and preserved in a silo or pit.

entrepreneur. One who assumes the risk and management of a business or enterprise; a promoter who initiates development.

entrepreneurial incentive. *See* entrepreneurial profit.

entrepreneurial profit. A market-derived figure that represents the amount an entrepreneur expects to receive in addition to costs; the difference between total cost and market value. *Also called* entrepreneurial reward.

environment. The social, physical, political, and economic characteristics of the area surrounding a property, which have an effect on its value.

environmental deficiency. Conditions, circumstances, and influences that surround and affect the development of an area, promoting blight and deterioration; e.g., overcrowding or improper location of structures on the land, excessive dwelling unit density, conversion of buildings to incompatible uses, obsolete buildings, detrimental land uses, unsafe or congested streets, inadequate utilities or community facilities.

environmental impact study (EIS). An investigation to assess the comprehensive, long-range environmental effects of a proposed land use.

environmental obsolescence. *See* external obsolescence.

Environmental Protection Agency (EPA). An independent agency of the executive branch of the federal government with broad powers to control and prevent water, air, and noise pollution and to protect the nation's environment in general.

EPA. *See* Environmental Protection Agency.

equalization. The process in which a government body attempts to ensure that all property under its jurisdiction is assessed at the same assessment ratio or at the ratio or ratios required by law.

equipment. Fixed assets other than real estate; e.g., office equipment, automotive equipment; as distinguished from fixtures, assets that are physically or legally attached to the real estate. *See also* chattel.

equitable ownership. The estate or interest of a person who has a beneficial right in property that is legally owned by another; e.g., the beneficiary of a trust has an equitable estate or interest in the trust property.

equity. The net value of a property, calculated by subtracting all liens or other charges against the property from its total value; the value of an owner's interest in property in excess of all claims and liens.

equity buildup. An increase in the equity investor's share of total property value that results from gradual debt reduction through periodic repayment of principal on a mortgage loan, an increase in total property value, or both.

equity-debt ratio. The ratio of the equity value or equity capital invested in a property to the amount of debt incurred on that property.

equity capitalization rate (R_E). A rate that reflects the relationship between a single year's pre-tax cash flow expectancy or an annual average of several years' pre-tax cash flow expectancies and the equity investment; used to convert pre-tax cash flow into an equity value indication; usually considered a pre-tax measure.

equity dividend. *See* pre-tax cash flow (*PTCF*).

equity dividend rate. *See* equity capitalization rate (R_E).

equity fund. A limited partnership or real estate investment trust (REIT) formed to purchase equities in real estate; typically formed to develop projects and purchase equity in existing projects. [1]

equity kicker. An interest in the equity of a property given to the mortgage lender to obtain a mortgage on the property. [5]

equity of redemption. The right of a mortgagor by absolute deed to redeem the property by paying the debt; exercised after forfeiture, but before sale under foreclosure, transfer of title, or expiration of this right under the statute of limitations.

equity participation. The right of a lender to receive a share of the gross profit, net profit, or cash flow from a property on which it has made a loan; an additional return to the lender to compensate for unusual risk or the effect of inflation on the real value of the return on capital. [3]

equity ratio. The ratio of down payment to total price; the fraction of an investment that is unencumbered by debt.

equity yield. The dollar return on equity from all sources, i.e., the annual equity dividend including any gain or loss in the original equity investment at termination.

equity yield rate (Y_E). A rate of return on equity capital; the equity investor's internal rate of return.

erosion. The wearing away of surface land by natural causes, e.g., running water, winds. *See also* gully erosion; rill erosion; sheet erosion.

escalation clause. A clause in an agreement that provides for the adjustment of a price or rent based on some event or index; e.g., a provision to increase rent if operating expenses increase.

escalation income. Income that is generated from an escalation clause in a lease.

escape clause. A provision that permits tenant cancellation of a lease under circumstances that would not ordinarily justify lease cancellation.

escarpment. A long, precipitous face of rock or land.

escheat. The government right that gives the state titular ownership of a property when its owner dies without a will or any ascertainable heirs.

escrow. Property or evidences of property, e.g., money, securities, instruments, deposited by two or more persons with a third person, to be delivered under a certain contingency or on the completion of specified terms. [5]

esker. A ridge of sandy or gravelly material deposited in a stream channel beneath a glacier, which indicates a meandering course.

estate
1. A right or interest in property; e.g., fee ownership interest, lease interest for a number of years. An estate in land is the degree, nature, or extent of interest that a person has in it.
2. The property of a deceased person.

estate at will. The occupation of lands and tenements by a tenant for an unspecified period, which can be terminated by one or both parties. [2]

estate for years. A leasehold interest in land established by a contract for possession for a specified period of time. [2]

estate in possession. An estate that entitles the owner to the immediate possession, use, and enjoyment of the property. [2]

estate in reversion. The residue of an estate left by operation of law in the grantor, the grantor's successors, or the successors of a testator, who can possess the estate on the termination of some particular estate granted or devised.

estate of inheritance. An estate that can be passed on to heirs, i.e., all freehold estates, except estates for life. [2]

estate tax. A tax on the estate or wealth of a deceased person that is usually computed as a percentage of the market value of the assets of the estate.

estimate
1. In appraising, an opinion based on an analysis of adequate data by one qualified to develop such an opinion.
2. A preliminary opinion of the cost of doing work.

estoppel. A legal doctrine under which one is precluded and forbidden to deny his or her own act or deed. [2]

estoppel certificate. A statement of material facts or conditions on which another person can rely because it cannot be denied at a later date.

Eurodollars. Dollars deposited outside the United States.

evaluation. A study of the nature, quality, or utility of a parcel of real estate or interests in, or aspects of, real property, in which a value estimate is not necessarily required.

evaluation process. A systematic procedure employed to provide the answer to a client's question about the nature, quality, or utility of an interest in or aspect of identified real estate.

eviction. The ouster of one or more persons from a property; a legal process for the recovery of property by virtue of a paramount right recognized by law or for a default. [6]

examination of title. An interpretation of the condition of the title to real property based on a title search or abstract. [1]

exception. In contracts, a clause in a deed in which the lessor denies or negates something granted elsewhere in the deed; the exclusion of something from the effect or operation of the deed or contract that would otherwise be included.

excess income. *See* excess rent.

excess land. Surplus land that is not needed to accommodate a site's highest and best use.

excess rent. The amount by which contract rent exceeds market rent at the time of the appraisal; created by a favorable lease and may reflect a locational advantage, unusual management, or lease execution in an earlier, stronger rental market. Due to the higher risk inherent in the receipt of excess rent, it may be calculated separately and capitalized at a higher rate in the income capitalization approach.

exchange. The trading of equities in certain types of properties, usually to defer the capital gains tax liability incurred in an outright sale.

exchange value. The value, in terms of money, of real estate in a typical market.

exclusionary zoning. The effect of intentionally or unintentionally excluding racial minorities and low-income persons from a community. [2]

exclusive agency listing. A contract to sell property that states that only one agent is hired to sell the property, but the seller can sell through his or her own efforts without paying a commission; also, a property so listed.

exclusive right to sell listing. A contract to sell property that states that the agent, or listing broker, is entitled to the commission regardless of who sells the property, including the owner.

exculpatory clause. A provision in an agreement that limits the recourse of one party against the other party in the event of default; e.g., a nonrecourse mortgage limits recovery to the property itself. [5]

execution sale. A legal procedure that enforces a payment judgment; property is sold to obtain the amount owed.

executor. An individual or trust institution designated in a will or appointed by a court to settle the estate of the deceased.

executor's deed. A transfer of real estate in which the grantor is the executor of the granting estate.

exemption. *See* tax exemption.

expansion joint. A bituminous fiber strip used to separate units of concrete to prevent cracking due to expansion resulting from temperature changes. [2]

expense ratio. The ratio of total expenses, excluding debt service, to either potential or effective gross income. [1]

expenses. *See* operating expenses.

expert. One who is presumed to have special knowledge of, or skill in, a particular field due to education, experience, or study.

expert testimony. Testimony of persons who are presumed to have special knowledge of, or skill in, a particular field due to education, experience, or study.

expert witness. One qualified to render expert testimony.

exponent. The number that indicates the number of times the base is to be used as a factor; e.g., in $x^3=(x)(x)(x)$, x is the base and 3 is the exponent.

expressway. A highway with full or partial control of access where major crossroads are separated in grade from the pavement for through traffic of all types.

expropriation. A British and Canadian term synonymous with eminent domain in the United States.

extension agreement. An instrument that grants further time to pay an obligation or to fulfill the requirements of a contract. [1]

extensive farming. The use of comparatively small amounts of labor and working capital per acre of land.

exterior finish. The outside finish of a structure that includes roof and wall covering, gutters, and door and window frames; any protective outer cover.

exterior fixture. An outside item, e.g., areaway, canopy, marquee, platform, loading dock, that is permanently attached to and part of the building structure.

exterior wall. Any outer wall, except a common wall that serves as a vertical enclosure of a building.

external conformity. The compatibility between a property and its surroundings.

externalities. The principle that economies or diseconomies outside a property may have a positive or negative effect on its value.

external obsolescence. An element of accrued depreciation; an incurable defect caused by negative influences outside the property itself.

extraction method. The method of estimating land value in which an appraiser estimates the contribution of the improvements to the improved property and deducts this amount from the total sale price to arrive at an estimated sale price for the land; most effective when the improvements contribute little to the total sale price of the property.

extrapolation. Calculating or estimating a quantity beyond the range of the data on which the calculation or estimate is based; projections into the future that presume a continuation of observed trends, patterns, or relationships.

F

FAA. *See* Federal Aviation Administration.

facade. The principal, exterior face of a structure; usually the front face or front elevation of a building.

facade easement. A restriction that prohibits the fee owner of a property from altering the facade, or exterior, of an existing improvement on his or her land; generally imposed on historically significant structures to ensure their preservation.

face
1. The most important side of a structure; the front or facade.
2. The exposed surface of an object, e.g., the earth, a structure, a wall, a panel.

face brick. A better grade of brick used for an exterior wall of a building, often only on the face.

faced wall. A wall, usually of masonry, that has an exterior face of a different material; the two materials are bonded so that they serve as a single load-bearing unit.

face value. The value of securities, e.g., bonds, stocks, mortgages, as set forth in the documents themselves.

factor
1. One of the elements that contributes a given result; e.g., land as a contribution to the value of an improved property.
2. One of two or more numbers that, when multiplied together, produce a given number; e.g., 2 and 5 are factors of 10; also, a divisor.
3. Arithmetically, the reciprocal of a rate; a multiplier or coefficient.

factors in production. *See* agents in production.

factory and shop lumber. Lumber that is cut up for use in manufacturing; graded on the basis of the percentage of area that will produce a limited number of cuttings of a specified or given minimum size and quality.

fair housing laws. Federal, state, and local laws that guarantee persons the right to buy, sell, lease, hold, and convey property without discrimination on the basis of race, color, religion, gender, sexual preference, or national origin.

fair market value. *See* market value.

fair rental. *See* market rent.

fairway
1. A part of a golf course between the tees and putting greens where the grass is kept very short.
2. An unobstructed, navigable channel in a river or harbor for the passage of vessels; the usual course taken by ships.

falling ground. The ground on which trees will land after they are felled; its condition, slope, and configuration must be considered in making a mill-cut cruise of redwood timber because the trees are large and the timber is brittle.

fallow
1. Land, ordinarily used for crops, that is allowed to lie idle during the growing season.
2. The tilling of land without sowing it for a season.

family room. An informal living room, usually the center of family activities.

fan window. *See* circlehead window.

Fannie Mae. *See* Federal National Mortgage Association (FNMA).

Farm and Land Institute (FLI). The organization of real estate professionals active in land brokerage and agribusiness; confers the AFLM designation.

farmland. Land devoted to agricultural production; usually refers to the land comprising a farm, including tillable areas, untillable areas, and woodlots.

farmstead. The site and location of farm buildings; the focal point of farm operations.

farrowing house. A building used for housing hogs that are giving birth.

fascia. A long, flat construction member or band; the horizontal division of an architrave; the finishing board used to conceal the ends of rafters.

FCC. *See* Federal Communications Commission.

FDIC. *See* Federal Deposit Insurance Corporation.

FEA. *See* Federal Energy Administration.

feasibility. An indication that a project has a reasonable likelihood of satisfying explicit objectives; analyzed by testing a selected course of action in a context of specific constraints and limited resources; in a real estate project, usually related to economic potential.

feasibility study
1. An analysis that determines whether a project will fulfill the economic requirements of the investor.
2. An analysis of the profitability of a specific real estate undertaking in terms of the criteria of a specific market or investor.

Fed. A shortened term for the Federal Reserve System.

Federal Advisory Council. A committee of the Federal Reserve System that advises the Board of Governors on major developments and activities.

Federal Aviation Administration (FAA). The agency in the U.S. Department of Transportation that regulates civil aviation to promote its development and safety and provide for the safe and efficient use of the airspace by both civilian and military aircraft. [4]

Federal Communications Commission (FCC). A government agency that regulates interstate and foreign commerce by wire and radio and consults with other government agencies and state regulatory commissions on matters involving telegraph, telephone, and radio communications. Its jurisdiction now includes radio, television, wire, cable, microwave, and satellite communication. [4]

federal debt limit. A legal ceiling on the aggregate face amount of outstanding obligations issued, or guaranteed as to principal and interest, by the U.S. government; guaranteed obligations held by the Secretary of the Treasury are exempt. [4]

federal deficit. A public or federal debt; the difference between government revenue and expenditures.

Federal Deposit Insurance Corporation (FDIC). A government body that insures the deposits of all banks entitled to insurance under the Federal Reserve Act, including all national and state banks that are members of the Federal Reserve System and many mutual savings banks. [4]

federal discount rate. The interest rate charged by the Federal Reserve for funds borrowed by member banks.

Federal Energy Administration (FEA). A federal agency that develops and implements federal energy policy, including the allocation of resources. [4]

Federal Farm Loan Act. Legislation that provides long-term credit and capital for agricultural development, creates standard forms of investment based on farm loans, establishes a market for U.S. bonds, and creates government depositaries and financial agents for the United States. [4]

federal funds. Funds available at a Federal Reserve Bank, including excess reserves of member banks and checks drawn in payment for purchases of government securities by the Federal Reserve Bank. [4]

federal funds rate. The interest rate charged on loans made by banks with excess reserve funds to banks with deficient reserves; an early indication of major changes in the national economy.

federal government securities. All obligations of the U.S. government. *See also* Treasury bill.

Federal Home Bank. One of 11 regional banks established in 1932 to encourage local thrift and home financing during the Depression; now owned jointly by various savings and loan associations. The Federal Home Loan Bank Board serves as a management body. [4]

Federal Home Loan Bank System. A system established in 1932 to serve as a mortgage credit reserve system for home mortgage lending institutions; members may obtain advances on home mortgage collateral and may borrow from home loan banks under certain conditions. [4]

Federal Home Loan Mortgage Corporation (FHLMC). An agency that aids secondary residential mortgages sponsored by the Veterans Administration and the Federal Housing Administration, as well as residential mortgages that are not government protected. [4]

Federal Housing Administration (FHA). The government agency that carries out the provisions of the National Housing Act by promoting homeownership and the renovation and remodeling of residences with government-guaranteed loans to homeowners. [4]

Federal Housing Administration mortgage. A mortgage that is made in conformity with the requirements of the National Housing Act and is insured by the Federal Housing Administration.

Federal Housing FHA insured loans. Insured mortgages from private lending institutions designed to stimulate homeownership and rental opportunities for American families; interest rates on these loans are set by the FHA.

Federal Intermediate Credit Banks. Regional banks created by Congress to provide intermediate credit for ranchers and farmers by rediscounting the agricultural paper of financial institutions. [4]

Federal Land Bank (FLB). One of 12 banks that offer long-term credit to farmers and are supervised by the Farm Credit Association. Strictly speaking, these banks compete with thrift institutions, but regulations limit their participation in housing loans to 15% of their total investments and their money is available only to farmers and ranchers. [4]

Federal National Mortgage Association (FNMA). An independent agency that purchases mortgages from banks, trust companies, mortgage companies, savings and loan associations, and insurance companies to help distribute funds for home mortgages. [4]

Federal Open Market Committee (FOMC). The Federal Reserve System's most important policy-making group, which creates policy for the system's purchase and sale of government and other securities in the open market; composed of the Board of Governors of the Federal Reserve System and five representatives of the 12 Federal Reserve Banks. [4]

Federal Power Commission (FPC). An agency that regulates the interstate operations of private utilities, i.e., the issuance of securities, setting of rates, and location of sites. [4]

Federal Reserve Bank. One of 12 banks created and regulated by the Federal Reserve System. *See also* Federal Reserve Board Bank. [4]

Federal Reserve Bank account. An account kept by all member banks, as required by Federal Reserve regulations, that clears member banks with a Federal Reserve Bank in their districts, showing the cash balance due from a reserve bank to guarantee that the member bank has sufficient reserves on hand. [4]

Federal Reserve Bank collections account. An account that shows the sum of monies for out-of-town checks distributed for collection by a Federal Reserve check collection system; the funds are not presently available in reserve but are being collected. [4]

Federal Reserve Board. The seven-member governing body of the Federal Reserve System that regulates all national and state-chartered banks belonging to the Federal Reserve System, has jurisdiction over bank holding companies, and sets national money and credit policy; the governors serve for 14 years and are appointed by the President of the United States, subject to Senate confirmation. [4]

Federal Reserve Board Bank. One of the 12 Federal Reserve District Banks, which are: 1st District, Boston; 2nd District, New York; 3rd District, Philadelphia; 4th District, Cleveland; 5th District, Richmond; 6th District, Atlanta; 7th District, Chicago; 8th District, St. Louis; 9th

District, Minneapolis; 10th District, Kansas City; 11th District, Dallas; and 12th District, San Francisco.

Federal Reserve Bulletin. A monthly journal, issued by the Board of Governors of the Federal Reserve System, that deals with issues in banking and finance. [4]

Federal Reserve Chart Book. A quarterly publication of the Board of Governors of the Federal Reserve System that contains charts of interest to the financial community. [4]

Federal Reserve credit. The credit supply that Federal Reserve Banks have added to member bank reserves; composed primarily of earning assets of the Federal Reserve Banks. [4]

Federal Reserve notes. Notes that are issued by the Federal Reserve Banks when certain areas require large volumes of currency or when the public demand for currency is very heavy; as the need for currency relaxes, Federal Reserve Banks retire these notes; issued to member banks in denominations of $1 to $10,000, providing elastic currency with full legal tender status. [4]

Federal Reserve notes of other banks. The total amount of Federal Reserve notes held by reserve banks other than the bank that issued them.

Federal Reserve System. The central banking system of the United States that regulates money supply, determines the legal reserve of member banks, oversees the mint, effects transfers of funds, promotes and facilitates the clearance and collection of checks, examines member banks, and serves other functions; consists of 12 Federal Reserve Banks, their 24 branches, and national and state banks that are members of the system. All national banks are stockholding members of the Federal Reserve Bank of their district; membership for state banks and trust companies is optional.

federal rule. *See* before-and-after rule.

Federal Savings and Loan Association. One of the associations, established by the Home Owner's Loan Act of 1933 and amended in the

Home Owners Loan Act of 1934, that brought existing and newly formed mutual savings banks and building and loan associations under a federal charter. [4]

Federal Savings and Loan Insurance Corporation (FSLIC). An organization that insures the shares and accounts of all federal savings and loan associations and any state-chartered savings and loan associations that apply for insurance and meet the requirements of the corporation.

Federal Savings Association. A savings association chartered and regulated by the Federal Home Loan Bank Board.

fee. *See* fee simple estate.

feed bunk. A wooden or concrete trough from which livestock and poultry feed.

feeder. A prefabricated container from which animals or birds feed.

feeder cattle. A market classification for cattle raised on feed, from yearlings to mature cattle, which have not reached a finished or prime condition for slaughter.

feedlot. An enclosed area where feeder cattle are finished for the market; usually equipped with feed/hay bunks or self-feeders, watering facilities, paving, and adjacent shelter.

feed value. The amount of nutrients found in dairy cattle feed, usually measured in total digestible nutrients (TDN), digestible energy (DE), metabolizable energy (ME), or net energy (NE). In calculating these measures of energy, the energy content of the feed and the feces, urine, gases, and heat produced by the animal are measured.

fee on condition. *See* fee simple conditional.

fee on limitation. A fee simple estate that is automatically terminated on the occurrence of a specified event, which may occur at any time or not at all. [2]

fee simple conditional. A fee simple estate that may be terminated on the occurrence of a specified event, which may occur at any time or not at all. The breach of the condition does not automatically terminate the estate; the grantor, the heirs, or a designee must act to terminate the estate. [2]

fee simple estate. Absolute ownership unencumbered by any other interest or estate; subject only to the limitations of eminent domain, escheat, police power, and taxation.

fee timesharing. *See* timesharing.

felt. A nonwoven fabric of wool, fur, hair, or vegetable fibers that are matted together by heat, moisture, and pressure.

felt paper. Paper used for sheathing on walls and roofs that serves as a barrier against heat, cold, and dampness; covered with tar or asphalt and surfaced with gravel on certain types of roofs, e.g., flat roofs.

fenestration. The design and arrangement of windows and other openings in a building wall.

FF&E. Furniture, fixtures, and equipment.

FHA. *See* Federal Housing Administration.

FHLMC. *See* Federal Home Loan Mortgage Corporation.

fiberboard. A prefabricated building material made of wood or other plant fibers compressed and bonded into a sheet.

fiberglass. Finespun filaments of glass that are made into yarn and used in batts as insulation; added to gypsum or concrete products to increase tensile strength.

fiduciary. A relationship between two individuals in which one is charged with the duty of acting for the benefit of the other, e.g., between guardian and ward; the person so charged.

field appraiser. An appraiser who conducts primary and secondary research, analyzes researched data, forms opinions, and prepares appraisal reports.

field box. In agriculture, a unit of measure applicable to harvested fruit crops; quantity varies with the variety and locality. *Also called* field lug.

field crop. In agriculture, an annual crop that is planted and harvested by mechanical means.

field tile
1. Porous tile placed around a building's foundation to drain off excess water and prevent seepage into the foundation.
2. A system of drain tiles buried well below the field's surface or ground to drain the subsoil.

fill. The use of added material to equalize topography or raise land to a desired grade; in highway construction, the use of stones and earth to fill low sections of the right-of-way; the material used for this purpose.

fill slope. The portion of a roadway that lies between the outer edge of a road shoulder and the toe of the slope at a different elevation.

final reconciliation. *See* reconciliation.

final value estimate. A range of values or a single dollar amount that an appraiser derives in the reconciliation of value indications and states in the appraisal report.

financial corporation. A corporation engaged primarily in some form of banking; e.g., a bank, trust company, insurance company, savings and loan association.

financial management rate of return (*FMRR*) procedure. A type of adjusted internal rate of return analysis in which an explicit reinvestment rate is assumed and positive cash flows are substituted to offset negative cash flows at the reinvestment rate. Remaining positive cash flows are compounded forward to arrive at a terminal value based on the minimum rate of return for projects of a particular risk class.

financial statement. A statement that reflects the economic status of an individual or entity.

financial structure. The character and extent of distributed ownership and control of assets in a corporation, particularly the setup of bonds, preferred stock, and common stock under qualified rights.

financing costs. The cost of acquiring capital to finance a project.

financing statement. An instrument that conveys a security interest in chattels and equipment, recorded in chattel records and indexed in land records.

finder's fee. A fee, usually expressed in points, that is paid to a banker, a broker, or an intermediary who locates debt or equity capital for a developer. [1]

fine sandy loam. A soil containing much sand, but enough silt and clay to make it cohesive; contains more fine sand than sandy loam.

fine-textured soil. A soil with a high percentage of fine particles, 0.005 millimeter in diameter or less. *Also called* clay soils.

finish floor. The top flooring of hardwoods, linoleum, terrazzo, or tile, laid over the subfloor.

finish hardware. *See* hardware.

fireback. *See* chimney back.

firebrick. A brick made of fireclay that is capable of resisting high temperatures and used to line heating chambers and fireplaces.

fire cut. A diagonal cut made across a horizontal, wood-supporting member at the end that is framed into a masonry wall. The cut, made from the top of the member and slanted toward the outside wall, that allows the member, in the event of failure from fire or any other cause, to collapse without causing the wall to collapse as well.

fire doors and walls. Doors and walls constructed of fire-resistive materials and designed to prevent the spread of fires.

fireproof construction. *See* fire-resistive construction.

fireproofing. The use of incombustible materials to protect the structural components of a building so that a complete burnout of its contents will not impair its structural integrity.

fire-resistive construction. Construction designed to withstand a complete burnout of the contents of the structure without impairing its structural integrity; not combustible at ordinary fire temperatures; capable of withstanding ordinary fire conditions for at least one hour without serious damage to the structure.

fire-retarding material. Material that tends to inhibit combustion.

fire stops. The use of incombustible material to block air spaces in a structure through which flames could travel.

fire wall. An incombustible wall built between two buildings, or between two parts of one building, as a fire stop.

first bottom. The normal plane of a stream, part of which may be flooded at times. *See also* floodplain; second bottom.

first mortgage. A mortgage that has priority over all other liens on a property.

first-user depreciation. In taxation, a determination of whether a property is considered new or used in the possession of the taxpayer. [1]

fiscal year. Any 12 months selected as an accounting period; may or may not coincide with the calendar year.

fixed assets. Permanent assets that are required for the normal operation of business; usually not converted into cash after they are declared fixed assets; e.g., furniture, fixtures, land, building, machinery.

fixed capital. Capital invested in property in a stationary form that may be used many times in production; permanent assets, e.g., land; ordinarily, but not necessarily, tangible assets.

fixed capital goods. *See* durable capital goods.

fixed disbursement schedule. A disbursement system on a construction loan in which the lender and borrower agree on the number and timing of payments to be made during the construction period; as distinguished from the voucher system, in which only actual costs are reimbursed. [1]

fixed expenses. Operating expenses that do not vary with occupancy; must be paid whether or not the property is occupied.

fixed-fee contract. A type of construction contract in which the contract price is a specific sum. [1]

fixed liabilities. Long-term debts; debts payable more than one year hence, as distinguished from current liabilities.

fixed-rate mortgage. A standard mortgage with an interest rate that does not vary over the life of the loan.

fixed window. A window that does not open; e.g., fixed bay window, fixed bow window, picture window.

fixture. An article that was once personal property but has since been installed or attached to the land or building in a rather permanent manner; regarded in law as part of the real estate.

flagstone. A flat, irregular slab of stone, usually sandstone or shale, used for paving walks, patios, terraces, and planter boxes.

flange. A projecting edge, ridge, rim, or collar used to attach an object to another object to keep it in place; e.g., the projecting horizontal portions of an I beam.

flank. The side of a building or an arch.

flashing. Strips of sheet metal, copper, lead, or tin used to cover and protect structural angles and joints from water seepage.

flat
1. A floor or story in a building.
2. An apartment on one floor.
3. A multifamily, residential structure containing a limited number of units, each with a separate, outside entrance.

flat coat. The first coat of paint applied to a finished surface.

flat cost. In the building trades, the cost of labor and materials only.

flat rental. A specified level of rent that continues throughout the lease term.

flat roof. A roof with just enough slope to provide for proper drainage; one with a pitch that does not exceed 20 degrees.

flat slab construction. A method of construction in which a concrete floor slab is supported by columns, not beams; requires a thicker slab.

FLB. *See* Federal Land Bank.

flexible conduit. A conduit made of flexible material, e.g., fabric, spiral metal strip.

Flexible Loan Insurance Plan (FLIP). An alternative mortgage instrument; a graduated-payment mortgage that combines graduated payments for the home buyer, level payments for the lender, and conventional underwriting.

FLI. *See* Farm and Land Institute.

flight pattern. The zone of approach or departure of aircraft from airport runways.

FLIP. *See* Flexible Loan Insurance Plan.

flitch beam. A beam consisting of an iron plate bolted between two timber beams.

float. A valve-like device, e.g., a hollow ball, that uses its buoyancy to automatically regulate the supply, outlet, and level of a liquid, e.g., in a toilet tank.

float finish. A concrete surface that is finished by continuously spreading the material with a flat board.

floating capital. Capital invested in current assets, e.g., inventory, receivables.

floating foundation. A mat, raft, or rigid foundation consisting of concrete slabs four to eight feet thick over the entire foundation area with reinforcing bars closely spaced at right angles to each other within the slab; used when the bearing power of the soil cannot support spread footings and the use of piles is not advantageous or necessary.

floating rate. A variable interest rate charged for the use of borrowed money; set at a specific percentage above a fluctuating base rate, usually the prime rate of major commercial banks.

floating zone. A provision in a zoning ordinance that permits the planned development of a tract of land, usually subject to binding, prearranged controls, for a use not normally permitted in the zone where the land is located; ordinarily requires the approval of a regulatory body but does not constitute an exception, variance, or change in zoning.

flood irrigation. An irrigation method in which water is applied to the land surface directly.

floodplain. The flat surfaces along the courses of rivers and streams that are subject to overflow and flooding.

floor
1. The lower, horizontal surface of a specific floor; the total area of all floors in a multistory building, computed from the outside building walls of each floor with balcony and mezzanine areas computed separately and added to the total.

2. The different stories of a structure; e.g., ground floor, first floor.
3. The horizontal structure dividing a building into various stories.

floor area. The total horizontal surface of a specific floor; the total area of all floors in a multistory building, computed from the outside building walls of each floor with balcony and mezzanine areas computed separately and added to the total.

floor-area ratio. The relationship between the aboveground floor area of a building and the area of the plot on which it stands; in planning and zoning, often expressed as a decimal; e.g., a ratio of 2.0 indicates that the floor area of a building is twice the total land area.

floor furnace. A metal, box-like, warm-air furnace installed directly under the floor so that its grilled upper surface is flush with the finished floor of the room above.

floor joists. Horizontal framing lumber to which flooring is attached.

floor load. The live weight-supporting capabilities of a floor, measured in pounds per square foot; the weight, in pounds per square foot, that can be safely placed on the floor of a building if it is uniformly distributed. *See also* dead load; live load.

floor loan. A part of a total loan that is disbursed when the physical improvements are complete; the balance of the loan is disbursed when the other requirements of the lender are met, e.g., rent roll achievement. *See also* ceiling loan.

floor of forest. The dead vegetative matter on the ground in a forest, including litter and unincorporated humus. In fire control, it is called *duff*. *See also* litter.

flowage easement. The perpetual right, power, and privilege to overflow, flood, and submerge land owned by another, reserving for the landowner all rights and privileges that do not interfere with or abridge this right; may be either permanent or occasional.

flow line. A profile of the low point of a drainage channel or structure, measured at the low point of the inside of the watercourse.

flue. A passage that removes smoke from a chimney; any duct or pipe for the passage of air, gases, smoke, etc.

flue lining. The tile or pipe inside a chimney.

flume. An artificial open channel used to carry water; e.g., a channel by which logs are transported; may or may not be supported by a trestle at points in its course.

fluorescent lighting. Lighting fixtures consisting of glass tubes with an inside coating of fluorescent material that produces light when subjected to a stream of electrons from the cathode.

flush siding. A level siding of tongue and groove boards laid flush on the sidewalls.

FNMA. *See* Federal National Mortgage Association.

fodder. Coarse food for horses, cattle, or sheep.

FOMC. *See* Federal Open Market Committee.

footcandle. A measure of the amount of illumination produced by a lighting fixture, recorded at desk level using a light meter.

footing. The base of a foundation wall or column. [2]

footings. Support parts used in building construction to prevent excessive settlement or movement.

forage. All browse and herbaceous food that is available to livestock or game animals; used for grazing or harvested for feeding.

forage acre. A unit of measure equal to an acre totally covered with vegetation that is usable to livestock; this factor times the number of surface acres indicates the total forage acres in a plot.

forage-acre factor. A factor obtained by multiplying the weighted use factor by the forage density; a forage index indicating the part of a range that is covered with available vegetation that can be entirely eaten by livestock without causing damage to the range. *See also* weighted use factor.

forage crop. A member of the grass family; e.g., corn or grain sorghum; often harvested and stored in silos as reserve food for livestock.

forage density. The part of the total vegetative density that is within reach of livestock, generally four feet for sheep and five feet for cattle.

forbearance. Refraining from taking legal action on a mortgage that is in arrears; usually granted when a mortgagor makes a satisfactory arrangement to pay the arrears at a future date. [1]

forbs. Herbs other than grass.

forced price. The price paid in a forced sale or purchase, i.e., a sale in which a reasonable time was not allowed to find a purchaser or the purchaser was forced to buy.

forced sale
1. Offering and transferring property for a valuable consideration under conditions of compulsion.
2. A sale at public auction made under a court order.

forecasting. Predicting a future happening or condition based on past trends and the perceptions of market participants, tempered with analytical judgment concerning the continuation of these trends and the realization of these perceptions in the future.

foreclosure. The legal process in which a mortgagee forces the sale of a property to recover all or part of a loan on which the mortgagor has defaulted.

foreshore. The land, in its natural condition, between mean high water and mean low water along a shore.

forest. A large tract of land covered with trees.

forestation. The establishment of a forest in an area where no forest existed before, e.g., abandoned or submarginal farmland.

forest permit. A permit issued by the U.S. Forest Service to a stock raiser that permits the grazing of a specific number of animals on a national forest for a particular period or season.

forfeiture. A means by which the property of a citizen reverts back to the state through the violation of law; in the United States, occurs only when the property is seized for taxes.

form class. In forestry, the relationship between the diameter outside a tree's bark at breast-height (DBH) and the diameter inside the bark at the top of the first 16-foot log; represents a percentage of taper or form; e.g., if DBH is 24 inches and top diameter is 12 inches, the form class is 12 divided by 24, or .5 times 100, or form class 50.

formica. A trade name for a plastic material used primarily on counter tops, but also on wallcovering, plywood panels, and wallboard, where a fire-resistive material is desirable; similar materials are produced under other trade names.

form report. An appraisal report presented on a standard form, as required by financial institutions, insurance companies, and government agencies.

forms. Temporary panels, usually of wood, plywood, or steel, that form the shape of poured concrete while it hardens.

formula rules. Formulas used to estimate the amount of board feet in a log from its diameter and length, allowing for waste in saw kerf and slabs; must be used very carefully. *See also* Humboldt rule; log rules; Scribner rule; Spaulding rule.

FORTRAN. Formula translator; a computer programming language used for problem solutions that can be expressed algebraically.

foundation. The base on which something is built; the part of a structure on which the building is erected; the part of a building that is below the surface of the ground and on which the superstructure rests.

foyer. A lobby of a theater or hotel; an entrance hall in a house.

FPC. *See* Federal Power Commission.

fractional assessment. A property's assessed value, computed by multiplying its full value by a specified percentage. [10]

fractional interest. *See* partial interest.

frame. The load-bearing skeleton of a building.

frame construction. *See* wood frame construction.

framing. A system of joining structural members that provides lateral, longitudinal, transverse, and vertical support for a building.

framing line. The outside, vertical plane of exterior wall framing.

franchise. A privilege or right that is conferred by grant on an individual or a group of individuals; usually an exclusive right to furnish public services or to sell a particular product in a certain community.

free and clear. Describes the title to a property that is unencumbered by mortgages or other liens. [2]

free bord. An allowance of land outside the property fence that may be claimed by the owner; in some places, the area extends two and a half feet outside the boundary or enclosure.

free good. A useful thing so plentiful that it is available without any effort; e.g., climate, fresh air, sunshine.

freehold. *See* fee simple estate.

free switching. The handling of freight by a railroad for no charge in certain switching districts or in areas where reciprocal switching is provided.

free switching limits. The specified boundaries that designate an area where a railroad will switch carload freight on which it receives a line haul, without further charge, to or from private spur tracks or its own team tracks; also, competitive traffic on which the line haul carrier absorbs the charge of the switching line.

freeway. A multilane highway with full control of access where intersecting roads are separated in grade from the pavements for through traffic. *See also* expressway; superhighway; toll road; turnpike.

French architecture. Any of several styles of architecture that originated in France. A common example is the small, formal house, perfectly balanced, with a steep roof hipped at the ends, plastered walls on the first floor, and second-floor dormer windows. The French farmhouse style is informal, of stone, painted brick, or plaster, and sometimes accented with half-timbering. Norman French architecture is large scale and distinguished by the use of a round tower.

french curve. A stencil-like device used by a draftsman to draw curves other than circles or arcs.

french doors or windows. A pair of glazed doors that are hinged at the jamb and function as both doors and windows.

Freon. A trade name for a group of nontoxic, nonflammable refrigerants used in air-conditioning systems.

frequency distribution. In statistics, a system for analyzing data that condenses it into a more easily interpreted form. The formation of a distribution involves three steps: 1) determine the range of data, 2) divide the range into a workable number of class intervals of a standard size, and 3) determine the number of observations falling into each interval using a tally or score sheet. [10]

fresco. A method for painting a mural using watercolors on freshly plastered walls.

friable. Easily crumbled; not plastic.

frieze. A horizontal trim piece immediately below the cornice soffit.

front. The primary face of a structure, usually containing the principal entrance. *See also* facade.

frontage road. A local street that parallels a limited-access highway, services abutting properties, and gathers and controls vehicles entering or leaving the major traffic artery.

front elevation. The front view of a building.

front foot. A land measure one foot in width taken along the road or water frontage of a property.

front foot cost. The cost of a parcel of real estate expressed in terms of front foot units.

front money
1.   The cash outlay required to launch a project.
2.   Money that must be spent before financing is available.

frost line. The depth of frost penetration in the soil, which varies throughout the United States; footings should be placed below this depth to prevent movement of the structure. [8]

FSLIC. *See* Federal Savings and Loan Insurance Corporation.

full covenant and warranty deed. A deed conveying real property in which the grantor usually warrants the title, making the five covenants of seisin, quiet enjoyment, against encumbrances, further assurances, and warranty or defense. [2]

full-cut lumber. Lumber that is cut to full dimension.

full-value assessment. An assessment that is theoretically based on 100% of the property's market value. [10]

fully amortizing mortgage loan. A loan with equal, periodic payments, usually on a monthly basis, that provide for both a return on investment, or interest, and a return of investment, or recovery of principal, over the term of the loan.

functional inutility. An impairment of the functional capacity or efficiency of a property or building according to market tastes and standards;

equivalent to functional obsolescence because the ongoing change makes layouts and features obsolete.

functional obsolescence. *See* curable functional obsolescence; incurable functional obsolescence.

functional utility. The ability of a property or building to be useful and to perform the function for which it is intended, according to current market tastes and standards; the efficiency of a building's use in terms of architectural style, design and layout, traffic patterns, and the size and type of rooms.

furring. Strips of wood or metal applied to a rough wall or other surface to form an air space or to provide a level surface for the application of a finish material.

fuse. An electrical safety device consisting of or including a wire or strip of fusible metal that melts and interrupts the circuit when the current exceeds a particular amperage.

fuse box. The container housing the fuses that control the electric circuits of a structure.

future worth of one. *See* amount of $1 ($S^n$).

future worth of one per period. *See* amount of $1 per period ($S_{\overline{n}}$).

G

gable. The end of a building, generally triangular in shape; the vertical plane that lies above the eaves and divides the slope of a ridged roof.

gable roof. A ridged roof, the ends of which form a gable.

GAFO. General merchandise, apparel, furniture, and other retail goods; identifies the type of retail goods sold in regional and super-regional shopping centers.

gallery
1. A covered walk or corridor that extends from an upper story of a building and runs along the exterior or interior wall.
2. The highest balcony in a theater.
3. A room for art exhibitions.

gambrel roof. A ridged roof with a side that has two slopes, with the lower slope the steeper.

gap loan. An interim loan.

garden apartments. An apartment development of two- or three-story, walk-up structures built in a garden-like setting; customarily a suburban or rural-urban fringe development.

garnishment. A statutory proceeding in which the property, money, or credits of a debtor in the possession of another are seized and applied to pay the debt. [1]

garret. *See* attic.

gathering pen. A corral or pen that is usually constructed on the range at some distance from the ranch headquarters to facilitate the gathering of herds for shipping, branding, or other purposes.

GBA. *See* gross building area.

general benefits. In eminent domain takings, the benefits that accrue to the community at large, to the area adjacent to the improvement, or to other property situated near the taken property. *See also* benefits; set-off rule; special benefits.

general contractor. A person or business entity that supervises the erection of structures or other improvements. [1]

general partner. The entity or individual in a limited partnership who has full management responsibility and assumes all personal liability for partnership debt. *See also* limited partnership.

general partnership. An ownership arrangement in which all partners share investment gains and each is fully responsible for all liabilities.

general warranty deed. A covenant of warranty inserted in a deed which binds the grantor and heirs to defend the title conveyed to the grantee and heirs against the lawful claims of all persons. *See also* quitclaim deed; special warranty deed. [1]

genesis of soil. The origins of the soil, particularly the processes responsible for developing the solum from unconsolidated parent material.

gentrification. A phenomenon in which middle- and upper-income people purchase neighborhood properties and renovate or rehabilitate them.

geocode. A code used to locate or identify a point geographically, e.g., the center of a parcel of real estate; usually expressed in coordinates relative to a standard point of reference.

geodetic system. The United States Coast and Geodetic Survey System; a network of bench marks located by latitude and longitude, that cover the entire country; initiated to identify tracts of land owned by the federal government, but gradually extended throughout the nation.

geographical sequence. A method for filing appraisal data by location; in assessing, the system in which property record cards are filed first by lot number, then by blocks, and finally by subdivisions.

geometric average. The nth root of the product of n items; dependent on the size of all values, but less affected by extreme values than the arithmetic average; useful in computing index numbers when all values are positive. *Also called* mean average.

geometric progression. A sequence in which the ratio of any item to the preceding item is constant; e.g., 2, 4, 16, 64, 256.

geomorphic. Resembling the earth in form; describes designs or forms that fit into the landscape where they are built. [6]

Georgian architecture. An architectural style, popular in the 18th century and still used in residences, that is a combination of popular English styles; characterized by regularity of form, horizontal lines, and classical proportions and featuring pitched roofs, central entrances, balanced windows, doors, and chimneys, and first-floor windows that extend to the ground.

gift deed. A deed given without consideration. [2]

gift tax. A graduated tax, imposed by the federal government and some states, on gifts of property during the donor's lifetime; under the law, gifts may include irrevocable living trusts.

GI loan. A mortgage loan granted to veterans that is guaranteed by the Veterans Administration and subject to its restrictions. [2]

gingerbread work. Describes excessive ornamentation in architecture, especially in a house.

Ginnie Mae. *See* Government National Mortgage Association (GNMA).

girder. A principal, horizontal structural member or beam that supports lesser beams, joists, or walls.

girt. A horizontal framing member that extends between columns or studs to stiffen the framework or carry the siding material.

GLA. *See* gross leasable area.

glacial soil. Parent material of soil that has been moved and redeposited by glacial activity.

glass block. A hollow building block of translucent glass that admits light, but provides privacy and sound-insulating qualities; not intended for use in a load-bearing wall.

glass wool insulation. Material made of glass fibers, usually in the form of blankets wrapped in heavy asphalt-treated or vapor-barrier paper. *See also* mineral wool.

glaze. To fit, furnish, or cover with glass; to produce a glassy or glossy surface.

glazed brick. A dress brick with a glossy surface made of glass.

glazed facing tile. A hollow, clay tile with one or two glazed surfaces.

glean. The gathering of grain or other produce left in fields by combines; accomplished by grazing livestock or hand picking.

GNMA. *See* Government National Mortgage Association.

GNP. *See* gross national product.

going-concern value. The value created by a proven property operation; considered a separate entity to be valued with an established business.

going value. *See* going-concern value.

good. In economics, a material or immaterial thing that satisfies human desire and is external to humans; divided into two categories, free goods and economic goods.

goodwill. A salable business asset based on reputation, not physical assets.

gore. A small, triangular piece of land.

government lots. In the government survey system, land areas that are not divided into sections and quarters due to location or size; usually lie along the edge of rivers or lakes and extend from the waterline to the first section boundary.

Government National Mortgage Association (GNMA). A federally owned and financed corporation under the Department of Housing and Urban Development that subsidizes mortgages through its secondary mortgage market operations and issues mortgage-backed, federally insured securities. *See also* Federal National Mortgage Association (FNMA).

government survey system. A ground survey system used in Florida, Alabama, Mississippi, and all states north of the Ohio River or west of the Mississippi River (except Texas); divides land into townships approximately six miles square, each containing 36 sections of 640 acres. *See also* legal description.

GPM. *See* graduated-payment mortgage.

grace period. A period of time, usually measured in days, during which the borrower under a mortgage or other debt instrument may cure a default without incurring a penalty or triggering foreclosure or other remedies by the creditor. [2]

grade
1. The slope of a surface, e.g., a lot or road, with the vertical rise or fall expressed as a percentage of horizontal distance; e.g., a 3% upgrade indicates a rise of 3 feet for each 100 feet of horizontal distance.
2. The level or elevation of a lot; e.g., rough grade is the level, slope, or general elevation of the land surface on which topsoil will be placed in landscaping; finish grade is the final level, slope, or elevation of a lot.
3. Sometimes used to mean on or at the same level; e.g., a crossing at street grade; a lot at street grade.
4. To provide a parcel of land with the desired contour and drainage.
5. A letter, number, or word that denotes the quality of construction materials.

grade beam. A horizontal, load-bearing foundation member that is end-supported like a standard beam, not ground-supported like a foundation wall.

graded tax. A local tax designed to impose an increasing burden on land values and a decreasing burden on improvements; differential is achieved by varying the assessment or the tax rate.

grade separation. A structure used to separate two intersecting roadways vertically; permits traffic on one road to cross traffic on another road without interference.

gradient. The rate of the rise or fall of land; i.e., the degree of inclination.

graduated-payment adjustable mortgage loan. A mortgage instrument, approved for use by federal savings and loans, that is a combination of the graduated-payment mortgage and the adjustable mortgage loan; monthly payments increase over the graduation period, which is limited to 10 years, and the interest rate changes with movements in a specified index. No limits are placed on the frequency of payment adjustments during the graduation period or on the frequency or amount of interest rate changes during the term of the mortgage.

graduated-payment mortgage (GPM). A mortgage designed to aid borrowers by matching mortgage payments to projected increases in income; the monthly payments start out low and gradually increase. Because payments in the early years of the loan are not sufficient to amortize the mortgage, the homeowner is actually borrowing the difference between the payments and the current interest due.

graduated rental lease. A lease that provides for specified changes in rent at one or more points during the lease term.

grain elevator. *See* elevator.

grand list. In New England, the tax roll or assessment list of a community.

grant. The act of transferring property or an interest in property.

grant deed. A deed in which the grantor warrants that he or she has not previously conveyed or encumbered the property; does not ensure that the grantor is the owner of the property or that the property is unencumbered; conveys any after-acquired title of the grantor, unless a different intent is expressed. [1]

grantee. A person to whom property is transferred by deed or to whom property rights are granted by a trust instrument or other document.

grant-in-aid. The allowable contribution made by local parties, in cash or its equivalent, as part of the local share in an urban renewal project.

grantor. A person who transfers property by deed or grants property rights through a trust instrument or other document.

granular structure. Soil aggregates of up to two centimeters in diameter that are of medium consistency and are somewhat rounded. Coarse granular describes aggregates close to maximum size; fine granular refers to aggregates under five millimeters in diameter.

graph. A diagram that represents the variation of a variable in comparison with one or more other variables; the collection of all points whose coordinates satisfy a given funtional relation.

grasses. Plants with hollow, jointed stems and leaves that grow in two rows on the stems; veins in leaves are parallel.

grassland. A type of range vegetation that includes all lands bearing grasses, except meadows; perennial grasses predominate, but forbs and browse may be present.

grazing capacity. The maximum number of animals that can feed in an area without damaging the vegetation or related resources. *Also called* grazing potential.

grazing land. Rangeland with an understory of vegetation that provides forage for grazing animals; includes natural grasslands, shrublands, savannas, most deserts, tundra, coastal marshes, and wet meadows.

grazing season. A period of grazing that makes optimum use of forage resources; on public lands, an established period for which grazing permits are issued.

grazing unit. An area of public or private rangeland that is grazed as a single entity.

greasewood. A type of range vegetation that includes areas where greasewood (*sarcobatus*) is the predominant vegetation.

great soil group. A group of soils with common internal characteristics; includes one or more families of soil.

green. An irregularly shaped area of nearly perfect turf where a golfer finishes the hole and putts the ball into the cup.

greenbelt. A band of countryside surrounding a development or neighborhood on which building is generally prohibited; usually large enough to protect against objectional property uses or the intrusion of nearby development. [6]

green lumber. Lumber that has more moisture than air- or kiln-dried lumber; unseasoned lumber.

grid
1. A grating of crossed bars.
2. A pattern composed of parallel lines that intersect at right angles.
3. A chart used to rate a property, a neighborhood, comparables, etc.

gridiron. The rectangular pattern of streets in a city or subdivision development.

grid system. The rectangular subdivision of property used in many American cities; designed to make a minimum amount of road surface accessible to a maximum number of individual parcels. [9]

grillage. A system of beams that are laid crosswise to form a foundation that evenly distributes imposed loads.

groin
1. A structure placed on a beach to act as a breakwater; usually made of piling, sometimes with a stone apron at the end.
2. In architecture, the curved line or edge formed by the intersection of two vaulted or arched surfaces.

gross building area (GBA). The total floor area of a building, excluding unenclosed areas, measured from the exterior of the walls; superstructure floor area plus substructure or basement area.

gross income. Income from the operation of a business or the management of property, customarily stated on an annual basis. *See also* effective gross income (*EGI*); potential gross income (*PGI*).

gross income multiplier (GIM). The ratio between sale price or value and potential or effective annual gross income; used to estimate value as a multiple of the specified gross income. *See also* effective gross income multiplier (*EGIM*); gross rent multiplier (*GRM*); potential gross income multiplier (*PGIM*).

gross leasable area (GLA). The total floor area designed for the occupancy and exclusive use of tenants, including basements and mezzanines; measured from the center of joint partitioning to outside wall surfaces and expressed in square feet. [13]

gross lease. A lease in which the lessor is obligated to pay all or most property charges, e.g., real estate taxes, insurance, structural repairs.

gross living area. A measurement of residential space.

gross national product (GNP). The monetary value of all final goods and services produced by a nation's economy, before deducting depreciation and allowances for the consumption of durable capital goods.

gross rent multiplier (*GRM*). The relationship or ratio between sale price or value and gross rental income.

gross sales. The total amount of invoiced sales, before deducting returns, allowances, etc.

ground area. The area in a building computed from the exterior dimensions of the ground floor.

ground beam. In construction, a horizontal member of iron, steel, or stone that is located on or near the ground and used to support the superstructure and distribute its load.

ground coverage. The percentage of ground area covered by ground floor building improvements.

ground floor. The floor of a building that is approximately level with the ground.

ground lease. A lease that grants the right to use and occupy land. [5]

ground rent. Rent paid for the right to use and occupy land; the portion of the total rent allocated to the underlying land.

grounds. Strips of wood placed around wall openings to indicate the finish level for plaster or concrete.

ground water. All water that has seeped down beneath the surface of the ground or in the subsoil; water from springs or wells.

grout. A thin, fluid mortar used to fill small joints and cavities in masonry work.

grove. A planting of uniformly spaced fruit- or nut-bearing trees; commonly applied to citrus plantings, but also applied to plantings of walnuts or other specialty nut crops.

guaranteed mortgage. A mortgage in which a party other than the borrower assures payment in the event of default; e.g., a VA-guaranteed mortgage. [2]

guaranteed title. A title whose validity is insured by an abstract, title, or indemnity company.

guide meridian. *See* meridian.

gully erosion. Rill erosion that continues over a period of time, cutting through the soft, tilled earth and into the firm, subsoil structure; in time, its depth becomes a barrier that is not easily crossed with farm tools or normal equipment. *See also* rill erosion.

gumbo soil. A silty, fine-textured soil that becomes very sticky and greasy when wet.

gunite. A trade name for a cement-like compound dispensed from a gun under pneumatic pressure.

gutter
1. A channel running along the length of a building that carries off rainwater, usually by means of downspouts.
2. A ridge formed where the edge of a street meets a raised sidewalk, or a depressed ridge on a road's shoulder, that controls the flowage of storm water.

gypsum. A common mineral, hydrated calcium sulphate, in the form of colorless crystals or masses that are easily crumbled; an ingredient of plaster of paris and Keene's cement.

gypsum blocks. A friable building material that is not suitable for load-bearing walls.

gypsum sheathing board. A prefabrication material made of set gypsum covered with water-repellent paper; replaces sheathing and sheathing paper in construction.

gypsum wallboard. A type of wallboard used as a substitute for plaster in drywall construction; a prefabricated sheet of gypsum covered with paper to which paint or wallpaper can be applied.

H

habendum clause. A clause in a real estate document that specifies the extent of the interest to be conveyed, e.g., life, fee.

half shrub. Semiwoody perennials of low stature; e.g., *aplopappus, gutierrezia, artemisia frigida, eriogonum wrightii*; a woody caudex that produces herbaceous stems that die back each year.

half-timbered. Describes house construction with exposed timber wall framing over masonry or lath and plaster; simulated half-timbering uses boards on plaster walls. Half-timbering is a distinguishing characteristic of Elizabethan architecture.

hall
1. A room at the entrance of a building or a passage that provides access to various parts of a building.
2. A large room used for public gatherings.

hand-move sprinkler. Portable irrigation sprinkler system constructed from aluminum pipe and moved by hand to various irrigation settings.

hard copy. In computer usage, any data or text printed on paper. [16]

hard disk. In computer usage, a rigid, magnetic storage medium that holds a great deal of information that can be accessed more quickly than data on a floppy disk. [16]

hard dollars. The portion of the total, initial consideration paid for the acquisition of property that cannot immediately be deducted by the buyer for income tax purposes. [1]

hard goods. A class of merchandise composed primarily of durable items; e.g., hardware, machines, heavy appliances, electrical and plumbing fixtures, farming machinery and supplies. *Also called* hardlines. [17]

hard finish. The smooth, finished coat of plaster that is applied over rough plastering.

hardpan. Silt, clay, or any soil material that is cemented together; a hardened soil horizon that will not dissolve in water; may be of any texture, compacted by iron oxide, organic material, silica, calcium carbonate, or other substances.

hardware
1.   The metal fittings of a building; e.g., hinges, locks, lifts, door-knobs. *Also called* builders' hardware or finish hardware.
2.   In computer usage, the physical components or equipment that make up a computer system. [16]

hardwood. Lumber cut from broad-leaved trees, e.g., oak, mahogany, walnut, birch, that is used for interior finishing and flooring; refers to a type of tree, not the hardness of the wood.

hatchway. A lifting or sliding door in a ceiling that gives access to an attic; a similar door in a floor, giving access to a cellar. *Also called* scuttle.

hay. Meadow grasses that are cut and cured for livestock feed.

haymow. The part of a barn where hay or straw is stored.

hazards. Sand bunkers, traps, ponds, and other obstacles on a golf course.

H beam. An H-shaped, steel structural member, frequently used as a column.

head

1. A body of water kept in reserve at a height, including the containing bank, dam, or wall.
2. The difference in elevation between two points in a body of fluid; the resulting pressure of the fluid at the lower point expressed as this height.
3. The source of a river or stream.
4. The topmost framing member of a window or door.

header. In masonry, a brick or stone laid across the thickness of a wall with one end toward the face of the wall; in carpentry, a wood beam set at right angles to the joists to provide a seat or support; a wood lintel.

head jamb. A piece of finish material placed across the underside of the top of a door or window opening.

head room. The distance between the top of a finished floor and the lowest part of the floor structure above.

headway. The time interval between two vehicles traveling in the same direction on the same route.

health-related facility. A facility designated, staffed, and equipped to accommodate individuals who do not need hospital care, are generally ambulatory, and require a minimum of supervision and assistance.

hearsay evidence. Testimony as to an event or fact about which the witness does not have firsthand knowledge; he or she relates what was reported by a person purporting to have direct knowledge.

hearth. The floor of a fireplace. The front hearth extends out into the room and may be of brick or decorative stone; the back hearth is inside the fireplace and usually made of firebrick. [8]

heating system. Any device or system for heating a building; usually, a furnace or boiler used to generate steam, hot water, or hot air; a burner or air device that uses coal, oil, gas, or electricity to heat water or air that is then circulated through the system. Types of heating systems include warm air, hot water, direct steam, radiant, and electric.

heating, ventilation, and air-conditioning system (HVAC). A unit that regulates the distribution of heat and fresh air throughout a building.

heat pump. A reverse cycle refrigeration unit that can be used for heating or cooling.

heavy industry. Describes industries that are physically extensive or complex and usually require large tracts of land; e.g., steel mills, refineries, foundries, packing plants; also, industrial operations that produce hazards or nuisances, e.g., objectionable fumes, pollution, noise, vibration.

heavy soil. A clay soil. *See also* clay; fine-textured soil.

heavy steel frame. A building with framing members of heavy steel, e.g., beams, girders, columns, that can carry heavy loads and absorb shocks and vibrations.

hedgerow planting. The planting of trees or vines in rows with little space between individual plants to increase production or decrease costs; usually permits more mechanization in harvesting, pruning, or other cultural operations; may affect the economic life of the trees or vines involved.

hedging. In agriculture, the trimming or mechanical pruning of permanent plantings, e.g., orchards, groves.

heel. In construction, the part of a framing member that rests on the wall plate.

height density. A zoning regulation that controls use or occupancy within a given area by designating the maximum height of structures.

heir. A person who inherits real or personal property; a person legally designated to inherit the estate of one who has died intestate.

hereditaments. All inheritable property, e.g., real, personal, corporeal, incorporeal.

highest and best use
1.   The reasonable and probable use that supports the highest present value of vacant land or improved property, as defined, as of the date of the appraisal.
2.   The reasonably probable and legal use of land or sites as though vacant, found to be physically possible, appropriately supported, financially feasible, and that results in the highest present land value.
3.   The most profitable use.

Implied in these definitions is that the determination of highest and best use takes into account the contribution of a specific use to the community and community development goals as well as the benefits of that use to individual property owners. Hence, in certain situations the highest and best use of land may be for parks, greenbelts, preservation, conservation, wildlife habitats, and the like.

high-rise apartment building. An indefinite term popular since World War II that is used to distinguish the modern, elevator apartment building from its prewar counterpart; usually a high building, but this standard varies in different areas.

high water line. The point on the shore to which the tide normally rises; varies with seasons, time, wind, and other causes. *See also* mean high water line.

highway capacity. The capacity of a roadway to accept traffic, expressed as a number; controlled by the types of vehicles using the highway, the number and width of travel lanes, the allowable speed, road curvature and topography, and the limitations of access and development controls of adjacent real estate.

highway easement. A right granted or taken for the construction, maintenance, and operation of a highway; in the case of a public thoroughfare, the abutting landholders are ordinarily assumed to own the fee to the center line of the right-of-way.

highway frontage. Land that is adjacent to and abuts a highway right-of-way.

highway line. The outside limits of a highway right-of-way; as distinguised from the limits of actual construction, e.g., curbs, shoulders, slopes. *Also called* right-of-way line.

hilly land. Uneven land with dominant slopes between 16% and 30%.

hindsight rule. A rule that permits the admission of evidence relating to events subsequent to the date of taking to prove or disprove the validity of any claim of value.

hip. The inclined ridge formed by the intersection of two sloping roof surfaces with unparallel eave lines.

hip roof. A roof with sloping sides and end slopes that are connected by a ridge, the length of which is called a run; distinguished from a pyramid roof in which all slopes meet so that virtually no ridge remains.

histogram. A set of vertical bars that are proportionate in size to the frequencies represented. *See also* frequency distribution.

historical cost. The cost of a property when it was originally constructed; as distinguished from original cost, the actual cost to the present owner, who may have purchased at a price greater or less than historical, or first, cost. In assembled property, e.g., a public utility, the first cost as defined, plus subsequent additions and betterments, minus deductions.

historic district. An area designated by municipal zoning to retain and preserve its historic quality.

historic preservation. The preservation of historic sites and districts by regulation or rehabilitation.

historic site. A parcel that is distinguished because an important historic event occurred on or near the site.

hog factory. In agriculture, a hog-feeding facility where hogs are confined to grow from farrowing to slaughter size under controlled conditions.

holdback. A portion of a loan commitment that is not funded until an additional requirement is met, e.g., rental and completion of a project.

hold harmless agreement. A legally binding agreement in which the liability of one party is assumed by another.

holding period. The term of ownership of an investment. *See also* projection period.

holdover tenant. A tenant who remains in possession of the leased real estate after the lease has expired; in many states, the lease is automatically renewed if the lessor accepts a rent payment after the expiration of the lease.

hollow-newel stair. A circular stairway with a well hole in the middle.

hollow wall. A wall, usually of masonry, that consists of two vertical components with an air space in betweeen.

homestead. The fixed residence or dwelling of the head of a family, including the principal house, other buildings, and the surrounding land.

homestead exemption
1. The lawful withdrawal of a property occupied by the head of a family from attachment by the occupant's creditors or forced sale for general debts.
2. A release from assessment or property tax, or the application of a lower tax rate, on property designated as a family homestead.

homogeneous. Describes an area or neighborhood where the property types and uses are similar and the inhabitants have compatible cultural, social, and economic interests.

hood. A canopy over a casement window; the part of a fireplace that projects over the hearth; a chimney cap that eliminates down draft; a canopy over a cooking appliance that is usually ventilated to control and disperse heat or offensive odors.

hopper. A device used on the sides of hospital windows to prevent drafts.

hopper window. *See* hospital window.

horizon. A layer of soil approximately parallel to the land surface that has more or less well-defined characteristics produced through soil-building processes. *See also* A horizon; B horizon; C horizon; D horizon.

horizontal control network. A national system of interrelated monument points that is used primarily to survey extremely large areas. [10]

horizontal subdivision. The division of a tract of land into smaller parcels for sale or lease.

Hoskold factor. A multiplier that is calculated from special tables and used to capitalize the income produced by a wasting asset; provides for recapture with actual or hypothetical contributions to a sinking fund that grows with compound interest at a safe rate and for return on the investment at a higher, speculative rate.

hospital. An institution where ill or injured persons receive short-term medical, surgical, or psychiatric treatment, nursing care, food, and shelter; provides complete medical and surgical services.

hospital window. A window that is hinged at the bottom and opens inward with draft-preventers, or hoppers, on the sides.

hotel. A facility that offers lodging accommodations and a wide range of other services, e.g., restaurants, convention facilities, meeting rooms, recreational facilities, commercial shops; usually located in an urban area.

hotel/motel unit. The smallest accommodation that can be sold to a patron; must contain one full bath, sleeping accommodations, and an entrance door with a key.

hot water system. A heating system consisting of a boiler, radiators, an expansion tank, and interconnected piping filled with water that circulates from the boiler through pipes to radiators where heat is released before the water returns to the boiler; classified as gravity or forced circulation systems, with one or two pipes and open or closed expansion tanks.

hour-inch. A measure that equals water flowing at a miner's inch for one hour; ⅟₅₀th of a cubic foot per second in Southern California, Arizona, Montana, and Oregon.

house. A dwelling; may be single or double; e.g., duplex, townhouse, row house, split-level ranch.

household. All persons who occupy a group of rooms or a single room that constitutes one housing unit. [17]

household size. The total number of related or unrelated persons residing in a household unit. [17]

house sewer. The drain pipe system or pipes that connect with the main sewer in the street. *See also* lateral.

housing starts. Newly constructed housing units, including both single-family and multifamily domiciles. [2]

housing stock. The total inventory of dwelling units, including both owned and rented property. [2]

HUD. *See* Department of Housing and Urban Development.

human ecology. The study of the relationship between man and the environment; when focused on the urban environment, it involves the spatial distribution of people, groups, and institutions in a community, the relationships among them, and the changes in the distribution caused by adaptation, competition, and accommodation.

Humboldt rule. A form of the Spaulding rule that measures old growth redwood logs and provides for their numerous invisible defects with a blanket 30% deduction; can produce a large overrun if the amount of defects is small; sometimes used to scale Douglas fir, although this practice is not recommended. *Also called* Humboldt scale. *See also* log rules.

hummocks. Low mounds in swamp soils formed by the wind or by pasturing.

humus. The well-decomposed, relatively stable part of the soil's organic matter; keeps the soil soft and granular and increases its capacity to hold water and plant food.

hundred percent location. Describes a location in the central business district that commands the highest land value or rent.

hunting leases. Agreements in which a private property owner grants the right to hunt natural game on his or her land; sometimes necessitate additional land management.

hutch. A type of housing used for domestic rabbit production.

HVAC. *See* heating, ventilation, and air-conditioning system.

hydraulic cement. A type of cement that hardens under water.

hydroelectric plant. A plant designed to generate and distribute electrical power produced by falling water; includes building(s), engines, dynamos, etc.

hydrograph. A chart that shows the quantity of flowing water in a stream at specific intervals over a period of time.

hydroponics. The science of growing plants in liquid mineral solutions that provide all plant nutrients artificially.

hypothecate. To pledge as security while retaining possession. [1]

hypothesis. In inferential statistics, a statement to be proved. One begins with a null hypothesis, a statement of what one chooses to accept in the absence of sufficient evidence to the contrary, specifies the alternative hypothesis to be proved, and analyzes the available data to determine if the null hypothesis can be rejected and the alternative hypothesis accepted with some confidence.

I

I beam. A steel beam that resembles the letter I in cross section.

igneous rock. A rock created by the cooling of melted, mineral material. *Also called* fire rock.

illiquidity. Describes the condition of assets that are not readily converted into cash.

illuviation. The process in which soil material from an upper horizon is deposited in the horizon below.

immature soil. A young or imperfectly developed soil without individual horizons.

impact printer. In computer usage, a type of printer that transfers information to paper by striking a ribbon against a sheet of paper, like a typewriter. [16]

impervious soil. Soil that does not allow the passage of water, air, or plant roots.

impounds. Payments made to a fiduciary, usually a lender, for items such as property taxes, assessments, and insurance; often imposed by government agencies on the sale of interests in real estate syndications. The agency may require that subscription funds be placed in a special escrow account until a specific number of subscriptions has been paid. Then the funds are returned to the syndicate for use in purchasing the subject property or other activities defined in the offering circular and application for qualification. [1]

improved land. Land that has been developed for some use by the construction of improvements; also, land that has been prepared for development by grading, draining, installing utilities, etc., as distinguished from raw land.

improvements. Buildings or other relatively permanent structures or developments located on, or attached to, land.

inadequate improvement. *See* underimprovement.

incentive zoning. An agreement between public officials and private developers concerning rentable building bulk and the minimum building bulk specified by the zoning ordinance. In this arrangement, a desirable public improvement or open-space objective is established by government officials and developers are offered an incentive, greater usable building bulk, to provide the desired amenity. Planned unit developments and voluntary cluster developments are forms of incentive zoning. [9]

incinerator. A device that burns waste material and rubbish.

income. Money or other benefits that are assumed to be received periodically.

income approach. *See* income capitalization approach.

income capitalization approach. A set of procedures in which an appraiser derives a value indication for income-producing property by converting anticipated benefits into property value. This conversion is accomplished either by 1) capitalizing a single year's income expectancy or an annual average of several years' income expectancies at a market-derived capitalization rate or a capitalization rate that reflects a specified income pattern, return on investment, and change in the value of the investment; or 2) discounting the annual cash flows for the holding period and the reversion at a specified yield rate.

income participation. The right of the mortgagee to share some portion of the future income generated by the property, usually over the term of the underlying mortgage. *See also* equity participation.

income-producing life. A period of time that begins when a plant or crop achieves peak production and ends when production declines; refers specifically to orchard or vineyard crops that require a long start-up period before cash flow is realized; varies with the type of crop and the effectiveness of management.

income-producing property. A type of property created primarily to produce monetary income.

income tax liability
1. An obligation to federal, state, or local government based on the marginal tax rate and taxable income of an individual or corporation.
2. In income-producing properties, net operating income less deductible items, e.g., interest on debt, allowable depreciation, times the appropriate marginal tax rate.

increasing and decreasing returns. The concept that successive increments of one or more agents of production added to fixed amounts of other agents will enhance income, in dollars, benefits, or amenities, at an increasing rate until a maximum return is reached. Then, income will decrease until the increment to value becomes increasingly less than the value of the added agent or agents.

increasing annuity. An income stream of evenly spaced, periodic payments that increase in a systematic pattern.

incubator building. An industrial property that is subdivided into low-rent space and leased to fledgling business or manufacturing firms in the hope that they will grow and require additional space.

incurable depreciation. *See* incurable functional obsolescence; incurable physical deterioration.

incurable functional obsolescence. An element of accrued depreciation; an incurable defect caused by a deficiency or superadequacy in the structure, materials, or design.

incurable physical deterioration. An element of accrued depreciation; a defect caused by physical deterioration that is impractical or uneconomic to correct.

indemnity. Recovery of sustained loss.

indenture. A deed or other instrument involving two or more parties that enumerates the reciprocal and paralleling rights and obligations of each party.

indexed mortgage. *See* price level-adjusted mortgage (PLAM).

index lease. A lease, usually for a long term, that provides for periodic rent adjustments based on the change in a specific index, e.g., the cost of living index.

index number. A measure of the differences in the magnitude of a group of related variables compared with a base period, which is typically valued at l00; usually, index numbers show the change in the prices of specific commodities or group averages over a period of time.

indirect costs. In construction, expenditures for items other than labor and materials; e.g., contractor's overhead and profit; administrative costs; professional fees; financing costs; taxes, interest, and insurance during construction; lease-up costs. *Also called* soft costs.

indirect lighting. Reflected or diffused lighting achieved by directing the light toward the ceiling, the walls, or some other surface.

industrial park. A controlled, park-like development that is designed to accommodate specific types of industry; provides the required appurtenances, e.g., public utilities, streets, railroad sidings, water and sewage facilities.

industrial plant. A single location where industrial operations are performed; includes all structures on the site. [11]

industrial property. Land and/or improvements that can be adapted for industrial use; a combination of land, improvements, and machinery integrated into a functioning unit to assemble, process, and manufacture products from raw materials or fabricated parts; factories that render service, e.g, laundries, dry cleaners, storage warehouses, or produce natural resources, e.g., oil wells.

industrial siding. A spur track running along an industrial site where a railroad delivers and removes freight cars.

industrial tax exemption. An exemption from local property taxes granted, for a specific period, to attract new industries to the community or to encourage the expansion of existing industry.

inferential statistics. A branch of statistics that attempts to predict the values of many observations of a variable from a few observations of that variable and related facts; the statistics calculated in such predictions.

inflation. An erosion of the purchasing power of currency. [2]

infrastructure
1. In planning, used to describe services and facilities that are integral parts of urban community life.
2. In a group of buildings or a complex, the core of development that is the source of all utilities and support services.

ingress. A means of entering; an entrance. [2]

inheritance tax. A tax on the right to receive property by inheritance; as distinguished from estate tax.

in lieu tax. A tax that substitutes for property taxes. *Also called* in lieu payments or payments in lieu of taxes.

in personam. Against a person, not a thing.

in rem. Against a thing, not a person. [1]

in rem note. A nonrecourse note.

inside lot. A lot that is removed from a street intersection and unaffected by corner influence.

installment contract. A type of purchase contract in which payment is made in prescribed installments that are usually forfeited if default occurs; in the sale of real property, title is not normally transferred until all payments under the contract are made.

installment note. A promissory note that provides for payment of the principal in two or more specific installments at stated times. [1]

installment sale. A sale in which the proceeds are to be received in more than one payment. [1]

Institute of Real Estate Management (IREM). The organization of real estate professionals concerned with property management. The institute confers the CPM and AMO designations.

institutional property. Property of a public nature owned and operated by the government or by nonprofit organizations; e.g., hospitals, orphanages, private and public educational facilities, correctional facilities, museums; also describes properties of a private nature, e.g., banks, insurance companies.

instrument. In real estate, a formal, legal document; e.g., a contract, deed, lease, will.

insulating board. A building board made of compressed plant fibers, e.g., wood, cane, corn stalks, dried and pressed to a specified thickness.

insulation. Any material used to reduce the transfer of heat, cold, or sound.

insurable value. The value of the destructible portions of a property, which determines the amount of insurance that may, or should, be carried to indemnify the owner in the event of loss.

insurance. A personal contract to indemnify the insured for a potential loss; specific coverages relate to the asset insured or the potential hazard; e.g., property insurance, boiler insurance, storm insurance, title insurance, mortgage insurance, rent loss insurance, fire insurance, plate glass insurance, extended coverage insurance, contents insurance, comprehensive insurance, scheduled insurance.

insurance rate. The percentage relationship between the insurance premium and the coverage it buys.

insured mortgage. A mortgage in which a party other than the borrower assures payment on default by the mortgagor in return for the payment of a premium; e.g., FHA-insured mortgages, private mortgage insurance (PMI). [2]

intangible assets
1. Items of personal property; e.g., franchises, trademarks, patents, copyrights, goodwill.

2.   Deferred items such as a development or organization expense.

intangible property. *See* intangible assets.

intangible value. A value that cannot be imputed to any part of the physical property; e.g., the excess value attributable to a favorable lease, the value attributable to goodwill.

intensity. In agricultural land use, a reflection of the expenditure of labor and capital per unit of land area; relates to physical development, not maximum economic potential or highest and best use of the land.

intensive farming. The use of comparatively large amounts of labor and working capital per acre of land; generally implies maximum productivity.

intercept. In graphic analysis, the point at which a line, e.g., the regression line, intercepts the axis on which the dependent variable is plotted; the value of the predicted variable when the value of the predictor variable is zero; the coefficient a or b_o.

interchange. A system of underpasses and overpasses that routes traffic on and off highways without disrupting through traffic; may link two or more highways.

interchange ramp. A traveled way that allows traffic to change from one roadway to another.

interest. Money paid for, or earned by, the use of capital; a return on capital as distinguished from a return of capital.

interest-only loan. A nonamortizing loan in which the lender receives only interest during the term of the loan and recovers the principal in a lump sum at the time of maturity. *Also called* straight loan. *See also* balloon mortgage.

interest rate. A rate of return on capital; usually expressed as an annual percentage of the amount loaned or invested.

interim financing. A temporary or short-term loan that is secured by a mortgage and generally paid off from the proceeds of permanent financing. *See also* construction loan. [2]

interim use. The temporary use to which a site or improved property is put until it is ready to be put to its highest and best use.

interior lot. *See* inside lot.

interior trim. The finish on the interior of a building; e.g., casing, molding, baseboard.

interjurisdictional equalization. The application of multipliers or factors to each assessment comprising the assessment base to ensure a common level of assessment in all taxing jurisdictions in a state or county; may include the adjustment of individual assessments and the ordering of reassessments.

intermediate-term credit. Credit extended for expensive items, e.g., equipment, feeder and breeding livestock, dairy cattle, that are used for more than one farm season and financed for five to ten years; may also be used to refinance short-term debts; personal property is ordinarily used as collateral.

internal conformity. The condition that exists when labor, capital, coordination, and land are appropriately combined in a property.

internal rate of return (*IRR*). The annualized rate of return on capital that is generated or capable of being generated within an investment or portfolio over the period of ownership; similar to the equity yield rate; often used to measure profitability after income taxes, i.e., the after-tax equity yield rate; the rate of discount that makes the net present value of an investment equal to zero; discounts all returns from an investment, including returns from its termination, to equal the original investment.

internal supports. The beams, columns, flooring system, and ceilings of a structure.

International style. An architectural style popular from 1930 to 1970 and characterized by skyscraper construction, no cornices, ornamentation, and terra-cotta exteriors; emphasized a streamlined appearance, with curtain wall and flush windows.

interpolation. The calculation or estimation of a quantity within the range of data on which the calculation or estimate is based; the approximation of a value that falls between the tabular entries in a set of tables.

intersection. The point at which two lines cross; the crossing of two streets at grade.

interstate highway system. A network of limited-access, divided highways within the United States that link principal metropolitan areas and industrial centers, serve the national defense, and connect with principal intercontinental routes in Canada and Mexico.

intestate. The condition of dying without leaving a valid will.

intractability. The characteristic that describes a soil that is difficult to work.

intrinsic value. The inherent worth of a thing.

inventory value. *See* book value.

inverse condemnation. A legal process in which an owner can claim damages from a loss in property value and receive compensation when the proposed condemnation action has not been instituted by the condemning body.

invested capital. The original capital, or equity, invested in an enterprise plus any accumulated profits that are not withdrawn, but allowed to remain and augment the initial investment.

investment. Monies placed in a property, usually with the expectation of producing a profit; assumes a reasonable degree of safety and the ultimate recovery of principal; for long-term use, as distinguished from speculation.

investment analysis. A process in which the attractiveness of an investment is measured by analyzing ratios, e.g., multipliers, financial ratios, profitability, that reflect the relationship between the investment's acquisition price and its anticipated future benefits; may analyze in terms of alternative investment opportunities or specific investor criteria.

investment builder. A company primarily engaged in the construction of residential, commercial, and industrial buildings to be retained as investments. [1]

investment property. Property that constitutes a business enterprise consisting of all tangible and intangible assets assembled and developed as a single unit of utility for lease or rental, in whole or in part, to others for profit; normally purchased in expectation of annual net income and/ or capital gain.

investment tax credit. A direct credit against federal income tax, equal to a percentage or portion of the investment in a qualified property, that can be taken when certain depreciable property with a useful life of at least four years is placed in service during the taxable year.

investment value. The value of an investment to a particular investor, based on his or her investment requirements; as distinguished from market value, which is impersonal and detached. *See also* market value.

investment yield. *See* internal rate of return (*IRR*).

involuntary conversion. The conversion of property when it is destroyed, in whole or in part, stolen, seized, requisitioned, condemned, or threatened by imminent requisition or condemnation; as a result, property is converted into money or other, similar property through insurance proceeds or condemnation awards. [1]

Inwood annuity. A traditional technique in which present value factors, or Inwood coefficients, from standard compound interest tables are used to discount a stream of level income to present worth; an annuity that can be capitalized with an Inwood factor, or coefficient. *Also called* Inwood annuity capitalization.

Inwood factor. A factor that reflects the present worth of $1 per period for a given number of periods, discounted at a given discount rate;

obtained by calculation or from standard compound interest tables; one of the six functions of $1. *Also called* Inwood coefficient.

IREM. *See* Institute of Real Estate Management.

irregular curve. *See* French curve.

irrigation. The artificial application of water to the soil for full crop production; used in arid regions or when rainfall is not sufficient.

irrigation district. An agency established by local government that has the authority to implement and operate an irrigation system for the district and to levy taxes to finance its operations.

island. In highway construction, the land area between opposing traveled ways that is designated for their control or for the safety of pedestrians.

island zoning. In planning and zoning, the placement of a property or a small group of properties in a permitted use category that does not conform to the zone classification and general character of the neighborhood; substantially equivalent to the legal concept of spot zoning.

isohyetal line. An imaginary line that connects areas on the earth where the quantity of annual rainfall is about the same; delineates zones of different rainfall.

Italianate style. An architectural style popular from 1850 to 1870 and often used in urban commercial buildings; characterized by flat roofs with projecting cornices, arches and columns framing windows, cast iron ornamentation on the facade, and red S-shaped roof tiles.

iteration. A series of repetitive computations; a mathematical process used to solve for an unknown quantity by trial and error, starting with a trial quantity and testing various quantities in a series of repetitive calculations until the error is negligible.

iterative routine. A computer subroutine that establishes a repeated calculation; used to derive a required value through repeated approximations.

J

jack rafter. A short roof rafter that extends from another structural framing member, not from the top of the exterior wall.

jack stud. An extra vertical supporting member in a frame wall or partition over a door, window, or archway.

jalousies. Adjustable glass louvers in doors or windows that regulate light and air or exclude rain.

jamb. The side framing or finish of a doorway or window.

jetty
  1. A structure of stones, piles, etc., that projects into a body of water to protect a harbor; e.g., a pier.
  2. In construction, the projecting parts of a structure; e.g., a bay window, a balcony.

J **factor.** An income adjustment factor used to convert a changing stream of income to its level equivalent.

joint. The point where two objects or surfaces meet; the space between units in a masonry wall that is occupied by mortar or bonding material *See also* butt joint; lap joint.

joint and several obligation. A situation in which each signing party is liable for his or her share of a debt or obligation plus the shares of all other signing parties; as distinguished from several obligation in which each signatory is responsible only for his or her liabilities.

joint probability. The probability that two or more events will both occur.

joint tenancy. Joint ownership by two or more persons with right of survivorship. [1]

joint venture. A commercial undertaking related to a specific project that involves two or more partners; a limited arrangement which the associates have no intention of developing into a permanent partnership. *See also* partnership.

joist
1. The lumber in a rectangular cross section of a building, two to five inches thick and four or more inches wide.
2. Any of the small, horizontal timbers or beams that support a floor.

judgment creditor. A person who has received a decree or judgment from the court against his or her debtor for money due. [2]

judgment debtor. A person against whom a judgment has been issued by the court for money owed. [2]

judgment lien. A statutory lien on the real and personal property of a judgment debtor; created by the judgment itself. [2]

judgment sampling. A sample selected according to personal judgment; subjective, but often less costly than probability samples and, in certain instances, superior, e.g., in small-scale surveys, in pilot studies, in constructing index numbers.

judicial sale. A court action that enforces a judgment lien by selling property to pay a debt. [2]

junction box. A box in an electrical system where main circuits are connected or smaller circuits join the main circuit.

junior department store. A store that is classified between a full department store and a variety store in terms of its size and selection of merchandise. [17]

junior lien. A lien placed on the property after a previous lien has been made and recorded; a lien made secondary to another by agreement.

junior mortgage loan. *See* junior lien.

jurisdiction. The extent or range of power, authority, or control; the physical territory over which power, authority, or control is exercised.

just compensation. In condemnation, the amount of loss for which a property owner is compensated when his or her property is taken; should put the owner in as good a position pecuniarily as he or she would be if the property had not been taken; generally held to be market value, but courts have refused to rule that it is always equivalent to market value.

K

kalamein. Trade name for the galvanized sheet steel that covers solid core wooden doors.

kame. A short, irregular ridge, hill, or hillock of stratified glacial drift; usually hilly and interspersed with depressions, providing no surface drainage.

Keene's cement. A white, hard-finished plaster that sets quickly and produces an extremely durable wall; used for bathrooms and kitchens; made of plaster of paris soaked in a solution of borax or alum and cream of tartar.

keystone. A wedge-shaped or trapezoidal structural piece that forms the center unit at the top of a masonry arch.

K factor
1. An income stabilization factor used to convert a stream of income changing at a constant ratio into its stable equivalent.
2. A measure of heat transmission used to measure the insulating value of materials.

kicker. Payments made to a lender over and above debt service. *See also* equity participation.

kick plate. A metal strip placed at the lower edge of a door to protect the finish.

kiln. An oven-like chamber that bakes, hardens, or dries material, e.g., green lumber, bricks.

kiln-dried lumber. Lumber that is dried in a kiln to reduce its moisture content. [2]

kilobyte (K). In computer usage, one thousand bytes in the base two numbering system; actually, 1024 bytes.

kilowatt-hour (kwh). A common unit of electrical energy consumption equivalent to the total energy consumed when 1,000 watts are drawn for one hour.

king post. The vertical member at the center of a triangular truss.

kip. A unit of weight equal to 1,000 pounds that is used to express dead load.

kite winder. A triangular or kite-shaped step in a circular stairway that occurs where the direction of the stairway changes.

knee. A brace placed diagonally at the juncture of a post and a beam to provide rigidity.

knob insulator. A porcelain knob to which electric wires may be fastened in a single-line, open wiring system; rarely used in building, but common on pasture fences that carry low voltage current to confine animals.

knock down. Describes prepared construction materials that are delivered to the building site unassembled, but complete and ready to be assembled and installed, e.g., a window.

knot. A defect in lumber caused by cutting through a limb where it joins the trunk or cutting through a knot embedded in a tree.

L

laches. An established doctrine of equity in which courts discourage delay in the enforcement of rights and decline to try suits that are not brought within a reasonable time, regardless of statutory limitations. [2]

lacustrine soil. Soils formed from materials deposited by the waters of lakes and ponds; usually fine-textured and heavy.

laissez-faire. Let things proceed without interference; a doctrine opposing governmental interference in economic affairs beyond the minimum necessary for the maintenance of peace and property rights; the belief that an individual is most productive when allowed to follow his or her own interests without external restrictions.

lally column. A steel column, usually filled with concrete, that supports beams and girders.

lambing ground. In sheep raising, a specific area where the ewes are held for grazing at lambing time; usually offers good protection and fresh water.

lamella roof structure. An arched, roof-framing structure composed of planking arranged in diamond shapes.

laminate. To build up with layers of wood that are held together in a single unit; used to produce plywood and laminated beams. One layer is called a lamination or ply.

laminated floor. A floor deck made by gluing or spiking two-by-fours or planks together.

laminated wood. Wood that is laminated with the fibers or grains of the plies running parallel; as distinguished from plywood in which the grains of the plies run crosswise and only the fibers of the exterior plies are parallel.

land

1. The earth's surface, both land and water, and anything that is attached to it; all natural resources in their original state; e.g., mineral deposits, wildlife, timber, fish, water, coal deposits, soil.
2. In law, the solid surface on the earth; as distinguished from water.

land bank. A stockpile of land; created when an investor or developer buys land and holds it for future use. [6]

land/building ratio. The proportion of land area to gross building area.

Land Capability Classification System. A system developed by the Soil Conservation Service to classify agricultural land use based on a soil's limitations, not on its potential yield; indicates risk of damage to soil, soil needs, and response to management. The system includes land capability classes that group soils with similar limitations and restrictions in use, but different productive capabilities; subclasses that identify important limitations such as wetness or climate; and capability units that identify soils within a subclass that have similar risks and productivity and require similar management.

land capitalization rate (R_L). A rate that reflects the relationship between land income and land value; used in certain residual techniques to convert land income into an indication of land value.

land classification. *See* Land Capability Classification System.

land contract. A contract in which a purchaser of real estate agrees to pay a small portion of the purchase price when the contract is signed and additional sums, at intervals and in amounts specified in the contract, until the total purchase price is paid and the seller gives a deed; used primarily to protect the seller's interest in the unpaid balance because foreclosure can be exercised more quickly than under a mortgage. *Also called* contract for deed.

land court. A court that has jurisdiction over issues concerning real property and interests in real property.

land development. The improvement of land with utilities, roads, and services, which makes the land suitable for resale as developable plots for housing or other purposes. [6]

land economics. A branch of economics that deals with the use of land resources in attaining objectives set by society. [2]

L and H hardware. Door hinges and latches in L and H patterns, designed to create a colonial atmosphere.

land improvements. Relatively permanent structures built on, or physical changes made to, a property to increase its utility and value.

landing
1. A floor or platform at the head or foot of a flight of stairs; used to break the rise or change the direction of the stairway.
2. A place or platform where goods or persons land, e.g., from a boat.

land loan. A loan made to finance the purchase of raw land. [1]

landlocked parcel. A parcel of land that has no access to a road or highway.

landlord. The owner of real estate that is leased to others. [2]

landmark. A monument or erection that serves as a boundary dividing two adjoining parcels. [2]

landowner's royalty. An interest in unsevered oil, gas, coal, and other mineral rights that is retained or reserved by the landowner when he or she relinquishes interest in the real property involved.

land patent. A legal document in which the federal government conveys the title to land to an individual.

land planner. An individual who studies and evaluates the appropriateness of a property's location within the larger community; integrates a development and its facilities into the larger community; and makes recommendations concerning various development standards, e.g., density, community service, functional design, environmental safety and health. [1]

land planning. The discipline concerned with the design of land area uses, road networks, and utility layouts to ensure efficient use of real estate resources. [2]

land reclamation. Adaptation of land to a more intensive use by changing its character or environment through drainage, the provision of water, etc.

land registration. The recording of deeds, mortgages, and other instruments in a public office to evidence one's rights in real property and protect against fraud and questions regarding the title to, or interest in, property. [6]

land residual technique. A capitalization technique in which the net operating income attributable to the land is isolated and capitalized to indicate the land's contribution to total property value.

landscape
1. A relatively extensive view of rural scenery.
2. The natural or man-made elements that characterize an area of land.
3. To improve the natural environment by modifying its features to achieve beautiful or unusual effects.
4. The natural setting for a structure.

landscape architect. One who designs ground forms by selecting plant materials, creating open space areas around buildings, and planning recreational space and other use areas. [13]

landscaping. Modifying an area or tract of land by adding land improvements, e.g., trees, shrubs, lawns, paths, gardens; the improvements so added.

land service road. A road that is used primarily for access to land.

land surveying. The location and identification of a parcel of land by a professional surveyor or engineer.

land trust. A legal vehicle for partial ownership interests in real property in which independently owned properties are conveyed to a trustee to effect a profitable assemblage.

land use. The employment of a site or holding to produce revenue or other benefits; also, the designation by a governing authority of the use to which land may be put to promote the most advantageous development of the community, e.g., designation of industrial, residential, commercial, recreational, and other uses under a master plan. [6]

land use map. A comprehensive map of a community or section of a community that shows the character of all land uses and the extent and density of each use.

land use model. A simplified representation of a planner's understanding of the land development process; normally in the form of mathematical models or sets of equations.

land use planning. The development of plans for land uses that will best serve the general welfare over the long term and the formulation of ways and means to achieve these uses.

land use regulation. Any legal restriction, e.g., a zoning ordinance, that controls the use to which land may be put; may include controls established by restrictive covenants or contained in redevelopment or urban renewal plans approved by local governing bodies.

land use study. A complete inventory of the parcels in a given community or area, classified by type of use; may include an analysis of the patterns of use revealed by the inventory.

land utilization and marketability study (LUMS). An analysis of the potential uses of a parcel of land that is to be acquired in an urban renewal project; considers the entire market to be served by the area and the effect of the project on the area; used to determine what the highest and best use of the land will be when the development project is completed.

land value map. An assessment map that shows the value of land by location, expressed as value per square foot, per acre, etc., depending on the type of land involved.

lap joint. The overlapping of two adjoining pieces of timber, wallpaper, or other material. *See also* butt joint.

lap siding. Siding used to finish the exterior surface of a house or other structure. *Also called* ship lap siding.

large-lot zoning. The practice of zoning large lots for single-family residence only; used mainly in rural and suburban areas to restrict the local environment and protect existing real estate values. [9]

larger parcel. In condemnation, the portion of a property that has unity of ownership, contiguity, and unity of use, the three conditions that establish the larger parcel for the consideration of severance damages in most states. In federal and some state cases, however, contiguity is sometimes subordinated to unitary use.

late charge. A penalty that a borrower or tenant must pay for failing to make a regular payment when due. [1]

latent defects. Physical weaknesses or construction defects that cannnot be detected in a reasonable inspection of the property. [2]

lateral. Of or pertaining to a side; anything situated at, proceeding from, or directed to a side; any line that branches off or extends from a main line; e.g., the laterals of a septic system, an irrigation distribution ditch or pipe.

lath. Material used as a base for plaster; e.g., wood lath, gypsum lath, wire lath, metal lath.

latitude. The distance of a point on the earth's surface north or south of the equator; measured on the meridian through that point and expressed in degrees.

lattice. An openwork screen of crossed strips, rods, or bars of wood or metal.

lavatory. A place where washing is done; a wash bowl; also, a room fitted with a wash bowl and toilet facilities.

layout. An arrangement or plan of the details of a room; the arrangement of partitions and areas that constitutes the floor plan of a building.

leaching. Removal of material from the soil by percolating liquid.

leaching trenches. Trenches that carry waste liquids from sewers; may be constructed in gravelly or sandy soils that allow liquids to percolate into surrounding soils, or dug into firm ground and filled with broken stones, tile, gravel, and sand through which liquids leach.

leach line. In sewage disposal, a loose tile or perforated pipeline used to distribute sewage effluent throughout the soil.

leader. A length of metal pipe that carries rainwater from the gutter to the ground or another place of disposal. *Also called* rain leader.

lean-to. A small structure with a pitched roof, usually erected against the outside wall of a larger structure.

lean-to roof. A sloping roof that is supported on one side by the wall of an adjoining building.

lease. A written document in which the rights to use and occupancy of land or structures are transferred by the owner to another for a specified period of time in return for a specified rent.

leaseback. An arrangement in which the seller of a property is obligated to lease the property from the buyer under terms and conditions that are not negotiable. *See also* sale-leaseback. [1]

leased fee. *See* leased fee estate.

leased fee estate. An ownership interest held by a landlord with the right of use and occupancy conveyed by lease to others; usually consists of the right to receive rent and the right to repossession at the termination of the lease.

leasehold. *See* leasehold estate.

leasehold estate. The right to use and occupy real estate for a stated term and under certain conditions; conveyed by a lease.

leasehold improvements. Improvements or additions to leased property that have been made by the lessee.

leasehold loan. A loan received by the lessee on improvements and the leasehold interest in leased property; may or may not subordinate the lessee's interest in the land. [1]

lease interest. One of the real property interests that results from the separation of the bundle of rights by a lease, i.e., the leased fee estate or the leasehold estate.

lease rollover. The expiration of a lease and the subsequent re-leasing of the space.

leaves. The sliding, hinged, or detachable parts of a folding door, window, shutter, or table top.

legal access. The right of an adjacent owner whose property abuts a highway to use the highway for property ingress and egress. *See also* access rights.

legal description. A description of a parcel of land that identifies the parcel according to a system established or approved by law; a description that enables the parcel to be located and identified.

legally nonconforming use. A use that was lawfully established and maintained, but no longer conforms to the use regulations of the zone in which it is located because of a subsequent change in a zoning ordinance; a legally nonconforming building or portion of a building constitutes a nonconforming use of the land on which it is located; generally precludes additions or changes without municipal approval.

legal notice

1. Notice to be given in a particular circumstance, as required by a statute; e.g., notice required prior to a public sale of foreclosed real estate.

2. Notice that is legally considered to have been given as a result of specified circumstances, although there is no proof that the involved parties were actually notified; e.g., recording a deed in the proper records office constitutes public notice of the facts contained in the deed. [3]

legal owner. The owner of title, as distinguished from the holders of other interests, e.g., beneficial or possessory interests.

legal rate of interest. The maximum rate of interest that may be charged under state law. [2]

lender. Any individual or institution that extends funds at interest; any institution that invests funds in mortgages; e.g., mutual savings bank, life insurance company, pension or other trust fund, commercial bank, savings and loan association. [1]

lender participation. A financing arrangement in which the mortgage lender shares in the income or ownership of a real estate venture as a condition of the loan.

lessee. One who has the right to use or occupy a property under a lease agreement; a tenant.

lessee's interest. *See* leasehold estate.

lessor. One who holds property title and conveys the right to use and occupy the property under a lease agreement; a landlord.

lessor's interest. *See* leased fee estate.

letter of credit. A letter issued by a financial institution that certifies that the person named is entitled to draw on the institution or that the institution will honor his or her credit up to a certain sum. [1]

letter of intent. A nonobligatory instrument that expresses an intent to invest, conditioned on the receipt and approval of further documentation or the issuance of a qualification permit. [1]

letter report. A brief appraisal report that contains only the conclusions reached in the appraiser's investigation and analysis.

levee. An embankment that prevents a river from overflowing; one of the small, continuous ridges that surround irrigated fields.

level annuity. An income stream consisting of equal payments that are equally spaced.

leverage.
1. The use of fixed-cost funds to acquire an income-producing asset in expectation of a higher rate of return on the equity investment; produced by trading on equity.
2. Magnification of profits through the use of borrowed funds.

LHA. *See* local housing authority.

license
1. A formal agreement from a lawful source that allows a business or profession to be conducted; e.g., a franchise.
2. Government permission to conduct an activity.

licensee. A person or corporate body that is granted a license or franchise to conduct a business or profession.

lien. A charge against property in which the property is the security for payment of the debt.

lien release. Written release given by laborers, materialmen, and subcontractors to the developer waiving their rights under any mechanic's lien laws; usually given at the time of progress payments and upon completion of their work. [1]

life annuity. An annuity that continues only during the lifetime of the recipient; as distinguished from an annuity certain, which continues for a specified period of time.

life-cycle cost. The total cost of owning, operating, and maintaining a building or item of capital equipment over its useful life, including its fuel and energy costs.

life-cycle costing. An analysis of the cost of an investment over its economic or useful life; often related to building energy costs. Life-cycle costs are based on the discounted present value of the aggregate future payments or benefits derived from current investments; life-cycle costing illustrates the trade-offs between additional dollars invested today and reduced costs incurred in the future.

life estate. The total rights of use, occupancy, and control, limited to the lifetime of a designated party. *See also* life tenant.

life interest. *See* life estate.

life tenant. One who owns an estate in real property for his or her own lifetime, the lifetime of another person, or an indefinite period limited by a lifetime.

lift slab. A method of construction in which the floor and roof slabs are cast on top of one another at ground level, jacked into position, and fastened to the columns.

light. A window pane; a section of a window sash; a single pane of glass.

lighter. A large boat that is usually flat-bottomed and used in loading or unloading ships.

lighterage. The transfer of freight between a railroad terminal and various points by barges, floats, or lighters.

lighterage limits. Points in a harbor beyond which railroad companies will not deliver merchandise by lighter as part of the service included in the freight charge.

lighterage pier. A structure, e.g., a dock, wharf, quay, equipped with railroad tracks to facilitate the direct transfer of freight between railroad cars and lighters, barges, or floats.

light industry. Industries with less extensive physical plant requirements than heavy industry and less objectionable operations. *See also* heavy industry.

light-textured soil. Describes sandy or coarse-textured soil.

light well
1. A well-like, open area within a building that provides light and ventilation to inside rooms.
2. An open, subsurface space around a basement window that provides light and air.

lime. One of the ingredients used in making plaster, mortar, and cement; produced by burning limestone; also, any calcium compounds used to improve lime-deficient soils.

limen. *See* threshold.

limestone. A sedimentary deposit formed by the accumulation of the calcareous remains of organisms, e.g., shells; composed essentially of calcium carbonate; used extensively for building and the production of lime.

liming. The application of ground limestone to an agricultural field.

limited-access highway. *See* controlled-access highway.

limited market property. A property that has relatively few potential buyers at a particular time.

limited partner. A passive investor in a limited partnership who has no personal liability beyond his or her investment. *See also* limited partnership. [5]

limited partnership. An ownership arrangement consisting of general and limited partners; general partners manage the business and assume full liability for partnership debt, while limited partners are passive and liable only for their own capital contributions. *See also* partnership. [5]

line fence. A fence on the boundaries or perimeter of a property, e.g., a farm, ranch.

line-of-sight easement. A right that prohibits using lands within the easement area in any way that obstructs the view of some distant area or object.

lining. A layer of material within another layer; the covering on the interior of a building, as distinguished from the covering on the exterior, or the casing.

linkages. Time and distance relationships between a particular use and supporting facilities; e.g., between residences and schools, shopping, and employment.

linoleum. A floor covering made of burlap or canvas coated with a combination of powdered cork, powdered wood, linseed oil, pigments, and rosins, smoked and glazed under pressure, and cured by baking.

lintel. A piece of wood, stone, or steel placed horizontally across the top of a door or window opening to support the wall immediately above the opening.

liquid assets. Assets that can be immediately converted into cash and are immediately available to pay debts.

liquidated damages. An amount to be paid for a breach of contract; agreed upon by the parties in advance. [2]

liquidation
1. Forced or voluntary cash realization; the selling of real estate, stocks, bonds, or other investments, either to take profits or in anticipation of declining prices. [3]
2. The termination or conclusion of a business or real estate operation by the conversion of its assets into cash; the proceeds are distributed first to its creditors in order of preference, and the remainder, if any, is allocated to the owners in proportion to their holdings. [3]

liquidation price. A forced price obtained when a reasonable time is not allowed to find a purchaser.

liquidation value. The price that an owner is compelled to accept when a property must be sold without reasonable market exposure.

liquidity. An entity's cash position, based on assets that can be readily converted into cash. [1]

lis pendens. Notice of a suit pending.

listing. A written contract in which an owner employs a broker to sell his or her real estate.

litter. The uppermost layer of organic debris; composed of freshly fallen leaves or slightly decomposed organic material; commonly designated by the letter *L*.

littoral. Pertaining to the shore or the area between high and low water levels.

littoral rights. The right of an owner of land with a contiguous shoreline to use and enjoy the shore without a change in its position created by artificial interference; as distinguished from riparian rights and water rights.

live load. Any moving or variable superimposed load; expressed in pounds per square foot of floor and roof areas for various types of building occupancy; e.g., weight of people, merchandise, or stock on a floor, snow load or wind pressure on a roof; measurement may vary with local building code requirements. *See also* dead load; floor load; total load.

livestock share rent. A form of rent in which the landlord and tenant are equal owners of the livestock and share equally in the proceeds from sale; similar to crop share rent.

living trust. A trust that becomes effective during the lifetime of its creator; as distinguished from a trust under a will.

load

1. The weight supported by a structural part or member.
2. The power delivered by a motor, transformer, generator, or power station.
3. The electrical current carried through a circuit.

load-bearing wall. *See* bearing wall.

loading chute. An inclined chute attached to a holding pen or corral to permit livestock to walk from ground level to the dock where they are loaded onto trucks or rail cars.

loafing shed. An open shed near feed bunks that provides livestock shelter.

loam. A soil that is a mixture of different grades of sand, silt, and clay in which no one characteristic predominates; mellow with a gritty feel and slightly plastic when moist. *See also* clay loam; fine sandy loam; sandy loam; silt clay loam; silt loam.

loan commitment. A written promise from a lender to loan a specified sum at a certain rate of interest; usually a fee is paid for this commitment, which is good for a specific period of time.

loan constant. *See* mortgage constant (R_M).

loan fee. The fee paid to a lender for the use and forbearance of money or for service in making the loan; generally a percentage of the face amount of the loan. [1]

loan servicing. The administration and collection of monthly mortgage payments from homeowners and other borrowers; usually performed by a bank, mortgage broker, or real estate company acting for itself or the mortgagee. [6]

loan-to-value ratio. The ratio between a mortgage loan and the value of the security pledged; usually expressed as a percentage. Institutional lenders are subject to state laws that prescribe maximum loan-to-value ratios.

lobby. An interior entranceway to a theater, public building, hotel, or office building.

local area network. An interrelated system of microcomputers and peripherals linked at a single location. Local networks using phone lines are called *private branch exchange* (PBX) systems; networking allows users to share data files, printers, and mass-storage devices. [16]

local housing authority (LHA). A government entity or public body authorized to develop or operate low-rent housing; usually an independent corporate body authorized by local government pursuant to state or territorial law.

local public agency (LPA). An official body contracted by the federal government to assist in urban renewal projects; may be one or more state, county, municipal, or other government entities authorized to undertake a project for which federal assistance is sought.

location. The time-distance relationship, or linkage, between a property or neighborhood and all possible origins and destinations of residents coming to or going from the property or neighborhood.

locational obsolescence. *See* external obsolescence.

lock-in period. A period during which a lender prohibits the borrower from prepaying any or all of the balance and from selling or assigning the note. [1]

lodging
1. In the lodging industry, *see* hotel; motel.
2. The falling down of crops, particularly small grain and hay, due to excessive vegetative growth, rain, or wind.

loess. Windblown material that is uniformly silty, as distinguished from till and water sediment.

loft. An attic-like space below the roof of a house or barn; any upper story of a warehouse or factory.

loft building. A multistory building with an open floor design that is used for small, light manufacturing, warehousing, and sometimes offices.

log
1. To cut and deliver logs.
2. Tree segment suitable for lumber; e.g., butt log, peeler log, saw log.

logarithm. The power, or exponent, to which a fixed number, or base, is raised to produce a given number; e.g., 2^3 equals 8, so the logarithm of 8 in base 2 is 3.

log boom. A boom used to transport logs over water.

log deck. A storage area for logs.

log price conversion return. An indication of the stumpage value of timber made by deducting all costs necessary to fell a tree and deliver the logs to a mill from the market price of the logs.

log rules. Tables showing the calculated amount of lumber that can be sawed from logs of a given length and diameter; provide a means of measuring the actual board foot volume in logs by allowing for waste in slabs and sawdust. *See also* Humboldt rule; Scribner rule; Spaulding rule.

log scale. The measurement of felled trees, i.e., the length of a tree or log at a top, fixed diameter in relation to the diameter at the larger end, which is reflected in volume tables.

longitude. The distance of a particular point east or west on the earth's surface expressed in degrees; measured as the angle between the meridian of the point and the prime meridian in Greenwich, England.

longitudinal. Of or pertaining to longitude or length; running lengthwise.

long-lived item. A component with an expected remaining economic life that is the same as the economic life of the entire structure.

loss of access. Depriving an abutting owner of the inherent rights of ingress to and egress from the highway or street.

lot

1. A distinct piece of land; a piece of land that forms a part of a district, community, city block, etc.
2. A smaller portion into which a city block or subdivision is divided; described by reference to a recorded plat or by definite boundaries; a piece of land in one ownership, whether platted or unplatted.

lot and block description. *See* recorded map.

lot and block system. A legal description of a parcel of land that refers to the lot and block numbers that appear on maps and plats of recorded, subdivided land. *See also* legal description.

lot line. The boundary line of a plot of ground as legally described in the title to the property.

louver. A slat or fin over an opening that is pitched to keep out rain and snow; a finned sunshade on a building; the diffusion grill on a fluorescent light fixture.

low density recreational property. An area of homesites that ranges from three to forty acres located some distance from an urban center; provides relatively modest scenic and recreational amenities and appeals to urbanites because of its remoteness and lack of development.

lower low water. The lower of the two low waters on any tidal day; the mean value of the lower low waters over a considerable period of time is used as a plane of reference for hydrographic work on the coasts of the United States.

low frequency. An electric current that has a small number of cycles per second.

low water line. The point on the shore where the tide ebbs; varies with season, time, wind, and other changes. *See also* mean low water line.

LPA. *See* local public agency.

lumber. Wood that has been processed in saw and planing mills and receives no further processing by sawing, resawing, passing lengthwise through a standard planing mill, or crosscutting to length; classified as veneer when it is no thicker than ¼ inch and is to be used for veneering; e.g., boards, clear lumber, dimension lumber, factory and shop lumber, green lumber, joist, plank, scantling lumber, strip lumber, structural lumber, timber, and yard lumber.

luminous ceiling. A suspended ceiling of translucent materials installed below a system of fluorescent tubes, making the entire ceiling a source of light; used to reduce glare and shadows.

LUMS. *See* land utilization and marketability study.

M

machine shed. A farm building used to store farm machinery; usually has an open wall on one side.

magnesite flooring. A flooring composition made of calcined magnesite and magnesium chloride solution with a filler of sawdust, wood flour, ground silica, or quartz; floated in a 1½-inch layer over a concrete floor.

MAI®. Member, Appraisal Institute. *See also* American Institute of Real Estate Appraisers (AIREA).

main. A pipe, conduit, or circuit leading to or from the branches of a utility system; carries the combined flow of all the branches.

main circuit. Circuit that carries a heavy electrical load to the branch circuits of a distribution system.

mainframe. A large, stationary computer. [16]

maintenance. Keeping a property in condition to perform its function efficiently; expenditures made for this purpose; does not extend the useful life of the property or increase its book value. *See also* deferred maintenance; repairs.

mall. Originally, a shaded walk; designates an area in a retail section or center that is designed for pedestrian use only.

management. Directing or conducting affairs; one of the elements of overhead or undistributed construction costs.

management contract. An agreement between a management company, the operator, and a property owner or investor in which the operator assumes complete responsibility for the management of the property.

management fee. As expense item representing the sum paid or the value of management service.

management program. A program of defined goals in directing or conducting the management of a property and the manner or means by which these goals can be achieved.

manifold. Consisting of many different parts, elements, or features; e.g., the juncture of many small pipes with a larger pipe or main.

mansard roof. A roof with two slopes or pitches on each of the four sides, with the lower slopes steeper than the upper slopes; provides a good base when adding another story to a building.

mantel. The decorative facing placed around a fireplace; usually made of ornamental wood and topped with a shelf. [8]

mantissa. The numbers to the right of the decimal point in a logarithm; e.g., the natural logarithm of 70 is 4.248495, so 0.248495 is the mantissa. *See also* characteristic.

marginal
1. In economics, describes the supplying of goods at a rate that barely covers the cost of production.
2. In real estate, describes a property with an earned income that covers only operating costs.

marginal land. Land that barely pays the cost of working or using it because the costs of labor, coordination, and capital are approximately equal to the land's gross income. *See also* agents in production.

marginal probability. The probability that a single event will occur; determined as the sum of the joint probabilities involving that event.

marginal revenue. The additional gross revenue produced by selling one additional unit of production.

marginal tax rate. The income tax rate charged on the last dollar of income; the relevant tax rate for making investment decisions.

marginal utility. The addition to total utility made by the last unit of a good at any given point of consumption. In general, the greater the number of items, the lower the marginal utility; i.e., a greater supply of an item or product lowers the value of each item.

margin of security. The difference between the loan and the market value of the property. [1]

marina. A boat basin that provides dockage and other services to small craft.

marine soil. A soil that is formed from materials deposited by oceans and seas and later exposed by upward movement; e.g., the coastal plain soils of Maryland and Virginia. *See also* accretion.

market. A set of arrangements in which buyers and sellers are brought together through the price mechanism. *See also* real estate market.

marketability. The state of being salable.

marketability study. A process that investigates how a particular piece of property will be absorbed, sold, or leased under current or anticipated market conditions; includes a market study or analysis of the general class of property being studied. *See also* market study.

marketable title. A title not subject to reasonable doubt or suspicion of invalidity in the mind of a reasonable and intelligent person; one which a prudent person guided by competent legal advice would be willing to accept and purchase at market value.

market analysis. *See* market study.

market area. A geographic area or political jurisdiction in which alternative, similar properties effectively compete with the subject property in the minds of probable, potential purchasers and users.

market data approach. *See* sales comparison approach.

market participants. Individuals actively engaged in real estate transactions. Primary market participants are those who invest equity in real property or who use real estate, e.g., buyers, sellers, owners, lenders, tenants. Secondary market participants include those who advise primary participants, e.g., advisors, counselors, underwriters, appraisers.

market rent. The rental income that a property would most probably command in the open market; indicated by current rents paid and asked for comparable space as of the date of the appraisal.

market segmentation. The process of identifying and analyzing sub-markets within a larger market.

market share. The portion of a trade area's potential, e.g., retail sales to be generated, office space to be absorbed, that can be attributed to a proposed facility; based on known market strength and the property's position relative to comparable, competitive facilities. [17]

market study. The process of determining the general market conditions affecting the property to be marketed, including historical and potential levels of supply and demand; as distinguished from marketability study, which determines a property's capacity to be absorbed, sold, or leased. *See also* marketability study.

market survey. *See* market study.

market value

Market value is the major focus of most real property appraisal assignments. Both economic and legal definitions of market value have been developed and refined. Continual refinement is essential to the growth of the appraisal profession. The current economic definition of market value can be stated as follows:

> The most probable price in cash, terms equivalent to cash, or in other precisely revealed terms, for which the appraised property

will sell in a competitive market under all conditions requisite to fair sale, with the buyer and seller each acting prudently, knowledgeably, and for self-interest, and assuming that neither is under undue duress.

Fundamental assumptions and conditions presumed in this definition are

1. Buyer and seller are motivated by self-interest.
2. Buyer and seller are well informed and are acting prudently.
3. The property is exposed for a reasonable time on the open market.
4. Payment is made in cash, its equivalent, or in specified financing terms.
5. Specified financing, if any, may be the financing actually in place or on terms generally available for the property type in its locale on the effective appraisal date.
6. The effect, if any, on the amount of market value of atypical financing, services, or fees shall be clearly and precisely revealed in the appraisal report.

[American Institute of Real Estate Appraisers, *The Appraisal of Real Estate*, 8th ed. (Chicago: American Institute of Real Estate Appraisers, 1983), 33.]

Many of the legal definitions of market value are based on the following:

The highest price estimated in terms of money which the land would bring if exposed for sale in the open market, with reasonable time allowed in which to find a purchaser, buying with knowledge of all of the uses and purposes to which it was adapted and for which it was capable of being used. [*Sacramento Southern R. R. Co.* v. *Heilbron* 156 Cal. 408, 104 P. 979 (1909).]

Persons performing appraisal services which may be subject to litigation are cautioned to seek the exact definition of market value in the jurisdiction in which the services are being performed.

marquee. A permanent hood that projects over the entrance to a building and is not supported by posts or columns.

masonry. Anything constructed of stone, brick, tile, cement, concrete, or similar materials; work done by a mason.

masonry wall. A wall of stone, brick, tile, cement block, concrete, etc.

Massachusetts trust. A form of business organization, distinct from a corporation or partnership, that conducts its business through a trustee or trustees who hold legal title to the property of the business. Capital contributions are made to the trustees by beneficiaries, whose equitable title and interests in the property of the trust are evidenced by trust certificates. The beneficiaries receive the earnings of the trust and may enjoy limited liability, but control and management of the trust rest solely with the trustees.

mass appraising. The process of valuing a large number of properties as of a given date; conducted in uniform order, using standard methodology, common reference data, and statistical testing.

master plan. A comprehensive, long-range official plan that guides the physical growth and development of a community, combined with the basic regulatory and administrative controls needed to attain the physical objectives; includes land use plan, thoroughfare plan, community facilities plan, and public improvements program. *Also called* city plan, general plan, or comprehensive community plan.

mastic. An adhesive material used to cement two surfaces together; an elastic caulking compound.

matched boards. *See* tongue and groove.

material bond. A bond that assures the contractor that the material supplier will provide the materials necessary to complete the job. [1]

mat foundation. *See* floating foundation.

mature forest. A forest that has reached the age of maximum utilization; varies with the objectives of forest management.

maturity. The date when an obligation comes due. [1]

MBF. In forestry, an abbreviation for one thousand board feet.

meadow. A type of range vegetation that includes areas where sedges, rushes, and mesic grasses predominate; usually remains wet or moist throughout the summer.

mean. A measure of the central tendency of data; a calculated average. *See also* arithmetic mean; geometric average; median; mode; moving average; weighted average.

meander. A winding course.

meander line. A line that points out the curves and lines of a bank or shore; a survey line that establishes the bank or shoreline of a stream or lake.

mean deviation. *See* average deviation.

mean high water line. The point on the shore that is the mean distance between the points to which the tide rises; determined through long observation of the rise and fall of tides; often used as the seaward boundary line of privately owned uplands. *See also* mean low water line; ordinary high water mark.

mean low water line. The point on the shore that is the mean distance between the points to which the tide ebbs; determined through long observation of the rise and fall of tides.

mechanic's lien. A lien provided by statute for those who perform labor or services or who furnish materials in the improvement of real property.

median. The value of the middle item in an uneven number of items arranged or arrayed according to size; the arithmetic average of the two central items in an even number of items similarly arranged; a positional average that is not affected by the size of extreme values.

median strip. In highway construction, a strip in the center of the highway that divides opposing lanes of traffic; may be a narrow, concrete buffer or a wide, landscaped section.

medium-textured soil. Loams, fine sandy loams, and clay loams.

meeting rail. *See* check rail.

megalopolis. A large, urbanized area resulting from the gradual merging of many cities and metropolitan areas into one, great urban agglomeration. [6]

mellow. Describes a soil that can be easily worked due to its friable and loamy characteristics.

membrane. A thin sheet or film of waterproof material used to prevent moisture from penetrating a floor wall.

memory. The storage space of a computer, where instructions and data are kept during program execution. [16]

merchant builder. A company primarily involved in constructing residential and commercial buildings for sale. [1]

merchants' association. An organization that advances the common interests of shopping center tenants by planning advertisements, promotions, decorations, etc.

merge line. A line that divides into two parts a parcel that extends from one street to another street in the rear; designated so that the highest total value of the two parts will be developed, considering each part as a separate lot valued on the basis of its front foot value modified by the depth factor to the depth of the merge line.

merger
1. The absorption of two or more corporations into a single corporation by issuing stock in the controlling corporation to replace a majority of stock in the others; usually accomplished without dissolving the individual companies.
2. The creation of a common land ownership for adjacent properties that were formerly owned separately. *See also* assemblage.

meridian
1. A great circle on the earth's surface passing through the poles and any given point.
2. In the government survey system, the true north and south lines that run from a base line where they are 24 miles apart. *Also called* guide meridians. *See also* base line; range line; standard parallels.

mesquite. A type of range vegetation that includes areas where various species of mesquite (*prosopis*) predominate.

metal lath. A sheet of metal that is slit at intervals; when expanded, the grillwork forms a base for plaster.

metal valley. *See* flashing.

metamorphic rock. Rock that has undergone pronounced alteration from the combined effects of pressure, heat, and water; frequently is compact and crystalline.

metes and bounds description. A legal description of a parcel of land that refers to the parcel's boundaries, which are formed by the point of beginning and all intermediate points, the bounds, and the courses of each point, the metes. *See also* legal description.

metropolitan area plan. The extension and adaptation of general community planning to embrace an entire metropolitan area, or a group of municipalities and suburban neighborhoods.

Metropolitan Statistical Area (MSA). A city of at least 50,000 people; an urbanized area of at least 50,000 with a total metropolitan population of at least 100,000; designated under standards set in 1980 by the Federal Committee on MSAs; replaces the term *Standard Metropolitan Statistical Area* (SMSA). *See also* Consolidated Metropolitan Statistical Area (CMSA); Primary Metropolitan Statistical Area (PMSA); Standard Metropolitan Statistical Area (SMSA).

mezzanine. An intermediate floor with less area than the regular floors; in a theater, a shallow balcony between the main floor and the first balcony.

MGIC. *See* Mortgage Guarantee Insurance Corporation.

microprocessor. In computer usage, a central processing unit, or CPU, that consists of only one semiconductor chip.

microrelief. Surface irregularity; used by farm appraisers to describe slight land surface irregularities, e.g., smooth channels, hogwallows, low hummocks, high hummocks, dunes.

middle rail. In construction, the central, horizontal structural member.

mill. One-tenth of a cent; often used to express real estate taxes. [3]

millage rate. A tax rate expressed in tenths of a cent; e.g., a tax rate of one mill per thousand means $1 of taxes per $1,000 of assessed value. *See also* mill. [3]

mill construction. A type of construction in which substantial, self-supporting masonry walls carry the wood roof and thicker floor decks are supported by heavy timber framing; corners, projections, and small section members that ignite easily are avoided; the stories are separated by incombustible fire stops and elevator hatches and stairways are encased by incombustible partitions. *See also* slow-burning construction.

mill-cut estimate. *See* will-cut cruise.

millwork. All building materials made of finished wood and manufactured in millwork plants and planing mills; e.g., doors, window frames, door frames, sashes, blinds, porch work, mantels, panel work, stairways, special woodwork; does not include yard lumber, e.g., dimensional lumber, siding.

mineral deposit. An existing quantity of recoverable metallic or nonmetallic natural resources, usually subject to commercial exploitation.

mineral rights. *See* subsurface rights.

mineral wool. Insulating material made by blasting molten slag or rock with steam; e.g., rock wool, glass wool.

miner's inch. A flow of water of $\frac{1}{50}$th or $\frac{1}{40}$th of a cubic foot per second.

minimum lot. The minimum, acceptable size of lots that can be developed in an area or community, as established by zoning regulations.

minimum rental. The base, or fixed, payment in a lease.

Mission style architecture. An architectural style based on the characteristics of early California missions; these churches of stone or adobe had small window openings, one or more towers, and sometimes vaulted interiors; ornamentation varied from primitive to refined and roofs of wood or thatch were later replaced with the red tile roofs so prevalent in the Southwest.

miter. The angular shape produced by cutting the ends of two boards at an angle and fitting them together. [8]

mixed fund. An investment fund in which capital is subscribed before all of the property is selected. [1]

mixed-use zoning. Zoning that allows a mixture of land uses within a single space; often encouraged by offering incentives to private developers who provide a mixture of residential, commercial, and office space in a building in a specially zoned district. [9]

mobile home. A house trailer; a complete, livable dwelling unit equipped with wheels so that it can be towed from place to place by a truck or automobile.

mobile home park. *See* trailer park.

mobile ownership. A form of tenure in which a building is not affixed to the land, but remains personal property that may be moved by the building owner when the landowner demands possession or a rent that the tenant cannot afford. [6]

mobility. In real estate, the ease with which people can move from one location to another.

mode. The most frequent, or typical, value in an array of numbers; a positional average that is not affected by extreme items. It is the most descriptive average and easily identified when the number of items is small; however, if the sample is too small, none of the values may be repeated and no mode exists.

model house. A house used for exhibition to sell other houses. [2]

Modern Colonial architecture. A residential architectural style characterized by windows divided into small panes and a simple, two-story design, to which third-floor dormer windows may be added.

modernization. A type of renovation in which worn or outdated elements are replaced with their current counterparts.

modified economic age-life method. A method of estimating accrued depreciation in which the ratio of effective age to total economic life is applied to the current cost of improvements after curable physical and functional items are deducted.

modified internal rate of return (*MIRR*) procedure. A type of internal rate of return analysis in which all negative cash flows up to the first positive cash flow are treated as part of investment capital.

modular construction. Prefabrication in three dimensions. Entire rooms are built in a factory and shipped to their eventual location, where very little onsite labor is required.

module. A standard measure of any size used in construction and design; allows repetition in design and use and saves material and labor costs.

module width. The distance between window mullions, which determines the size of partitioned offices in a building.

moisture barrier. Insulating material placed in walls, floors, or other parts of a structure to block the passage of vapor or moisture and prevent condensation.

moisture equivalent. The percentage of water retained by a soil against a force 1,000 times stronger than gravity; an arbitrarily determined percentage that is correlated with other soil properties, e.g., moisture-holding capacity, wilting percentage, texture.

molded base. A two-member base consisting of a common base with molding above; a three-member base consisting of a common base with base mold above and shoe mold below. *See also* sanitary base.

molding. A finishing piece used to cover a joint, e.g., one formed by a ceiling and a wall; usually a long, narrow strip of plain or curved wood; may be ornamented.

monetary controls. The Federal Reserve's efforts to influence the level of economic activity by regulating the availability of money and the rate of interest.

money market. The interaction of buyers and sellers who trade short-term money instruments.

money market certificates. Certificates that pay interest equal to the average yield recorded in the weekly auction of six-month Treasury bills and have a minimum deposit that must be deposited for six months.

monitor. A raised structure on a roof with windows or louvers that ventilate or light the building; usually found on a factory or warehouse.

monitor roof. A type of framing that includes an elevated central section and provides better lighting and ventilation; generally found in industrial buildings.

monolithic concrete. Concrete that is poured continuously so that it has no separations or joints due to different setting times.

monopoly. A market in which one person or group controls the supply of a good and, therefore, its price.

monopoly property. A property used by an enterprise that, through franchise, license, zoning regulation, etc., has the exclusive right to conduct that enterprise.

Monterey architecture. A residential, two-story style adapted from the architecture prevalent in California in the early Spanish era; usually characterized by a balcony that runs across the entire face of the building.

monument. A stone or other fixed object used to establish real estate boundaries.

monuments description. A method in which property is described by reference to natural or man-made objects in the field.

mop board. *See* baseboard.

moraine. A mass of material deposited by a glacier; e.g., terminal moraine, deposited at the front of a glacier, and lateral moraine, deposited along the sides of a glacier; usually consists of an irregular ridge deposited by ice melting along the rim of the glacier at a rate equal to its forward flow.

moratorium. A temporary suspension in the enforcement of liability for a financial obligation; often required by statute. [2]

mortar. A pasty substance of lime and/or cement mixed with sand and water that hardens when exposed to air; used as a bonding material in brick and stone work.

mortgage. A legal document pledging a described property for the repayment of a loan under certain terms and conditions.

mortgage-backed securities. Bond-type securities backed by a pool of mortgages or trust deeds; generally not an obligation of the issuer. [1]

mortgage banker. A person or company that makes mortgage loans with its own funds on its own behalf, usually in expectation of reselling the loans to lenders at a profit and then servicing the loans.

mortgage broker. One who places mortgages, i.e., finds appropriate borrowers or willing lenders, for a fee, which is usually a percentage of the loan amount.

mortgage coefficient (*C*). A multiplier used in the Ellwood formula to compute a capitalization rate; a function of the terms of the mortgage loan, the projected ownership period, and the equity yield rate.

mortgage company. A firm that brings mortgagors and mortgagees together, for a fee, or one that acquires mortgages for resale.

mortgage constant (R_M). A rate that reflects the relationship between debt service and the principal amount of the mortgage loan; used to convert debt service into mortgage loan value.

mortgage correspondent. One who acts as an agent for national lenders, making loan commitments for them using their standards of acceptability; may also service loans for the lender for an additional fee.

mortgage deed. A deed that has the effect of a mortgage on the property conveyed and imposes a lien on the granted estate.

mortgaged fee interest. A fee simple estate or leased fee estate subject to a mortgage.

mortgagee. A party who advances funds for a mortgage loan and in whose favor the property is mortgaged; the lender.

mortgage equity analysis. Capitalization and investment analysis procedures that recognize the influence of mortgage terms and equity requirements in the valuation of income-producing property.

Mortgage Guarantee Insurance Corporation (MGIC). A secondary market for conventional, nonfederal mortgages. [1]

mortgage insurance premium. A percentage charged each year on the declining balance of the principal of a mortgage to insure the mortgagee against loss. [6]

mortgage note. A document or a clause in a document in which the borrower accepts personal responsibility for the repayment of a debt.

mortgage out. To finance a project without making a cash investment in it.

mortgage release price. A specified amount to be repaid to a lender to relinquish the lien on an individual parcel. [1]

mortgage requirement. The periodic level payment, or installment, required for debt service, i.e., interest plus principal, on a direct reduction loan. *See also* mortgage constant (R_M).

mortgage revenue bonds. Tax-exempt bonds sold by state and local governments or state housing finance agencies to finance the sale, repair, or construction of real estate. Because the interest earned by bondholders is exempt from federal taxation, the bonds are sold at a lower interest rate than taxable bonds; the interest rates to borrowers are below market level because the interest savings on the bonds are passed on to the borrowers. *Also called* mortgage subsidy bonds.

mortgage risk rating. A process in which the major risks undertaken in the making of a mortgage are thoroughly analyzed in accordance with the risk involved in the loan transaction or in connection with insurance of the mortgage; a basis for classifying mortgages as to their quality as investments.

mortgage term. The amount of time, specified in the mortgage contract, in which the mortgage loan must be paid off. *See also* amortization. [1]

mortgagor. One who gives a mortgage as security for a loan; the borrower.

mortise. A notch or hole that is cut in a piece of wood or other material to receive a projecting part, the tenon, of another piece in order to join the two.

mosaic. A decoration made of small pieces of glass, stone, ceramic, or other material laid in mortar or mastic to form a design.

most appropriate use. In planning and zoning, the land use that is in the best interest of the community as a whole and will promote the greatest good for the greatest number; may or may not be the highest and best use; may be a present use or a future use.

most probable selling price. The price at which a property would most probably sell if exposed on the market for a reasonable time, under the market conditions prevailing on the date of the appraisal.

motel. A building or group of buildings located on or near a highway designed to serve the needs of travelers by offering lodging and parking; may also provide other services and amenities, e.g., telephones, food and beverages, recreational areas, service station, shops.

mouse. An input device resembling an inverted track ball that allows a user to control a computer without using the keyboard. [16]

moving average. In statistics, successive arithmetic averages or arithmetic means developed by eliminating the first item in each averaged group and adding the next quantity in the series; used to reduce fluctuations in a graph or curve that reflects a pattern or trend.

M roof. A type of roof consisting of two double-pitch roofs; provides two advantages: uses shorter material for rafters and reduces the elevation of the building.

MSA. *See* Metropolitan Statistical Area.

MS-DOS. Microsoft's copyrighted disk-operating system. [16]

muck. Organic soil material that is fairly well decomposed, relatively high in mineral content, and dark in color; accumulates in areas with poor drainage.

mullion. A thin, vertical bar of wood, lead, or stone that divides multiple windows, panes of glass, wall panels, screens, etc.; as distinguished from a muntin.

multicollinearity. The phenomenon of two or more variables being correlated.

multileg intersection. A road intersection with five or more travel routes.

multiple dwelling. A building composed of three or more dwelling units, usually with common access, service systems, and use of land.

multiple listing. A listing that is not limited to one agent, but is offered by other agents who have agreed to cooperate in finding a purchaser for the property. *Also called* multiple listing service (MLS).

multiple regression analysis. A type of analysis that measures the simultaneous influence of a number of independent variables on one dependent variable.

multiple use
1. A combination of compatible land uses in an area.
2. A combination of compatible uses in a single building.

multiplier. A figure that is multiplied by income to produce an estimate of value; called a *gross income multiplier* when gross income is used, and a *net income multiplier* when net income is used; may be monthly or annual.

municipal notes. Short-term obligations of villages, cities, counties, etc., used to finance current operations until satisfactory long-term funds are obtained.

muntin. A slender, horizontal bar of wood or metal that divides panes in a window or panels in a door.

mutual saving bank. A financial institution owned by its depositors; a primary source of home mortgage funds.

N

NAR. *See* NATIONAL ASSOCIATION OF REALTORS®.

narrative report. The most complete type of appraisal report; includes an introduction, a factual description, an analysis of data and opinions, and sometimes addenda.

NATIONAL ASSOCIATION OF REALTORS® (NAR). The trade and professional organization that serves the real estate industry; includes the following organizations: American Institute of Real Estate Appraisers, American Society of Real Estate Counselors, Farm and Land Institute, Institute of Real Estate Management, REAL ESTATE SECURITIES AND SYNDICATION INSTITUTE®, REALTORS NATIONAL MARKETING INSTITUTE®, Society of Industrial REALTORS®, and Women's Council of REALTORS®.

national income. The total net earnings attributable to the various factors employed in the production of goods and services in a nation over a particular period.

National Register of Historic Places. An official listing of national historic and cultural resources that are considered worthy of preservation under the National Historic Preservation Act of 1966. [9]

national wealth. The total monetary value of all material economic goods possessed by residents of a given nation at a particular time.

native plants. Plants that are native to an area and have not been introduced by humans.

natural features. Elements of the physical environment that are the result of natural causes; e.g., rivers, plains, hills, valleys, minerals; as distinguished from those created or erected by humans.

natural resource property. A property with recoverable or adaptable natural resources that could be exploited commercially; contains natural deposits of valuable material, e.g., rock, sand, gravel, clay, oil, gas, coal, metals. An enterprise using these resources is called an *extractive industry*.

natural resources. *See* natural resource property.

natural seasoning. The drying of lumber by stacking, which permits free circulation of air around each timber.

navigable waters. Fresh or salt waters that, alone or with other waters, form a continuous waterway over which commerce may be conducted with other states or foreign countries.

navigable waters of the United States. Waters of the United States that are subject to the ebb and flow of the tide shoreward to the mean high water mark; waters that are, have been, or can be used in transporting interstate or foreign commerce.

negative amortization. The difference between required debt service and the actual debt service paid; unpaid interest is added to the outstanding loan balance so that the balance increases instead of decreasing over time. Mortgage instruments in which negative amortization occurs usually require larger down payments or higher interest rates.

negative easement. Property that is burdened by an easement. *Also called* the subserviant estate. *See also* affirmative easement.

negative leverage. The increasing financial losses that result from borrowing when the cost of capital exceeds the return on capital; reverse leverage. Negative leverage magnifies losses, and positive leverage magnifies profits.

negotiable order of withdrawal (NOW) accounts. Interest-bearing accounts with checking privileges.

neighborhood. A group of complementary land uses.

neighborhood shopping center. A shopping center that provides for the sale of convenience goods, e.g., food, drugs, sundries; and personal services, e.g., laundry, dry cleaning, barbering, shoe repair; to satisfy the daily needs of the immediate neighborhood; has a supermarket as the principal tenant. The neighborhood center is the smallest type of shopping center, with a typical gross leasable area of 50,000 square feet; however, it may range in size from 30,000 to 100,000 square feet.

net income before recapture. *See* net operating income (*NOI*).

net income multiplier. The relationship between price or value and net operating income expressed as a factor; the reciprocal of the overall rate.

net income ratio. The ratio of net operating income to effective gross income; the complement of the operating expense ratio.

net lease. A lease in which the lessee pays all property charges, e.g., taxes, insurance, assessments, maintenance, in addition to the stipulated rent.

net listing. A listing in which the broker is entitled to any proceeds in excess of a specified selling price. [1]

net operating income (*NOI*). The actual or anticipated net income remaining after deducting all operating expenses from effective gross income, but before deducting mortgage debt service.

net present value (*NPV*). The difference, if any, between the present value of expected benefits, or positive cash flows, and the present value of capital outlays, or negative cash flows.

net realizable value (*NRV*). Market value minus the cost of disposition.

net sales. Gross sales less returns and allowances, e.g., freights, trade discounts.

net sales area. The area in a department or retail store that is available for the sale of merchandise, excluding storage and equipment areas, rest rooms, etc; the actual floor area used for merchandising.

network. In computer usage, an interconnected group of computers or terminals that are linked together for a specific purpose, e.g., to share data files. [16]

net worth. The difference between total assets and total liabilities.

neutral soil. A soil that is not significantly acid or alkaline; has a pH between 6.6 and 7.3.

newel post. A vertical post that supports the handrail at the top or bottom of a stairway or at a landing turn; the post around which a circular stairway winds.

New England Colonial architecture. A residential architectural style developed to imitate classic motifs from brick and stone Georgian houses in wooden houses; characterized by white clapboard exteriors, shingle roofs, and openings embellished with moldings of refined detail.

new standard. A system for measuring office buildings based on typical floor plans, barring structural changes that materially affect the typical floor. The measurements stand for the life of the building, regardless of readjustments in tenant layout. In buildings designed for divided or multiple tenancy, this typical floor plan must permit subdivision to accommodate normal tenant requirements, with corridors that reach every office subdivision.

nogging
1. Brick that fills the spaces in a frame wall.
2. Pieces of wood inserted in a masonry wall to receive nails.

nominal interest rate (*I*). A stated or contract rate; an interest rate, usually annual, that does not necessarily correspond to the true or effective rate of growth at compound interest; e.g., a true or effective 1% monthly interest rate may be called a nominal, annual interest rate of 12%, although true growth with monthly compounding amounts to slightly more than 12.68% per year. *See also* effective interest rate (*i*).

nomogram. A diagram, chart, or arrangement of scales used in the graphic solution of problems with fixed numerical relationships.

nonapparent easement. An easement that is not obvious or ascertainable by cursory inspection of the premises. [7]

nonassumption clause. A conventional mortgage clause that states that the property of an owner-borrower cannot be sold or the mortgage assumed by a third party without the consent of the lender. *See also* due-on-sale clause.

nonbasic activities. In economic base analysis, activities producing outputs that are primarily consumed within the subject area or community.

nonbasic crops. Agricultural products that are entitled to government support, but are not basic to the areas in which they are grown; e.g., oats, barley, rye, some dairy products, honey, wool. *See also* basic crops.

nonbasic income. Income that comes from within the community.

nonbearing partition. A partition wall that divides space, but does not carry overhead partitions or joists.

nonbearing wall. A self-supporting wall that carries no vertical load.

nonconforming building. A building or portion of a building that was lawfully erected or altered, but no longer conforms to the use, height, or area regulations of the zone where it is located because of a subsequent change in a zoning ordinance. *See also* legally nonconforming use.

nonconforming use. *See* legally nonconforming use.

nonconventional mortgage. Mortgages that are insured or guaranteed by an agency of the federal government, e.g., Federal Housing Administration, Veterans Administration, or by a private insuring company.

nondurable goods. Short-lived consumer goods; e.g., food, clothing.

nonexclusive zoning. An ordinance that clearly defines and permits exceptions to a particular type of zoning.

nonfee timesharing. A limited interest in real property in which the purchaser receives only those rights specifically granted by the developer, usually the right to use a timeshare unit and the related premises; purchaser does not receive legal title in the property.

nonrecourse loan. Debt agreements secured by real estate that contain clauses providing that the lender has no claim against the debtor in the event of default, but can only recover the property. [5]

nonrecurring expense. An expense occasioned by a condition that is not regularly repeated in the ordinary course of business operations; e.g., a loss by fire or theft.

normal curve. In statistics, a symmetrical, bell-shaped curve that represents the distribution of a population of certain types of measurements or the frequency distribution of all possible means in large samples that may be drawn from almost any kind of population.

normal distribution. *See* normal probability distribution.

normal probability distribution. In statistics, a continuous distribution that is usually represented by a normal curve; a probability function that produces a symmetrical, bell-shaped curve.

nosing. The rounded, projecting edge of a stair tread or landing.

notary public. A public officer who is authorized to take acknowledgments and witness sworn affidavits. [2]

notice of default. A document filed with the county concerning a lien(s) on property that is in default; states that notice of default must be given to the person named in the document to validate subsequent foreclosure proceedings and give the person an opportunity to reinstate. [1]

NOW accounts. *See* negotiable order of withdrawal accounts.

noxious weeds. Unwanted plants that are considered agricultural hazards due to their vigorous growth or propagation.

nuisance. Something that interferes with the use and enjoyment of property or is a source of discomfort and annoyance to others; legally divided into two classes: public, or common, nuisances, which touch the public interest; and private nuisances, which destroy or injure an individual's property, interfere with its lawful use and enjoyment, or deny an individual common rights. [6]

nuisance value. The price that probably would be paid to avoid or relieve an objectionable condition.

null hypothesis. In statistics, a statement that there is no difference between two comparable and calculated statistics; tested against evidence found in samples.

nurse crop. A crop planted primarily to shelter less vigorous seedlings; e.g., when barley and alfalfa are planted to establish an alfalfa stand, barley is the nurse crop.

nursing home. A facility designated, staffed, and equipped to accommodate individuals who are not in need of hospital care, but require skilled nursing care and other medical services.

nutrients. Elements essential to plant growth in soil development; a factor in soil analysis.

O

oakum. Loose fiber obtained from hemp or rope; used to caulk joints.

O and D survey. *See* origin-destination survey.

observed condition. The condition of a property ascertained from a detailed inspection; physical condition.

observed condition method. *See* breakdown method.

obsolescence. One of the causes of depreciation; an impairment of desirability and usefulness caused by new inventions, current changes in design, improved processes for production, or external factors that make a property less desirable and valuable for a continued use; may be either functional or external. *See also* curable functional obsolescence; depreciation; external obsolescence; incurable functional obsolescence.

O.C. *See* on center.

occupancy. The state of being in possession.

occupancy cost. The periodic expenditure of money necessary to occupy a property, excluding expenses directly attributable to the operation of a business.

occupancy permit. Public acknowledgment that a building meets the requirements for use. *See also* certificate of occupancy (C of O).

occupancy rate. The relationship between the income received from the rented units in a property and the income that would be received if all the units were occupied.

Occupational Safety and Health Act (OSHA). An act that imposes federal safety standards on employers.

offer. To present a set of terms that will result in a contract if the other party accepts these terms.

offering circular. For an offering that must be qualified, a written description of the proposed offering that has been submitted and cleared by the proper agency; for an exempt offering, a brochure that describes the terms and conditions of the purchase in detail. *Also called* offering circular, for state qualification, and prospectus, for federal registration. [1]

offset
1. A ledge formed by a difference in the thickness of a wall. *See also* setback; set-off.
2. A deduction, usually from rent; e.g., an agreement in which a shopping center tenant is allowed to deduct a portion of the rent or escalation payments from the otherwise payable percentage or base rent.

offsite costs. Costs incurred for the improvement and development of a project, excluding actual construction costs of the buildings; e.g., costs for streets, sidewalks, curbing, traffic signals, water and sewer mains. *Also called* common costs or offsite improvement costs. [5]

offsite improvements. Improvements such as streets, sidewalks, curbing, traffic signals, and water and sewer mains.

old growth. Mature timber stands that remain in their natural condition; generally yield the highest volume and the best quality.

on center (O.C.). The distance from the center of one structural member to the center of a similar member, e.g., spacing studs, joists, girders.

onsite costs. Costs incurred for the actual construction of buildings and improvements on a particular parcel of land. [5]

open-beam construction. Frame construction in which the ceiling and ceiling joists are eliminated, exposing the beams and deck of the roof and treating them as elements of interior finish; usually structural members of the roof are heavier and on wider centers.

open-end mortgage. A mortgage in which the mortgagor is permitted to borrow additional sums on the condition that a stated ratio of assets to the debt is maintained or under other specified terms.

open listing. A listing contract that provides that the agent shall receive a commission if the property is sold through his or her efforts or if the agent produces a buyer under the terms of the contract before the property is sold.

open planning. House design in which few partitions divide different activity areas, e.g., living room, dining room, kitchen, family room.

open space. Land designated for nonbuilding uses; typically of three ownership types: private open space adjacent to dwellings owned by individual residents, public open space owned by government, and common open space owned by a community association and set aside for the use of residents. [13]

open space ratio. The ratio of open space to the total site or to the land area improved with buildings.

open steel construction. A type of construction in which a rigidly connected steel frame that is unwrapped, or without fireproofing, carries all loads directly to the foundation and footings; in a multistory structure, the exterior walls are carried on this framework, usually at each level.

open web joist. Lightweight, parallel trusses of prefabricated metal.

operating expense ratio (*OER*). The ratio of total operating expenses to effective gross income.

operating expenses. Periodic expenditures that are necessary to maintain the real property and continue the production of the effective gross income. *See also* fixed expenses; replacement allowance; variable expenses.

operating income. Income derived from the operation of a business; indicates a stage in the profit-and-loss account where all direct costs and income from the operation have been taken into account; as distinguished from net profit.

operating profit. Profit that arises from the regular operation of an enterprise that performs services, excluding income from other sources and expenses not related to direct operation.

operating standards. Standards of performance; derived by analyzing the operating expenses of comparable properties. *Also called* comparative standards.

operating statement. A statement that reflects the gross revenues, expenses, and net operating profit or loss of an investment over a fixed period.

opinion of title. A certificate pertaining to title in real property from an attorney or title insurance company.

opportunity cost. The cost of options foregone or opportunities not chosen.

optimum use. *See* highest and best use.

option. A legal contract that permits, but does not require, one to buy, sell, or lease real property for a stipulated period of time in accordance with specified terms; a unilateral right to exercise a privilege. [5]

option term. A stipulated time during which an optionee can exercise his or her rights under the option agreement. [1]

oral report. An unwritten appraisal report that includes a property description and all facts, assumptions, conditions, and reasoning on which the conclusion is based.

orchard. A planting of uniformly spaced fruit- or nut-bearing trees; normally spaced for easy equipment operation and to allow the highest production from a specific variety of tree. Some crops will require plantings of more than one variety for proper pollination.

ordinance. A public regulation, e.g., a law, usually local.

ordinary annuity. A common type of level annuity with income payments received at the end of each period.

ordinary high water mark. On nontidal rivers, the line on the shore established by the fluctuations of water and indicated by physical characteristics, e.g., a clear, natural line impressed on the bank, shelving, changes in the character of the soil, the destruction of terrestrial vegetation, the presence of litter and debris. *See also* mean high water line.

ordinary income. Income that is subject to income taxes at the taxpayer's regular rate; as distinguished from capital gains income, which may be taxed at a lower rate.

ordinate. In the rectangular coordinate system, the distance from a point to the horizontal x-axis; denoted by the second number in an ordered pair; e.g., in the expression (3,7), 7 is the ordinate.

organic matter. The relatively decomposed material of the soil that is derived from organic sources, usually plant remains.

organic soil. Any soil that is predominantly organic matter.

organization cost. The cost incurred in the formation of a functioning enterprise, excluding costs for promotion, obtaining capital, constructing the property, and acquiring the business.

organization fee. A one-time fee received by the promoter or general partner for organizing a syndicate. [1]

oriel window. A window that projects from the outer face of a wall, especially from an upper story, and is supported by brackets or a cantilever; as distinguished from a bay window, which is at first-floor level and usually supported by a foundation.

orientation. The positioning of a structure on a lot with regard to exposure to the sun and prevailing winds, privacy, and protection from noise.

original cost In accounting, the actual cost of a property to its present owner.

origin-destination survey. A traffic study technique in which the movement of people, vehicles, and goods in a given area is systematically sampled to determine where journeys begin and end, the purpose of journeys, the modes of travel, the time elapsed, and the land uses at the origin and the destination. [6]

OSHA. *See* Occupational Safety and Health Act.

overage income. *See* overage rent.

overage rent. The percentage rent paid over and above the guaranteed minimum rate.

overall capitalization rate (R_o). An income rate for a total property that reflects the relationship between a single year's net operating income expectancy or an annual average of several years' income expectancies and total price or value; used to convert net operating income into an indication of overall property value.

overbuilding. Building more structures of a particular type than can be absorbed by the market at prevailing prices. [2]

overflight. The air space over a property through which aircraft may pass so long as the property's occupants suffer no inconvenience beyond established standards.

overgrazing. The overstocking or overuse of a range, which causes better forage to disappear, secondary species to decline in vigor until they too are gone, and a change in the type and quality of forage.

overhang. A type of roof in which the rafters and roofing extend beyond the exterior walls of the structure; used to protect against precipitation and direct sunlight.

overhead. Expenses of direction and administration that are necessary to conduct a business.

overhead easement. The right to use space at a designated distance above the surface of the land; e.g., for power lines, avigation, air rights.

overhead irrigation. Sprinkler irrigation installed with tall rises that permit water to be delivered above crops; frequently installed in orchards, groves, and vineyards.

overimprovement. An improvement that does not represent the most profitable use for the site on which it is placed because it is too large or costly and cannot develop the highest possible land value; may be temporary or permanent.

overpass. A grade separation where a highway passes over another highway or a railroad; constructed to avoid surface intersections and traffic congestion.

overriding royalty. An interest in unsevered oil and gas that the lessee retains when executing a sublease or assignment.

overrun
1. Cost or expense in excess of budgeted cost.
2. The amount of lumber actually sawed from logs that is in excess of estimated volume; usually expressed as a percentage.

overstocking. Placing too many animals in a given area, which results in overuse at the end of a planned grazing period; distinguished from overgrazing because an area can be overstocked for a short period, but the animals may be removed before the area is overutilized. However, continued overstocking will lead to overgrazing.

overstory. The portion of a forest that contains the tallest trees, or the top canopy.

ownership of real property. The holding of rights or interests in real estate.

P

pad

1. An area in a mobile home park that is reserved for the exclusive use of mobile homeowners; as distinguished from commonly used areas. [1]
2. The land underlying a condominium unit or a store in a shopping center. [1]

paired data analysis. A procedure in which sales are compared in pairs to identify the effect of specific differences on sale price.

PAM. *See* pledged account mortgage.

panel. A section of a surface, e.g., a wall, ceiling, that is raised or recessed and usually enclosed in a frame-like border; prefabricated construction materials, e.g., gypsum board, plywood, fiberboard, plasterboard.

panel board. A panel to which electrical meters and control equipment are attached for electrical service distribution.

panel heating. A radiant heating system; one in which pipes or coils are embedded in walls or ceilings to serve as heating panels.

panel wall. A prefabricated section of wall that is erected in one piece. *See also* curtain wall.

par. Originally, denotes equality, or 100%, without a premium or discount, e.g., the par value of a mortgage is its face, or nominal, amount; more commonly used to describe the value imprinted on stock certificates or the principal amount at which bonds can be redeemed at maturity. [3]

parameter

1. A variable that can assume any of a given set of values.
2. A statistic that characterizes a population; usually unknown and must be inferred.

parapet. A low wall or railing along the edge of a roof, balcony, bridge, or terrace; constructed for protection, to control water resulting from rain or artificial flooding, or to insulate against the sun's rays.

parcel. A piece of land of any size that is in one ownership.

parent material. The unconsolidated mass from which the soil profile develops.

parent rock. The rock from which the parent material of soils is formed.

parging. A thin coating of mortar that is applied to a masonry wall; used on the exterior face of below-grade walls for waterproofing or to smooth rough masonry.

parity. The state of being equivalent; used to refer to federal price policies for agricultural products; e.g., policies are designed to bring farm income into parity with the incomes of other sectors of the national economy.

parking area. The area of a facility, e.g., a shopping area, industrial plant, supermarket, designated for the parking of customer and employee automobiles.

parking garage. A commercial facility where automobiles may be parked for a fee; may be either public or private.

parking ratio. The number of available parking spaces per rentable area, usually per 1,000 square feet of rentable area; a standard comparison that indicates the relationship between the number of parking spaces and the rentable area.

parkway. An arterial highway for noncommercial traffic with full or partial control of access; usually located in a park or park-like development.

parquet floor. A floor that is laid in rectangular or square patterns, not in long strips; often of prefinished, thin, fabricated wood blocks.

partial interest. Divided or undivided rights in real estate that are less than the whole. *See also* undivided partial interest.

partially amortizing mortgage loan. A loan that is not fully amortized at maturity; the outstanding principal must be repaid in one lump sum; often created by writing a loan for one maturity and calculating debt service payments based on a longer amortization period. *See also* balloon mortgage.

partial payment factor $(1/a_{\overline{n}|})$. The compound interest factor that represents the installment needed to repay $1 with interest at a specified rate for a specific number of periods; the reciprocal of the level annuity, or Inwood, factor; expressed annually, it is the mortgage constant or annual constant.

partial taking. The taking of part of any real property interest for public use under the power of eminent domain; requires the payment of compensation.

participation. *See* equity participation; income participation.

participation mortgage. A mortgage held by more than one lender.

partition
1. The division of real property into separately owned parcels according to the owners' proportionate shares; usually pursuant to a judicial decree; severs the unity of possession, but does not create or transfer a new title or interest in property. [3]
2. An interior wall that divides a building; e.g., a permanent, inside wall that divides a house into various rooms.

partnership. A business arrangement in which two or more persons jointly own a business and share in its profits and losses. *See also* general partnership; limited partnership.

party wall. A common wall erected along the boundary between adjoining properties; the respective owners have common right of use.

pasture. Land devoted to the production of tame or native forage that is harvested directly by livestock. [7]

patio. A courtyard; an open, paved area used for outdoor living; may or may not be partially or entirely surrounded by other parts of a building.

patio house. A type of single-family, attached house that is typically one story, L- or U-shaped, and without a basement. The entire lot area is used; the design is based on the lot line construction of a house with living area in the enclosure or garden court. *Also called* court garden. [13]

payback period. The length of time required for the cash flow stream produced by the investment to equal the original cash outlay.

PC-DOS. IBM's copyrighted disk-operating system; nearly identical to MS-DOS. [16]

peat soil. Unconsolidated soil material that consists mainly of undecomposed or slightly decomposed organic matter that has accumulated under excessive moisture.

pedalfers soil. A soil in which alumina and iron oxide have shifted downward in the soil profile, but with no horizon or carbonate accumulation.

pedestrian overpass. A structural grade separation, e.g., a bridge, that permits pedestrian traffic to pass over a highway.

pedestrian underpass. A structural grade separation, e.g., a tunnel, that permits pedestrian traffic to pass under a highway.

pedocal soil. A soil with a horizon of accumulated carbonates in the soil profile.

peeler log. A log that can be used for the manufacture of rotary cut veneer.

penetration ratio. The rate at which stores obtain sales from within a trade area or sector relative to the number of potential sales generated; usually applied to existing facilities. [17]

Pennsylvania Colonial architecture. An informal, residential architectural style characterized by a high roof line on the main section of the house, whitewashed or plastered exterior stone walls, simple details, and a roof of slate or wood shingles; a regional variation of Colonial architecture adapted for flat ground.

pension fund. Contributions from an employer and employees that are placed with a trustee, who must invest and reinvest prudently, accumulate funds, and pay plan benefits to retirees.

penstock. A conduit that conveys water to a power plant; a sluice-like device used to control the flow of water.

penthouse. A building on the roof of a structure that contains elevator machinery, ventilating equipment, etc.; a separate dwelling or apartment on the roof of an apartment house or other building; any roof-like shelter or overhanging part, e.g., a part that shelters a doorway.

per capita. By the head; according to the number of individuals. [2]

per capita income. The total personal income of area residents divided by the number of residents.

per capita retail sales. Total sales for retail categories as defined from universe; e.g., a metropolitan area, divided by the population of that area, and corrected for export and import. [17]

percentage-of-completion method. A method of recording income from construction contracts in which income is based on the percentage of construction completed. Performance is often measured on a cost-incurred basis. [1]

percentage rent. Rental income received in accordance with the terms of a percentage clause in a lease; usually includes a guaranteed minimum.

percolation. The seepage of water through soil; the soil's ability to absorb water or other liquid, e.g., effluent from a septic system.

percolation test. A test conducted by hydraulic engineers and others to determine the percolation rate of the soil; used by health departments to determine the amount of land area needed for an operational septic system.

perennial forb. A type of range vegetation that includes areas where perennial forbs predominate. True forb vegetation is rare because forb cover is usually temporary and replaced by more permanent vegetation when the disturbing factor is removed.

performance bond. A bond that guarantees completion of an undertaking in accordance with an agreement; e.g., a bond supplied by a contractor who guarantees to complete a building or road, a bond given to a municipality by a subdivider who guarantees proper completion, road construction, and utility installations. [2]

performance standards. Tests performed to determine whether a prospective land use will harmonize with the goals of applicable zoning; e.g., in an industrial area, performance standards would include tests of smoke control, noise levels, off-street parking and loading, expansion room for future utilization, and similar factors.

perimeter. The total length of the periphery of a given area; e.g., the distance around the outside of a building.

perimeter heating. Any heating system in which registers are located along the outside dimensions of a room, especially under windows.

periodic growth. Growth that occurs in periodic increments; e.g., financial growth at compound interest; as distinguished from continuous growth, as it occurs in nature.

peripheral. Any external device that communicates with a computer; e.g., a printer, a disk drive. [16]

permanent loan. A long-term loan used to finance the purchase and operation of a completed structure; as distinguished from a temporary loan, e.g., land and construction loans.

permanent monument. In surveying, a boundary line marker of some permanence; one that is not perishable. [7]

permeability. Describes the behavior of water in soil. A soil permeated by water is friable, deep, and without dense or compact horizons that would restrict the free movement of water.

perpetual easement. An easement in perpetuity; one that lasts forever. [7]

perpetuity. The state of being everlasting; e.g., an ordinary annuity that extends into the future without termination.

personal liability. The possibility of incurring a loss due to a legal claim. [1]

personal property. Movable items of property that are not permanently affixed to, or part of, real estate. *See also* real property.

personalty. *See* personal property.

pH. A measurement that designates the degree of acidity or alkalinity; technically, the common logarithm of the reciprocal of the hydrogen ion concentration of a system expressed in grams per liter.

phase soil. The part of a soil unit or soil type that exhibits minor variations from the characteristics normal for the soil type; variations, which may be of great importance, are mainly in external characteristics, e.g., relief, stoniness, accelerated erosion.

photogrammetry. The science, art, and technological skill involved in obtaining reliable measurements and quantitative information from photographs. [10]

physical age-life method. A method of estimating incurable physical deterioration based on physical age-life; assumes that deterioration occurs at a constant, average, annual rate over the estimated life of the improvements. Calculated physical incurable deterioration is deducted from current reproduction cost less physical curable deterioration to produce a cost estimate that reflects physical deterioration.

physical deterioration. *See* curable physical deterioration; incurable physical deterioration.

physical possession. The state or condition of being in occupancy.

picture window. A large window, usually a fixed pane of plate or insulating glass; sometimes divided into small panes; designed to command an interesting view or to allow more light into the interior of the building.

pier

1. A quay or wharf that extends seaward at an angle from the shore; provides a landing place on each side for vessels to receive and discharge passengers and cargo.
2. A square column.
3. A support placed where two abutting bridge spans meet.

pierhead line. *See* structure limit line.

pilaster. A rectangular, upright, architectural member; structurally used as a pier, but architecturally treated as a column.

pile. A wood timber; a round or square tube of solid or hollow steel that is filled with concrete and driven into the ground to support the foundation of a building, pier, or other structure.

pilings. Columns that extend below ground to bear the weight of a structure when the surface soil cannot; may extend down to bearing soil or support the load by skin friction; e.g., sheet piling is used to form bulkheads or retaining walls and to support docks or piers.

pinon-juniper. A type of range vegetation that includes pinon, juniper, and digger pine.

pipeline. A conduit of connecting pipes used to transmit liquids or gases.

pipeline easement. The right to construct, operate, and maintain a pipeline over the lands of others within prescribed geographical limits. The language of the easement determines the extent of the rights granted.

piping. A system that consists of pipes that carry water, and sometimes other fluids, under pressure and waste pipes that depend on the flow of gravity.

piscary. The right to fish in another person's waters; one of the burdens, or servitudes, that may be attached to land as a result of this right. [7]

pitch. The slope or incline of a roof; expressed in inches of rise per foot of length, or as the ratio of the rise to the span.

pivot sprinkler. An automatic irrigation system in which a mechanically moved main line rotates around a pivot point.

PLAM. *See* price level-adjusted mortgage.

plan. A horizontal cross section of any level of a structure that shows room arrangement, the location of doors, windows, etc; may also show the site and objects surrounding the building.

plank. A piece of unfinished lumber two to four inches thick and at least eight inches wide.

plank-and-beam framing. A type of frame construction in which heavier structural members are spaced farther apart than in other framing, and supporting posts, roof beams, and the roof deck are left exposed as part of the interior decor. [8]

planned unit development (PUD). A type of residential, commercial, or industrial land development in which buildings are clustered or set on lots that are smaller than usual, and large, open, park-like areas are included within the development. Individual properties are owned in fee with joint ownership of open areas or, if local law requires, open areas are deeded to the city.

planning districts. A geographical area that is planned using a system of zones in which each district is delineated according to population density.

plans and specifications. Working papers used in construction. Plans include all drawings pertaining to the property under consideration, e.g., building drawings, mechanical drawings, electrical drawings. Specifications are written instructions to the builder that contain information pertaining to dimensions, materials, workmanship, style, fabrication, colors, and finishes; they supplement the detail indicated on the working drawings. [1]

plant. In real estate, land, buildings, machinery, equipment, furniture, etc.; a portion of an assembled property, e.g., a power plant; the fixed property of an enterprise, e.g., an educational plant.

plantation. In forestry, an area planted to forest seedlings or seeded by broadcast methods. *Also called* tree farm.

planting easement. The right to use and control an area of land to establish and maintain plant growth for safety and beautification.

plaster. A mixture of lime, sand, and water that is used to finish walls and ceilings.

plaster ground. A narrow strip of wood or metal placed around openings and the perimeter of a room; may be at the base, at chair rail height, or at picture mold height; used as a nailing strip for trim and as a plane for plastering.

plaster of paris. Calcined gypsum, i.e., gypsum that has been converted into a fine, white powder by heat.

plastic. Synthetic substances that can be molded or shaped by heat.

plat
1. A plan, map, or chart of a city, town, section, or subdivision indicating the location and boundaries of individual properties.
2. A map or sketch of an individual property that shows property lines and may include features such as soils, building locations, vegetation, and topography.

plat book. A record showing the location, size, and owner of each plot of land in a stated area.

plate. A horizontal structural member that is laid across the top of a row of studs to serve as a frame for interior partitions and exterior walls; provides lateral rigidity for the wall by tying the studs together; serves as support for upper-story floor joists and as lower support for rafters. *Also called* top plate.

pledged account mortgage (PAM). A mortgage in which the borrower deposits a sum of money into a special savings account to cover any interest on the mortgage that is not covered by the monthly payment; a special type of adjustable rate mortgage or graduated-payment mortgage under which no negative amortization occurs.

plenum. The chamber in a warm-air furnace where air is heated before the ducts carry it to the registers. [2]

plex. A dwelling that is similar to a townhouse, but has many characteristics of single-family detached housing; may or may not occupy its own structure from ground to roof; has an outside entrance, is separated from other structures by open space, and is designed for occupancy by one or more families. A structure designed for occupancy by two families is a duplex; for three, a triplex; for four, a fourplex; and so on. The prefix identifies the number of dwelling units per building. [13]

plinth. A square block of trim material placed upright at the floor line on either side of the bottom of a door opening, or at the base of a column; meets the lower end of the door casing and the end of the baseboard. *Also called* plinth box.

plottage. An increment of value that results when two or more sites are assembled under a single ownership to produce greater utility. *See also* assemblage.

ply. Denotes the number of thicknesses or layers; e.g., three-ply; used for roofing felt, veneers, etc.

plywood. An assembled product constructed of three or more layers of veneer laid with the grain of adjoining plies at right angles and joined with glue; usually an odd number of plies is used for balanced construction.

PMI. *See* private mortgage insurance.

PMSA. *See* Primary Metropolitan Statistical Area.

POB. *See* point of beginning.

podzol. A zonal group of soils with an organic mat and a thin layer of organic mineral over a gray leached layer that rests on an alluvial dark brown horizon; developed under a coniferous or mixed forest, or under vegetation in a temperate-to-cold, moist climate.

point. A percentage of the loan amount that a lender charges a borrower for making a loan; may represent a payment for services rendered in issuing a loan or additional interest to the lender payable in advance.

point estimate. A final value estimate reported as a single dollar amount.

pointing. The process of removing deteriorated mortar from masonry and replacing it with new mortar; also, the final patching, filling, or finishing of mortar joints in new masonry work.

point of beginning (POB). A survey reference point that is tied into adjoining surveys. In a metes and bounds description, courses that connect monuments or points are generally described from this point. A course is described by length and bearing from the true north and south line; e.g., "north 50 degrees east" describes a line that runs 50 degrees east of north in an easterly direction; "south 30 degrees west" describes a line that runs westerly 30 degrees west of true south.

pole construction. A construction method in which poles or timbers are installed at intervals for structural support and no continuous foundations are used; frequently used in farm outbuildings.

pole line easement. An easement for the construction, maintenance, and operation of a pole line, usually for the transmission of electric power.

police power. The right of government under which property is regulated to protect public safety, health, morals, and general welfare; usually no compensation is provided for property owners whose property is affected.

pollution. The fouling of air, water, or soil by the introduction of injurious or corrupting elements. [6]

port authority. A commisssion or other agency with the power to coordinate land, air, and water traffic in and around a port.

porte cochere. A roof that extends from a building's entrance over an adjacent driveway to shelter people getting in or out of vehicles. [3]

portico. A roof supported by columns; either part of a building or standing alone. [2]

possessory interest. The right to the occupancy and use of any benefit in a transferred property, granted under lease, permit, license, concession, or other contract.

post. A vertical, structural member that carries stresses in compression; used where strength in bending is not required.

post-and-beam framing. A type of framing in which beams are spaced up to eight feet apart and supported on posts and exterior walls; framing members are much larger and heavier than those used in other framing systems.

posterior distribution. In Bayesian analysis, a decision-making distribution that represents the decision maker's uncertainty concerning the unknown value of the population mean after considering sample evidence.

posts and timbers. Lumber of square or approximately square cross section, five by five inches and larger; graded primarily for use as posts or columns carrying longitudinal load, but adapted for other uses where strength in bending is not important. *Also called* posts and pier.

poststressed concrete. Concrete that has been strengthened by placing reinforcing cables in metal sheaths in the wet concrete; the cables are stressed after the concrete sets and the sheathing is filled with grout. After the grout sets, the cables are released and the stress is transmitted to the concrete.

potential gross income (*PGI*). The total income attributable to real property at full occupancy.

potential gross income multiplier (*PGIM*). The ratio between sale price or value and potential gross income; used to convert a single year's potential gross income expectancy or an annual average of several years' potential gross income expectancies into an indication of property value.

power feed wiring. The main electric power line that enters a building from a utility or a private source; supplies electric power to machinery and equipment through main bus ducts or heavy wiring enclosed in conduit; does not include branch feed lines or controls from the main line to machinery.

power of attorney. A legal instrument in which a person authorizes another to act as his or her attorney or agent. [1]

power plant. A plant, within a structure or building, that generates power from coal, gas, oil, or water for its own use or for commercial distribution to others; includes engines, dynamos, etc. *See also* hydro-electric plant; water power plant.

practical capacity. The maximum number of vehicles that can pass a given point on a roadway in one hour without creating undue traffic density and unreasonable delay, hazards, or driving restrictions.

prairie. An extensive tract of level or rolling land that is originally treeless, grass-covered, and characterized by a deep, fertile soil.

Prairie School. A school of architecture prominent in the late 19th and early 20th centuries; used a style that emphasized strong horizontal and rectangular elements, unity between exterior structure and interior design, simplicity, and natural materials to create harmony between the architecture and its surroundings. Among the leaders of the Prairie School were Frank Lloyd Wright, George Grant Elmslie, and George Washington Maher.

prairie soils. A zonal group of soils with a dark brown or grayish brown surface horizon that grades through brown soil to lighter-colored parent material at two to five feet; develops under tall grasses in a temperate, relatively humid climate; does not include all dark-colored soils of treeless plains, but only those in which carbonates are not concentrated in any part of the profile.

precast concrete. Concrete structural components that are not poured in place, but are cast separately, on site or at another location.

pre-engineered building. A building constructed of predesigned, manufactured, and assembled units, e.g., wall, framing, floor, and roof panels that are erected at the construction site.

prefabricated house. A dwelling that is partially constructed in a factory and transported to the site for installation and final assembly.

prefabrication. The manufacture and assemblage of construction materials and parts into component structural units; e.g., wall, floor, and roof panels that are later erected at the construction site.

preferential assessment. A system in which farmland is taxed at the value of its productive capacity rather than its market value; the land must meet certain conditions to get reduced taxes, e.g., it must be in agricultural use for a specified number of years.

prepaid interest. Interest that is paid in one period but not due until a future period under the terms of the debt obligation. Under the accrual basis, prepaid interest is expended as incurred. [1]

prepayment penalty. An extra charge incurred by paying a mortgage or other debt instrument before its due date; provided for in the debt instrument and usually expressed as a precentage of the loan. [5]

prepayment privilege. A clause in a mortgage that allows the mortgagor to pay part or all of the mortgage debt before it becomes due. [1]

prescription. Legal title obtained by long possession; occupancy for a period prescribed by the Code of Civil Procedure bars any action for the recovery of the property and gives title by prescription.

prescriptive easement. *See* easement by prescription. [7]

present value (PV). The value of a future payment or series of future payments discounted to the current date or to time period zero.

present worth (PW). *See* present value (PV).

present worth of $1 (1/S^n). A compound interest factor that indicates how much $1 due in the future is worth today.

present worth of $1 per period $(a_{\overline{n}|})$. A compound interest factor that indicates how much $1 payed periodically is worth today. *Also called* ordinary level annunity.

preservation easement. A restriction that prohibits certain physical changes in an historic property; usually based on the property's condition at the time of acquisition of the easement or immediately after proposed restoration of the property.

prestressed concrete. Concrete that has been strengthened by stressing the reinforcements in the concrete before it sets and releasing them after the concrete has hardened.

pre-tax cash flow *(PTCF)*. Income remaining from net operating income after debt service is paid, but before ordinary income tax on operations is deducted.

price. The amount a particular purchaser agrees to pay and a particular seller agrees to accept under the circumstances surrounding their transaction.

price level. The average of the prices, usually at wholesale, of selected, representative commodities at a stated time; usually expressed as an index number.

price level-adjusted mortgage (PLAM). A mortgage in which the interest rate remains fixed, but the outstanding balance is adjusted according to price level changes. The interest rate on a PLAM is a real interest rate with no inflation premium. On each annual anniversary of the loan, the outstanding balance is adjusted for inflation and monthly payments are recomputed based on the new balance.

price supports. Various governmental programs designed to keep market prices from falling below a certain minimum level; e.g., agriculture is supported by outright subsidies or the purchase of crops at prices higher than market prices.

primary easement. An easement to which a secondary easement is attached; e.g., an easement in a ditch to which a secondary easement of access is attached for the purpose of cleaning out and repairing the ditch. [7]

Primary Metropolitan Statistical Area (PMSA). An area of more than one million population that consists of a large, urbanized county or a cluster of counties with very strong internal economic and social links; designated under standards set in 1980 by the Federal Committee of MSAs. *See also* Consolidated Metropolitan Statistical Area (CMSA); Metropolitan Statistical Area (MSA).

primary soil. A soil formed in place by the weathering of underlying rock and minerals.

primary trading area. The geographic area around a retail facility from which approximately 60% to 70% of the facility's customers come; geographic radii and driving times to the primary trading area vary with the type of facility. [17]

prime cost. The cost of direct labor and materials in any project.

prime rate. The interest rate that a commercial bank charges for short-term loans to borrowers with high credit ratings.

principal. A capital sum invested; a payment that represents partial or full repayment of the capital loaned or invested, as distinguished from the payment of interest; the unrecovered capital remaining in a loan or investment.

principal meridians. In land surveying, major north-south lines established as general reference points. There are about 25 principal meridians in the 48 contiguous states.

prior appropriation. A doctrine under which water is owned by the state and granted for beneficial use through appropriation; appropriative surface water rights are acquired by use and the performance of certain legal requirements, as directed by the state, the county, or an irrigation district. The owner of a water right may be entitled to surface water not contiguous to the land on which it is used.

prior distribution. In Bayesian analysis, a decision-making distribution that represents the decision maker's uncertainty about the unknown value of the population mean before a sample of the population is taken.

private alley. A narrow path that is not open to public use; its use is legally confined to a certain property owner or owners. [7]

private mortgage insurance (PMI). Insurance provided by a private mortgage lender to protect against loss caused by a borrower's default under a residential or commercial mortgage loan. [3]

private offering. An offering that is assumed to be exempt from securities registration. Those seeking a private offering exemption under federal securities law may follow Regulation D of the Securities Act of 1933 or may continue to claim the private offering exemption under judicial and administrative interpretations of Section 4(2) of the same act. [1]

private placement. An exempt placement of securities with an investor, usually an institution, under circumstances that do not constitute a private offering. *See also* private offering. [1]

private road. A road on private property that is maintained and kept open for use by the owner, the tenant(s), or their licensees, invitees, or guests; not open to the general public. [7]

private sector. The portion of the economy that produces goods and services; as distinguished from the governmental sector. [2]

private waters. Waters on land that is privately owned; subject to private control only; a stream that runs in a bed to which a riparian owner holds title. [7]

private way of necessity. An appurtenant easement that is granted to meet practical needs, e.g. to allow ingress and egress from a parcel of land that is legally landlocked.

probability. A number that represents the chance or likelihood that an event will occur; expressed as a decimal between zero and one.

proceeds of resale. Total property reversion; the transaction price minus selling expenses.

processor. The hardware that performs the actual arithmetic and logical operations of the computer system, using programs and data stored in the memory.

productivity
1. The capacity of a soil to produce crops in the existing environment under a specified system of management.
2. The amount of goods produced by labor, or other agents in production, per unit of time.
3. The net value of the services provided per unit of space.

productivity rating. The effect of surface soil texture, subsoil characteristics, topography, climate, drainage, soil, organic matter, and fertility on the productive capacity of a soil; used to determine the most suitable land use and cropping patterns for a property and as a basis for estimating yields and potential income.

profit
1. The amount by which the proceeds of a transaction exceed its cost.
2. In theoretical economics, the residual share of the product of enterprise that accrues to the entrepreneur after paying interest for capital, rent for land, and wages for labor and management.
3. In accounting, an increase in wealth that results from the operation of an enterprise. Gross profit usually is the selling price minus cost; items such as selling and operating expenses are deducted from the gross profit to indicate net profit. *See also* operating profit.

profitability index. The relationship, or ratio, between the present worth of the future benefits of an investment and the present worth, or cost, of the capital outlay.

profit and loss statement. *See* operating statement.

pro forma. According to form; a financial statement for real estate in which gross income, operating expenses, and net operating income for a future period, usually one year, are projected, based on specified assumptions. *Also called* pro forma statement. [3]

progress billing. A billing system in which a contractor sends bills before the work is complete; generally based on stages of completion, as laid out in the contract. [1]

progression. In appraisal, the concept that the value of an inferior property is enhanced by its association with better properties of the same type. *See also* regression.

project cost. The total cost of a project, including professional compensation, land costs, construction costs, costs for furnishings and equipment, financing, and other charges. [1]

projection. A process of extrapolation, extending the experience of the past into the future using a mechanical formula; may be a simple, straight-line projection or one based on a complex formula; based on the presumption that the conditions and rates of change of the past will continue in the future.

projection period. A presumed period of ownership; a period of time over which expected net operating income is projected for purposes of analysis and valuation.

proper stocking. Placing a number of animals in a specific area to make proper use of the forage over a planned grazing period; will lead to proper grazing.

property. *See* personal property; real property.

property brief. A description of a property for sale complete with details and pictures, in a form suitable for presentation to a prospect.

property line. The boundary between two parcels of land or between a property and a traveled way, e.g., a street, alley.

property residual technique. A capitalization technique in which the net operating income is attributed to the property as a whole, not to separate land and building components. In yield capitalization, the present value of the income stream is computed and added to the present value of the reversion at the assumed termination of the investment.

property tax. A tax levied on real or personal property.

property tax base. The assessed value of all property within a designated area, e.g., an assessment or tax district.

proprietary lease. A type of lease given to tenant-shareholders in a cooperative apartment corporation. In such a venture, a tenant purchases a specific number of shares of stock to obtain possession of an apartment and makes monthly payments to the corporation to cover his or her pro rata share of operating expenses and debt service.

pro rata share.
1. A share of a fund or deposit that is divided or distributed proportionately. [3]
2. A share of a burden or obligation that is divided proportionately; e.g., a tenant in a multitenant building or development may be required to pay a pro rata share of the building's operating expenses according to the number of square feet the tenant occupies. In a shopping center, the tenant's share of operating costs is often stated as a fraction, with the gross leasable area of the tenant's premises as the numerator and the gross leasable area or gross leased area of the entire shopping center as the denominator. [3]

prorates. Expenses that are prorated in escrow between the buyer and the seller based on the closing date, e.g., property taxes, interest. [1]

proscenium. The portion of a stage that is in front of the curtain; sometimes includes the curtain and the framework that supports it; an arch or opening that separates the stage from the auditorium.

prospectus. *See* offering circular.

proximity damage. An element of severance damages that is caused by the remainder's proximity to the improvement being constructed, e.g., a highway; may also arise from proximity to an objectionable characteristic of a site or improvement, e.g., dirt, dust, noise, vibration.

pruning. The selective cutting or removal of branches or twigs from a tree, shrub, or vine.

public domain land. Land owned by the federal government.

public facilities. Facilities that are owned by the public or a municipality, and operated for public benefit. [13]

public good. An economic good that is furnished by government, e.g., a recreation park, public education, museums; as distinguished from free good.

public housing. Rental projects that are owned and managed by state or local government agencies and made available to low- and middle-income tenants at reduced rates.

Public Housing Administration. A unit of the Department of Housing and Urban Development that administers legislation providing loans and subsidies to local housing authorities to encourage the creation of low-rental dwelling units.

public lands. Lands owned by the government; public domain. In the United States, the federal government holds title to vast tracts, including Indian reservations, national parks and forests, and grazing lands.

public land system. A system in which a parcel of land is described by reference to its position in the public land survey, e.g., the NE¼ of the SW¼ of Section 4, in Township 5 South, Range 7 West, Mt. Diablo Base and Meridian. *See also* government survey system.

public utility property. A property that produces commodities or services for general community consumption; usually a monopoly or quasi-monopoly with or without benefit of franchise; ordinarily subject to some form of government regulation and control.

PUD. *See* planned unit development.

pulpwood. A forest product used in the pulp and paper industry.

purchase and leaseback. *See* sale-leaseback.

purchase money. Money that is paid for property; a debt created by a purchase.

purchase-money mortgage. A mortgage that is given by a purchaser to a seller as partial payment for the purchase of real property.

purlin. A structural member that is laid horizontally to support roof rafters or a roof deck; in mansard roof construction, a base that supports the rafters in the upper slope of a gambrel or mansard roof.

purpose of an appraisal. The stated scope of an appraisal assignment, i.e., to estimate a defined value of any real property interest, or to conduct an evaluation study pertaining to real property decisions.

pylon. A gateway; a marking post or tower in an airport; a post or marker that guides pilots over a prescribed course of flight.

pyramid roof. A roof with four sides and four ridges that resembles a pyramid; usually comes to a point in the center.

pyramid zoning. A system of zoning in which the uses permitted in more restrictive zones are permitted in less restrictive zones as well.

Q

quadratic mean. *See* standard deviation.

quantity survey method. A method in which the quantity and quality of all materials used and all labor required are estimated and unit cost figures are applied to arrive at a total cost estimate for materials and labor.

quarry tile. A hard-burned, unglazed ceramic tile.

quarter. In the government survey system, one-fourth of a section containing 640 acres, or 160 acres.

quarter round. A molding in the shape of a quarter of a circle. [8]

quartile. The item that divides a frequency distribution into four equal groups; there are three quartile points and the second is the median.

quay. A landing place that is built parallel to navigable water and used in loading and unloading vessels.

queen post. One of two vertical members in a triangular truss, which are equidistant from the apex.

question of fact. Questions arising from evidence given in court that are in opposition to law and must be decided by jury; based on absolute reality, i.e., events, actions, or conditions that actually occurred, or physical objects or appearances that actually existed, not on mere supposition or opinion.

question of law. Questions arising from evidence given in court that deal with the letter of the law and must be determined by the court; based on interpretation of legal principles, conceived law, and established rules of duty.

quick assets. *See* liquid assets.

quiet title. A legal action that establishes title to real property. [1]

quitclaim deed. A form of conveyance in which any interest the grantor possesses in the property described in the deed is conveyed to the grantee without warranty of title.

quotient. An answer or result obtained by dividing one number by another.

R

rabbet. A groove cut on the edge or end of a board or other timber to receive the edge of another board with a similar cut.

raceway. A slim, metal conduit that carries electric or telephone wires with convenience outlets at frequent intervals; a plug-in strip.

radial highway. A traffic artery that runs from an urban center to less densely developed suburban or rural areas.

radial plan. A development of roads radiating from a city center with urban accretions along the way; results from natural, uncontrolled growth; may lead to good planning if combined with concentric, or ring, roads to form a spider-web plan or a star-shaped plan with green wedges between urban areas.

radiant heating. A type of steam, electric, or hot water heat that uses pipes concealed in floors, ceilings, or walls. *Also called* concealed heating.

radiant heating system. A system in which floors or other surfaces are warmed with hot air or, more commonly, hot water; the pipes are embedded in the floor slab or in side walls, and the air or water is distributed by forced circulation.

radiation. The emission of heat or light rays; applied in heating systems by the use of radiators, convectors, etc.

radiator. An exposed fixture that heats with a combination of radiation and convection; e.g., the common, cast-iron radiator; as distinguished from convectors, finned heating elements that are concealed in walls or cabinets, e.g., baseboard heating.

rafter. Structural members, e.g., joists, beams, that shape and support the roof deck or sheathing and the roof covering.

raft foundation. *See* floating foundation.

rail. The horizontal piece in a door, window sash, or panel; the top, horizontal member of a balustrade. *See also* stile.

railroad grade crossing. The intersection of a traffic artery and a railroad at the same grade elevation.

railroad siding agreement. A contract between a railroad and another, usually adjacent, industry for the construction and maintenance of a sidetrack on either party's land. *See also* industrial siding.

rake. In construction, a board or molding placed along the sloping sides of a frame gable to cover the ends of the siding.

RAM

1. In appraising, *see* reverse annuity mortgage.
2. In computer usage, random access memory; high-speed, volatile memory where data and progams reside during program execution. The user can both enter and retrieve data from this portion of memory, but when power is cut off, this memory is lost. [16]

ramp. An inclined walk or roadway; in highway construction, the roadway used to enter or leave a controlled-access highway.

ranch. A facility for raising livestock under range conditions where forage grasses are the main source of feed; sometimes used synonymously with farm or homestead to describe a rural property.

ranch improvements. All places of habitation, fences, water developments, and corrals associated with a ranch.

ranch-style house. A rambling, one-story house that is low to the ground and has a low-pitched gable roof or roofs, an open interior design, and sometimes a basement.

ranch unit. In public domain states, an entire, operating ranch unit; a combination of fee-owned land, Taylor Grazing Act permit land, and/ or Forest Service permit land.

random. Without uniformity of dimension or design; e.g., a masonry wall with stones placed irregularly, not in a straight course.

random sample

1. In statistics, the chance selection of a number of observations from a universe; i.e., the selection of items from an entire aggregate of items at stated intervals.

2.   In forestry, a sample chosen so that each individual tree or stem in the population has an equal, or independent, chance of being included.

random shingles. Shingles of different widths.

range capacity. The grazing capacity of grassland that typically maintains a satisfactory grass cover; expressed as the number of acres of grass needed to carry one animal unit through one grazing season or other specified period.

range inventory. An itemized list of all the resources of a management area, e.g., range sites, range condition classes, range condition trends, range use, estimated proper stocking rates, physical developments, natural conditions.

range line
1.   An extensive stretch of grazing land that produces native forage plants.
2.   In the goverment survey system, one of a series of lines that extend due north and south at six-mile intervals and are numbered east or west from the principal meridian. Range lines form the east and west boundaries of townships.
3.   The region or area over which something is distributed or occurs.
4.   The difference between the smallest and largest items in a statistical distribution.

range management. The planning and directing of range use to obtain maximum, sustained animal production and perpetuation of the natural resources.

range of value. The range, or confidence interval, in which the final estimate of a property's value may lie.

range site. An area of land with a combination of edaphic, climatic, topographic, and natural biotic characteristics that is significantly different from adjacent areas. These areas are considered as units for purposes of discussion, investigation, and management, and present significant differences in potential forage production and management requirements for proper land use.

range states. The 17 western states, where most of the land is used to produce livestock from range.

range survey. The science of range reconnaissance in which data are assembled to estimate grazing capacity; consists of two phases: 1) the mapping of grazing types and any cultural and topographic features that may influence grazing value; and 2) an analysis of the density and species composition of the vegetation to determine its livestock grazing capacity.

range utilization. The extent to which animals have consumed the total, current herbage production of a range area; expressed in percentage by weight.

rate. The ratio of one quantity to another; e.g., the ratio of net operating income to sale price or value is the overall capitalization rate.

rate base. The total amount of value on which a public utility is permitted by law to earn a fair return.

rate of return. The ratio of income or yield to the original investment.

ratio. The relationship between two similar magnitudes with respect to the number of times the first contains the second, either integrally or fractionally; e.g., the ratio of three to four may be written 3:4 or ¾.

raw land. Land on which no improvements have been made. [1]

raw material. Nonfabricated material used in processing or manufacturing, during which its nature or form is changed; e.g., iron is a raw material used in the production of steel, steel is a raw material used in the manufacture of automobiles.

real estate. Physical land and appurtenances affixed to the land, e.g., structures.

real estate counseling. Advice, guidance, and support in real estate matters, e.g., acquisition planning, cost-benefit studies, development planning, disposition planning, feasibility analysis.

real estate investment trust (REIT). A method that allows small investors to combine their funds and protects them from the double taxation that is levied against an ordinary corporation or trust; designed to facilitate investment in real estate as a mutual fund facilitates investment in securities.

real estate market. The interaction of individuals who exchange real property rights for other assets, e.g., money.

real estate owned (REO). Denotes real estate that has been acquired by a lending institution for investment or through foreclosure of mortgage loans. *Also called* owned real estate (ORE). [3]

**REAL ESTATE SECURITIES AND SYNDICATION INSTITUTE®
(RESSI®).** An organization of professionals involved in the real estate securities and syndication field; confers the SRS designation.

real estate syndicate. A general partnership, limited partnership, joint venture, unincorporated association, or similar organization that is formed or operated solely as an investment in real property; including, but not limited to, a sale, exchange, trade, or development; offers investors the tax, legal, and practical advantages of real property investment. [1]

real estate taxation appraisal. An appraisal that is performed to estimate the value of real estate for taxation. *Also called* ad valorem appraisal.

real property. All interests, benefits, and rights inherent in the ownership of physical real estate.

REALTOR®. A registered trademark that identifies a member of the NATIONAL ASSOCIATION OF REALTORS®.

realty. *See* real property.

reassessment. The process in which all property within a taxing jurisdiction is revalued to assign new assessed values. *See also* revaluation.

REALTORS NATIONAL MARKETING INSTITUTE® (RNMI). An organization that offers education and training to individuals engaged in real estate brokerage, sales, investment, and marketing; confers the CCIM, CRB, and CRS® designations.

recapture rate. The annual amount that can be recovered, returned, or allocated to be returned from an investment, divided by the cost or the original amount invested; may be applied to the total investment or to a wasting asset.

receiver. A person who is appointed by a court to administer a property or business when it appears necessary, in the interest of justice, that a qualified and impartial person assume control.

recent soil. A secondary soil that has been so recently deposited that weathering and aging have produced little or no change in the soil profile.

recession. A mild form of depression; a period of reduced economic activity.

reciprocal. A number divided into one; e.g., ½ or .50.

reclamation. Any method that brings wasted natural resources into productive use; e.g., desert land may be reclaimed through irrigation, forestland may be restored by artificial planting and seeding, and fields that are not too badly eroded may be reclaimed through proper cultivation.

reconciliation. A step in the valuation process in which an appraiser considers alternate value indications and selects a final value estimate.

reconciliation criteria. The criteria that enable an appraiser to form a meaningful, defensible conclusion about a final value estimate; criteria are appropriateness, accuracy, and quantity of evidence.

reconditioning. *See* renovation.

reconstructed operating statement. A statement that reflects an opinion of the probable future net operating income of an investment.

recorded map. A map of a parcel of land that has been filed in the office of the county recorder.

recorded plat. *See* plat.

recording. The filing of a copy of a legal instrument or document, e.g., a deed, in a government office provided for this purpose; creates a public record of the document for the protection of all concerned and gives constructive notice to the public at large.

recourse debt. A debt agreement secured by real property that gives the lender legal rights against the debtor beyond the right to property value; equivalent to a general obligation of the debtor. [5]

Rectangular Survey System. *See* government survey system.

redevelopment. The development or improvement of cleared or undeveloped land in an urban renewal area; technically includes the erection of buildings and other development and improvement of the land by private or public redevelopers to whom the land has been made available; does not include site or project improvements that are installed by a local public agency to prepare the land for sale or lease.

regional resort. A resort that is popular in a particular season and is usually located within a three-hour traveling radius of a metropolitan area; most of its patrons travel by automobile from a nearby metropolitan area.

regional shopping center. A shopping center that provides a variety of general merchandise, apparel, furniture, and home furnishings and a range of services and recreational facilities; built around one or two full department stores of at least 100,0000 square feet; usually contains 400,000 square feet of gross leasable area and provides services common in a business district, but not as extensive as those provided by a super-regional shopping center.

registration. An application to the Securities and Exchange Commission (SEC) for an interstate sale. [1]

regression. In appraisal, the concept that the value of a superior property is adversely affected by its association with an inferior property of the same type. *See also* progression.

regrowth. The younger, smaller trees in a timber stand that have not yet reached minimum diameter at breast-height and are still growing. *Also called* reproduction.

rehabilitation. *See* renovation.

reimbursement rate. A rate, usually set by the State Department of Health, that represents a reimbursement to an owner-operator for the care provided in a skilled nursing home or health-related facility; usually refers to the rate paid for public assistance patients who qualify under Medicare/Medicaid programs.

reinforced concrete. Concrete that is strengthened by embedding iron or steel bars, rods, or mesh in it.

reinforced concrete construction. Construction in which reinforced concrete is used for foundations, frames, floors, roofs, or other structural members.

reinforcement. A system of steel rods or mesh that absorbs tensile and shearing stresses in concrete work; complements the inherent compressive qualities of concrete.

reinsurance. A reassignment of all or part of the insurance carried from one company to another.

reinvestment rate. An obtainable rate of return for capital recaptured from a prior investment.

reinvestment rate of return. A modified internal rate of return that assumes that cash flows from an investment can be reinvested at a specified rate. *See also* internal rate of return (*IRR*).

REIT. *See* real estate investment trust.

release clause. A clause stipulating that, upon payment of a specific amount of money to the holder of a trust deed or mortgage, the lien on a particular described lot or area shall be removed, i.e., from the blanket lien on the whole area. [2]

relief. The configuration or irregularities of a land surface; the topography of land.

relief map. A map representing the topographical relief of an area, usually with general contour lines.

relinquishment. The conveyance of a portion of a transportation facility from a state transportation agency to another government agency for transportation use.

relocation
1. The moving of individuals or businesses from one location to another.
2. A process in which a federal, state, or local public agency provides relocation services, moving cost payments, and related expenses to individuals, families, and businesses displaced by urban renewal projects or other federal or federally assisted programs; required by statute.

relocation payment. A cash amount paid by a federal, state, or local public agency to reimburse individuals, families, and businesses for reasonable moving and other expenses resulting from their displacement by urban renewal projects or other federal or federally assisted programs.

relocation plan. A program devised by governmental agencies to relocate residents of an urban renewal area who will be displaced by project activities or other government actions.

remainder
1. A future possessory interest in real estate that is given to a third party and matures upon the termination of a limited or determinable fee; e.g., A gives B a life estate in A's farm for B's lifetime. A also gives C an interest in the farm to take effect upon B's demise. C has a remainder interest.

2. In eminent domain condemnation, property remaining in possession of the owner after a partial taking.

remainderman. A person who is entitled to an estate after a prior estate or interest has expired. *See also* remainder.

remaining economic life. The estimated period during which improvements will continue to contribute to property value.

remnant. A remainder that has negligible economic utility or value due to its size, shape, or other detrimental characteristics. *Also called* uneconomic remnant. *See also* remainder.

remodeling. A type of renovation that changes property use by changing property design.

rendering
1. In perspective drawing, to finish with ink or color to bring out the effect of the design; e.g., an architect's rendering of a proposed project. [8]
2. A process used to convert a substance to industrial fats, oils, or fertilizer.

renegotiable rate mortgage (RRM). A rollover mortgage sponsored by the Federal Home Loan Bank Board; called an *adjustable mortgage loan* (AML) under current regulations.

renovation. The process in which older structures or historic buildings are modernized, remodeled, or restored. *See also* modernization; remodeling; restoration.

rent. An amount paid for the use of land, improvements, or a capital good. *See also* assart rent; contract rent; crop share rent; dead rent; ground rent; livestock share rent; market rent; percentage rent.

rentable area. The amount of space on which the rent is based; calculated according to local practice.

rental requirement. A condition in a commitment letter that stipulates that a certain amount of space must be rented at a minimum rental rate if the entire loan amount is to be funded. [1]

rental value. *See* market rent.

rent concession. A discount or other benefit offered by a landlord to induce a prospective tenant to enter into a lease; usually in the form of one or more rent-free months, but it may be expressed in extra services to the tenant or some other consideration. [3]

rent control. A legal regulation that specifies the maximum rental payment for the use of property. [2]

rent escalation. *See* escalation clause.

rent roll. A report that is prepared regularly, usually each month, and indicates the rent-paying status of each tenant.

rent-up period. A period of time during which a rental property is in the process of initial leasing; may begin before or after construction and lasts until a stabilized occupancy is achieved. [5]

REO. *See* real estate owned.

repairs. Current expenditures for general upkeep to preserve a property's condition and efficiency; may include renewal of small parts of any unit of a plant; does not include replacement, i.e., the renewal of any substantial part of the property, or a change in the form or material of the building. *See also* cost of repairs; maintenance.

replacement allowance. An allowance that provides for the periodic replacement of building components that deteriorate and must be replaced during the building's economic life.

replacement cost. The estimated cost to construct, at current prices, a building with utility equivalent to the building being appraised, using modern materials and current standards, design, and layout.

replacement reserves. *See* replacement allowance.

reproduction cost. The estimated cost to construct, at current prices, an exact duplicate, or replica, of the building being appraised, using the same materials, construction standards, design, layout, and quality of workmanship, and embodying all the subject's deficiencies, superadequacies, and obsolescence.

repurchase agreements and reverse repurchase agreements. Short-term financing arrangements made by securities dealers, banks, and the Federal Reserve System in which a person who needs funds for a short period uses his or her portfolio of money market investments as collateral and sells an interest in the portfolio with the obligation to repurchase it, with interest, at a specific future time.

reserve
1. An appropriation from surplus that is allocated to deferred or anticipated contingencies. In business, a credit account created to accumulate funds to retire indebtedness or to cover losses that are payable or expected to accrue in the future.
2. In natural resource property, the extent of proven or unproven, commercially available resources that are not required or involved in current operations.

reserve for depletion. In accounting, an amount set aside before determining net worth to offset the depletion of an asset, e.g., a mineral deposit that is carried on the accounts at a value assigned before the depletion occurred.

reserve for depreciation. In accounting, an amount set aside before determining net worth to offset the depreciation of fixed assets that are carried on the accounts at values assigned before they suffered depreciation. *Also called* provision for depreciation or allowance for depreciation. *See also* book value.

reserve for replacements. *See* replacement allowance.

reserve requirement. The Federal Reserve System's requirement that member banks keep part of their deposit liabilities frozen in reserve accounts.

reservoir. A natural or artificial place, e.g., lake, pond, tank, where water is collected and stored to supply a community, an irrigation system, or a power plant; the water above a dam that is used to control the flow of the stream.

residence. Any property used as a dwelling; in law, the legal domicile; used for owner's occupancy, not investment income.

residential building rate. The rate of housing starts per 1,000 population; used to determine the level of residential construction in a community.

residential property. A vacant or improved parcel of land devoted to or available for use as an abode; e.g., single-family homes, apartments, rooming houses.

residential restriction. A covenant or zoning ordinance that limits the construction of buildings in a subdivision or district to residences. [7]

residential square. A park-like city square; usually owned cooperatively by the occupants of row houses or townhouses that abut the square.

resident management. An additional expense to the project, over and above the off-premises management expense, that is incurred by employing a live-in manager. *Also called* on-premises management. [1]

residual. The quantity left over; used to describe capitalization procedures that develop the value of a property component based on its residual income. *See also* residual techniques.

residual soil. Soil formed in place by the weathering of mineral material or by the disintegration and decomposition of rock.

residual stands. Timber stands that have been partially logged, leaving some of the original old growth trees; tend to develop a young growth understory if not relogged.

residual techniques. Techniques that permit the capitalization of the income allocated to an investment component of unknown value after all investment components of known value have been satisfied; include both physical techniques, for land and buildings, and financial techniques, for mortgage and equity. *See also* building residual technique; land residual technique; property residual technique.

resort property. Types of property that are located in resort areas or devoted to public or private recreational use; e.g., summer homes, hotels, motels.

RESSI®. *See* REAL ESTATE SECURITIES AND SYNDICATION IN-STITUTE.

restaurant activity index. The ratio between an area's restaurant sales, expressed as a percentage of total U.S. restaurant sales, and the area's food store sales, expressed as a percentage of total U.S. food store sales; reflects the current level of restaurant activity, but does not indicate the cause of changes in activity.

restaurant growth index. The ratio between an area's daytime and nighttime population, expressed as a percentage of the total U.S. population, and the area's restaurant sales, expressed as a percentage of total restaurant sales.

restoration. A type of renovation in which a property is returned to its original appearance and condition.

restrictive covenant. A private agreement that restricts the use and occupancy of real estate that is part of a conveyance and is binding on all subsequent purchasers; may involve control of lot size, setback, placement of buildings, architecture, or cost of improvements.

resurvey. The surveying of a tract of land according to a former plat or survey; using the best evidence obtainable, the surveyor locates the courses and lines in the same places they were located by the first surveyor.

retail land developer. A person engaged in development for retail lot sales. Lots are usually sold before offsite improvements are completed, with small down payments and soft terms without recourse. [1]

retail lot sales. The sale of lots to ultimate owners on a volume basis; as distinguished from the sale of individual lots to an intermediate owner, e.g., a merchant builder. [1]

retainage. A portion of the amount due under a construction contract that is withheld by the owner until the job is completed in accordance with the plans and specifications. [3]

retaining wåll. A sloping or vertical structural support that confines or restricts the movement of adjoining earth or water.

retention basin. *See* retention pond.

retention pond. A man-made impoundment with a permanent pool of water that is used to reduce storm water runoff. [3]

retirement community. A life-care facility in which a resident purchases a living unit with an entrance fee and continuing monthly maintenance charges; provides for congregate living with persons occupying separate units; offers amenities geared to senior citizens and total nursing care facilities for residents when they are unable to care for themselves.

retrofit. A modification in the design, construction, material, or equipment of an existing building to reduce energy use.

reuse appraisal. An appraisal performed to estimate the value of vacant land or improved property in an urban renewal project area; conducted under the provisions of the National Housing Act of 1949, as amended, and subject to the restrictions and controls set forth in the urban renewal plan for the project area.

revaluation. The mass appraisal of all property within an assessment jurisdiction to equalize assessed values; the reappraisal of a previous assignment.

revaluation lease. A lease that provides for rent adjustments at periodic intervals based on a revaluation of the real estate.

revenue stamps. Stamps purchased from the state government and affixed, in amounts provided by law, to documents or instruments that represent original issues, sales, or transfers of stocks and bonds and deeds of conveyances; may provide an indication of sale price. *Also called* documentary stamps.

reverse annuity mortgage (RAM). A type of mortgage designed for retirees and other fixed-income homeowners who owe little or nothing on their homes; typically permits owners to use some or all of the equity in their homes as supplemental income, while retaining ownership. They are borrowing against the value of their homes on a monthly basis; the longer they borrow, the less equity they retain. The loan becomes due on a specific date or when a certain event occurs, e.g., the sale of the property or death of the borrower. [4]

reverse leverage. *See* negative leverage.

reversion. A lump-sum benefit that an investor receives at the termination of an investment. *Also called* reversionary benefit.

reversionary right. The right to repossess and resume full and sole use and ownership of real property that has been temporarily alienated by a lease, an easement, etc.; may become effective at a stated time or under certain conditions, e.g., the termination of a leasehold, the abandonment of a right-of-way, the end of the estimated economic life of the improvements.

reversion factor. A compound interest factor that is used to discount a single, future payment to its present worth, given the appropriate discount rate and discount period. *See also* present worth of $1 ($1/S^n$).

reverter clause. A clause that provides that title reverts to the grantor when a restriction set forth in a deed is violated; affects the marketability of the mortgagee's title and thus the value of the property.

review appraiser. An appraiser who examines the reports of other appraisers to determine whether their conclusions are consistent with the data reported and other generally known information.

ribbon board. A horizontal structural member that is let into outside wall studs to support upper-story floor joists that are being spiked to the studs in a balloon frame. *Also called* ledger or ledger board.

ribbon development. *See* roadside development.

ridge. The top, horizontal edge or peak of a roof.

ridge board. The horizontal structural member at the top of a roof against which the upper ends of the rafters are butted.

right of access. *See* access rights.

right of drainage. An easement that gives the owner of land the right to drain water through or from the land of another, from its source or from any other place. [7]

right of entry. The right to enter and begin construction on land that is in the process of being acquired.

right of first refusal. An option that gives the lessee the right to purchase a property before any offer to purchase by a third party.

right of immediate possession. The right to occupy property after preliminary steps for acquisition have been taken, but before final settlement.

right of redemption. The privilege of a property owner to reacquire foreclosed property by paying the mortgage debt or real estate taxes within a limited time after the final payment date. [2]

right of survivorship. Right to acquire the interest of a deceased joint owner, e.g., in joint tenancy. [1]

right-of-way. A privilege to pass over the land of another in some particular path; usually an easement over the land of another; a strip of land used in this way for railroad and highway purposes, for pipelines or pole lines, and for private or public passage.

rights. An enforceable, legal claim to title of, or interest in, real property.

right-to-farm legislation. Laws that protect agricultural owners from private nuisance lawsuits and new ordinances that would restrict normal farming practices, e.g., environmental or land protection laws; exist in different forms in several states.

rigid conduit. A rigid pipe used as a protective enclosure for electrical wiring.

rigid foundation. *See* floating foundation.

rill erosion. The loss of soil by heavy rains after fields are tilled. Small channels are cut into the soft, loose earth as the water races down a slope.

riparian. Pertaining to the bank of a river or other body of water.

riparian owner. The owner of riparian land, who is ordinarily entitled to the benefits of riparian rights. [7]

riparian rights
1.   The right of the owners of land bordering a lake or stream to the use and enjoyment of the water that flows across their land or is contiguous to it; entitles the user to reasonable use that does not materially diminish the quality or quantity of the water for other owners. The owners' rights are equal, regardless of their location along the stream or the time when each property was purchased.
2.   The right of an owner of land abutting a body of water to use the water area for piers, boat houses, fishing, boating, navigation, and the right of access for such purposes, limited by public need if on a navigable stream. In some states, the common law doctrine of riparian rights has been superseded by the doctrine of beneficial use. *See also* accretion; beneficial use; prior appropriation; water rights.

riprap. A foundation or wall of stones or rocks that are loosely placed together without order; usually constructed adjacent to deep water to prevent scour on the sides of bulkheads, or at river bends to prevent erosion from fast flowing water; may also be made of wood or concrete beams laid in regular patterns.

riser. The vertical part of a stair step that is in back of the tread.

risk. The possibility of loss; the chance of loss on an investment or from a particular hazard, e.g., fire, earthquake, wind.

risk factor. The portion of a given return or rate of return from capital invested in an enterprise that is assumed to cover the risks associated with the particular investment; as distinguished from, and in excess of, the return or rate obtainable from funds invested where the safety of principal is virtually assured.

risk premium. In risk or security analysis, the return over and above the risk-free rate.

risk rate. The annual rate of return on capital that is commensurate with the risk assumed by the investor; the rate of interest or yield necessary to attract capital.

river bed. The land between a river's banks that is worn by the regular flow of water.

rivulet. A small stream. [7]

RM. Residential Member, Appraisal Institute. *See also* American Institute of Real Estate Appraisers (AIREA).

RNMI. *See* REALTORS NATIONAL MARKETING INSTITUTE®.

roadside development. A residential, commercial, or industrial strip development that occupies the frontage properties abutting a highway leading from an urban community.

rock. Natural, consolidated or unconsolidated mineral matter of various compositions. *See also* igneous rock; metamorphic rock; sedimentary rock.

rock wool. *See* mineral wool.

roll. *See* tax roll.

rollover mortgage. A mortgage in which the terms, or interest rate, are reviewed and adjusted periodically according to contract. Technically, the outstanding principal balance is due on the renewal date, but lenders may extend the mortgage for a second renewal period or even renew the entire amount of the mortgage at the going market rate. Usually, only the interest rate is adjusted, and monthly payments are based on the remaining term for the following renewal period. *Also called* renewable mortgage.

roll roofing. A roofing material made of compressed fibers saturated with asphalt; supplied in rolls.

ROM. Read only memory; in computer usage, permanent, high-speed memory that usually contains a manufacturer's program; not used to record data; retained when power to a computer is shut off. [16]

roof. The top portion of a structure. Types include butterfly roof, double-pitch roof, flat roof, gable roof, gambrel roof, hip roof, lean-to roof, M roof, mansard roof, pyramid roof, sawtooth roof, semicircular roof, single-pitch roof.

roofer. A piece of lumber, usually one inch thick, that is fastened to the rafters; used to enclose the top of a building frame and to support the roof covering. *Also called* roof sheathing.

roofing felt. Sheets of felt or some other close-woven, heavy material that are placed on top of the roof boards for insulation and waterproofing; treated with bitumen or another tar derivative to increase its water resistance; applied with a sealing compound or with intense heat, which softens the tar so it adheres to the roof. [8]

roof pitch. The slope or inclination of a roof; usually expressed in inches; e.g., a 5-inch pitch, a 5-in-12 pitch, and a 5-to-12 pitch all mean that the roof slope rises five inches for every 12 inches of horizontal distance.

room count. The number of rooms in a building; a unit of comparison used particularly in residential appraisal.

room night. In the lodging industry, a unit of demand that denotes one room occupied for one night by one or more individuals.

root-mean-square average. *See* standard deviation.

root stock. The part of the tree or vine that includes the root system; may differ in type from the crown and trunk of the plant. A plant is budded or grafted to a different root stock to provide a root system that is more resistant to disease or nematodes, or to encourage rapid growth. The life span of the tree or vine depends upon the type of root stock.

rotary interchange. An intersection of multiple highways in which traffic interchange for entrance and exit is controlled in a circular traffic flow.

rotunda. A circular building or room that is covered by a dome.

rough. The 10- to 40-foot wide area on either side of a fairway that guides golfers and sets the direction for play; similar in character to the fairway, but with slightly longer grass.

roughage. Plant materials that contain a small proportion of nutrients per unit of weight and are usually bulky, coarse, high in fiber, and low in total digestible nutrients; may be classified as dry or green.

rough hardware. Metal ware, e.g., nails, screws, bolts, that is buried in construction and rarely exposed to view.

round timber. Timber used in the original round form; e.g., poles, pilings, mine timbers. *See also* lumber; timber.

row crop. Farm crops planted in rows to permit cultivation during growth; generally vegetables or produce for human consumption, but some seed crops are planted in rows.

row houses. Attached dwellings that have architectural unity.

row stores. *See* strip development.

royalty. In real estate, the money paid to an owner of realty for the right to deplete the property of its natural resource, e.g., oil, gas, minerals, stone, builders' sand and gravel, timber; usually expressed as a stated part or price per unit of the amount extracted; a combination of rent and depreciation, or depletion charge. *See also* landowner's royalty; overriding royalty.

RRM. *See* renegotiable rate mortgage.

rubble. Field stone.

rubblework. Masonry built of rubble or roughly dressed stones that are laid in irregular courses.

running lines. Set boundary lines; refer to the calls in the grant and field notes carried into the grant, or to the map or plan referred to in the conveyance. [7]

S

safe rate. The rate that can be obtained on an investment with maximum safety and minimum risk.

sagebrush. A type of range vegetation that includes all lands where species of sagebrush predominate.

sale barn. A livestock shed in an auction sale yard where livestock are exhibited as they are sold.

sale contract. A written document signed by a buyer and a seller who agree to the transfer of ownership interests in real estate.

sale-leaseback. A financing arrangement in which real property is sold by its owner-user, who simultaneously leases the property from the buyer for continued use.

sale price. *See* price.

sales-assessment ratio. A ratio derived by dividing sale price by assessed value.

sales commission. A fee paid to a salesperson or broker who arranges for the sale of property; generally expressed as a percentage of the sale price. [1]

sales comparison approach. A set of procedures in which an appraiser derives a value indication by comparing the property being appraised to similar properties that have been sold recently, applying appropriate units of comparison, and making adjustments, based on the elements of comparison, to the sale prices of the comparables.

sales-ratio analysis. A study of the relationship between assessed values, sale prices, and the deviations that result from differences between the two; used to determine the efficiency and fairness of assessment in a particular jurisdiction.

saline soil. A soil that contains enough common alkali salts to harm plant growth.

salt box architecture. *See* New England Colonial architecture.

saltbush. A type of range vegetation that includes areas where various salt desert shrubs, e.g., atriplex, predominate.

salvage value. The price expected for a whole property, e.g., a house, or a part of a whole property, e.g., a plumbing fixture, that is removed from the premises, usually for use elsewhere.

SAM. *See* shared appreciation mortgage.

sample. In statistics, a limited or finite number of observations selected from a universe and studied to draw qualified, quantitative generalizations with respect to the universe.

sampling error. The difference between a sample statistic and the characteristic that would have been found if the entire population had been tested.

sand. Small rock or mineral fragments ranging in diameter from 1 to 0.005 millimeters; e.g., coarse sand, 1 to 0.05 millimeters; sand, 0.50 to 0.25 millimeters; fine sand, 0.25 to 0.10 millimeters; very fine sand, 0.100 to 0.005 millimeters; soils that contain 90% or more of all grades of sand combined.

sandwich beam. *See* flitch beam.

sandwich lease. A lease in which an intermediate, or "sandwich," leaseholder is the lessee of one party and the lessor of another, i.e., the owner of the sandwich lease is neither the fee owner nor the user of the property; a leaseholder in a chain of leases, excluding the ultimate sublessee.

sandwich leaseholder. The lessor under a sandwich lease.

sandwich panel. A core of insulation that is covered on both sides with a material such as concrete, metal, or asbestos.

sandy loam. A soil that contains much sand and enough silt and clay to make it somewhat coherent; will form a weak cast when dry and squeezed in the hand.

sanitary base. A three-member base consisting of a common baseboard, a base mold above, and a shoe mold that is let up behind the common base. The shoe mold is fastened to the floor and the common base is nailed to the studs above it; in common and molded bases, the common baseboard rests directly on the floor.

sanitary district. An assessment district established with particular reference to improvements, e.g., sewers and sewage disposal plants, that are constructed in the interest of sanitation and health; a municipal corporation organized to secure, preserve, and promote the public health. [7]

sanitary landfilling. A waste disposal method in which solid waste is spread on land in thin layers, compacted to the smallest practical volume, and covered with soil at the end of each working day; used to protect the environment. [3]

sanitary sewer. A sewer that carries only sewage, not storm water runoff.

sash. The framework that holds the glass in a window or door.

satellite tenant. An independent, local merchant who leases a store in a shopping center, as distinguished from a major department store operator; attracted to the shopping center by the presence of a major tenant and the traffic that the major tenant will generate. [3]

satisfaction. The payment or discharge of a debt or obligation.

saturation zone. The lower, ground water zone; the area below the aeration zone that serves as a reservoir for ground water that feeds wells, streams, and springs.

savings and loan association. A financial intermediary that receives savings deposits, lends money at interest, and distributes dividends to depositors after paying operating expenses and establishing appropriate reserves.

saw log. A log that is large enough to be used for sawed lumber or other sawed products; its size and quality vary with regional use practices.

sawtooth roof. A roof consisting of a series of single-pitch roofs, usually found on factory buildings, garages, or similar structures; allows abundant light and ventilation.

scale
1. The estimated sound contents of a log or group of logs in terms of a given log rule; to estimate the sound contents of a log or group of logs.
2. A measured length on maps and engineered plans that is used to convert map measurements to actual measurements; e.g., one inch on a map may equal one foot in actual length.

scantling lumber. Yard lumber two inches thick and less than eight inches wide.

scatter diagram. A chart with data points plotted according to coordinates that represent two variables.

scenic easement. A restriction that is imposed on the use of the grantor's property to preserve the natural, scenic, or historic attractiveness of adjacent lands owned by the grantee, usually a city, a county, a state, or the federal government.

scheduled rent. Income due under existing leases.

scrap value. The price expected for a part of a property that is sold and removed from the premises to reclaim the value of the material of which it is made, e.g., plumbing fixtures sold for their metal content.

scratch coat. The first coat of plaster, which is scratched or scored to provide a proper base for the second coat.

Scribner rule. A diagram rule for measuring logs into 1-inch boards at least 4 inches wide, assuming a ¼-inch saw kerf; does not consider the taper of logs and gives a large overrun for small logs and logs longer than 16 feet; not recommended for logs less than 12 inches in diameter; generally used on fir and pine timber. *Also called* Scribner scale.

scuttle. A framed opening in a ceiling or roof that is fitted with a lid or cover.

seasonal dwelling. A dwelling not intended for year-round use; e.g., a beach house, a ski lodge.

seasonal stream. A stream that flows only during the rainy part of the year. [7]

SEC. *See* Securities and Exchange Commission.

secondary easement. The right of the owner of an easement to keep the easement in repair; includes the right to enter the servient estate at all reasonable hours to effect necessary repairs and maintenance, or to make original constructions necessary for the enjoyment of the easement; as distinguished from an ancillary easement, which is the right to go on another's land to carry off a profit à prendre.

secondary financing. A loan that is secured by a second mortgage or trust deed on real property or by another junior lien. [1]

secondary location. A location that is near or adjacent to the prime location; a second-best location; gains enhancement from proximity to the prime location.

secondary mortgage market. A market created by government and private agencies for the purchase and sale of existing mortgages; provides greater liquidity for mortgages. [3]

secondary soil. A soil that has been transported and redeposited by water or wind.

secondary trade area. The portion of a trade area that supplies additional support to a shopping center beyond that provided by the primary trade area. Secondary trade area patronage for a shopping center is primarily generated by the comparison shopping stores in the center; convenience shopping is usually done at neighborhood centers closer to home. [17]

second bottom. The first terrace level of a stream valley; lies above the floodplain and rarely, if ever, floods. *See also* first bottom; floodplain.

second foot. A measure that equals a flow of one cubic foot of water per second, or 449 gallons per minute.

second growth. Forest growth that comes up after the old stand is removed by cutting, fire, or other causes; smaller trees left after lumbering, or trees available for a second logging operation.

section
1. In the government survey system, one of the 36 sections, each one mile square, into which each township is divided.
2. In architecture, a detailed drawing that depicts a cross section of a building.

Section 8 housing. A federal program that provides assistance for lower-income households. The difference between the HUD-established allowable rent for each unit and the household's contribution is paid by HUD to the project owner or manager.

secular trend. In statistics, a long-term growth or decline established within the data; should not cover a period of less than 10 years.

securities. A class of investments represented by engraved, printed, or written documents that show ownership or creditorship in a corporation or other form of business organization; includes creditorship in public bodies; e.g., bonds, stocks, mortgages, notes, coupons, scrip, warrants, rights, options. [3]

Securities and Exchange Commission (SEC). A federal agency created by the Securities Exchange Act of 1934 to carry out the provisions of that act and to take over, from the Federal Trade Commission, the administration of the Securities Act of 1933. [3]

security. An asset that is deposited or pledged as a guarantee of the payment or fulfillment of an obligation or debt.

security agreement. An agreement between a secured party and a debtor that creates a security interest. [1]

sedimentary peat. A soil made up of finely divided plant, and sometimes animal remains. *See also* peat soil.

sedimentary rock. A rock composed of particles deposited after suspension in water; chief groups are conglomerates, from gravel; sandstones, from sands; shales, from clays; and limestones, from calcium carbonate deposits.

seed money. The money needed to initiate a project; e.g., funds needed to acquire or control a site, to obtain zoning, to perform feasibility studies. [2]

seepage. The loss of water from a natural or artificial watercourse or body of water by slow percolation or movement through the ground or the walls of a reservoir. [7]

segregated cost method. *See* unit-in-place method.

select lumber. Lumber, e.g., flooring, that is selected for length, color, grain, and the relative absence of imperfections; very similar to clear grade, usually containing a substantial quantity of it.

self-liquidating mortgage. A mortgage loan that will be completely repaid at maturity by amortization payments. If the installment payments are constant, it is a constant-payment loan; otherwise, it is a variable-payment loan. [3]

self-supporting walls. Walls that support their own weight, but do not carry the weight of the floors above or below, the roof, or the live load.

seller's market. An economic market in which sellers can obtain prices higher than those prevailing in the immediately preceding period; a market in which the few available properties are demanded at prevailing prices by many users and potential users. [2]

semicircular roof. A type of curved roof that is often used on farm barns.

senior mortgage. A mortgage that has preference over another mortgage. [2]

septic system. A private sewage system that usually consists of a septic tank, a distribution box, a septic field, and connecting pipes and laterals.

septic tank. A tank in which sewage is held until the organic matter decomposes by natural bacterial action and most of the solid matter dissolves into liquids and gases that flow into the septic field. *See also* cesspool.

service industry. An industry based on the sale of a service, e.g., insurance, banking, accounting, not a product.

service line. A pipeline that connects a public water or gas main with a property.

service road. *See* frontage road.

services
1. In economics, the contributions of business organizations or persons who render a service, e.g., teacher, accountant, rather than produce goods.
2. The facilities of a community that are provided by local government; e.g., police and fire protection, water and sewer systems.

service station. A commercial enterprise specifically designed to provide services and products for automobiles and trucks. *Also called* filling station, gasoline station, or gasoline service station.

setback
1. Zoning regulations that designate the distance a building must be set back from the front property line.
2. The height at which the upper floors of a building are recessed, or set back, from the face of the lower structure.

setback line. A line outside a right-of-way, established by public authority or private restriction; on its highway side, the erection of buildings or other permanent improvements is contolled.

set-off. A reduction in the thickness of a wall; a flat or sloping ledge or projection below the thinner part of a wall; also, a sunken panel or a recess of any kind in a wall.

set-off rule. In eminent domain, a rule governing the setting off of special benefits. Federal courts and some state courts allow benefits to be set off against both the value of the land taken and the damages to the remainder; in other jurisdictions, benefits are set off against damages to the remainder only.

severance
1. The act of removing anything attached or affixed to land, or a part of the land itself, that causes a change of its character from real property to personal property. [7]
2. The separation of mineral ownership from land ownership; a conveyance of land in which mineral rights are excepted or reserved. [7]
3. The termination of a joint tenancy or a tenancy in common. [7]
See also severance damages.

severance damages. In a partial taking, a decline in the market value of the remainder that arises as a result of the taking and/or the construction of the proposed improvement. *See also* just compensation; severance.

sewer. An underground system of pipes or conduits that carries sewage and/or rainwater from a point of reception to a point of disposal. *See also* combination sewer; sanitary sewer; septic system; storm sewer.

sewer line easement. An easement for the construction, maintenance, and operation of a sewage disposal line.

shake. A hand-split shingle that is usually edge-grained. [2]

sharecropper. A tenant farmer who receives land, living quarters, seed, stock, and implements from the owner and, in return, shares the crops produced.

shared appreciation mortgage (SAM). A mortgage in which the borrower receives assistance in buying the real property in return for a portion of the property's future appreciation in value. *Also called* shared equity mortgage.

sheathing. The first, tight covering applied to the outside of a building; in frame construction, the studs or rafters to which the outside covering is fastened.

sheathing line. The outer, vertical plane of exterior wall sheathing.

shed roof. *See* lean-to roof.

sheet erosion. The loss of surface soil by water, usually in even amounts over a given area.

sheet piling. Planking or steel shafts placed vertically and close together to form a temporary wall around an excavation.

shelter belt. A band or row of trees or large shrubs planted to protect farm buildings in open plains country from blizzards, snowstorms, and prevailing winds.

shingles. A surfacing material used on roofs or walls and composed of thin, small sheets of waterproof material, e.g., asphalt, wood, slate, tile.

shoe. A structural member that is laid horizontally on rough flooring to serve as a base for interior partition framing; found particularly in platform construction; also used as a base for bearing partitions on top of an I beam or steel beam where studs are let down to support the partitions.

shopping center. A tract of land, under single real estate ownership or control, improved with a coordinated group of retail buildings with a variety of stores and free parking. *See also* community shopping center; neighborhood shopping center; regional shopping center; super-regional shopping center.

shopping goods. Goods from variety, department, and general merchandise stores; e.g., clothing, furniture, appliances. [17]

shoreline. The land between high and low tide.

shoring. Temporary structural columns, beams, and braces that are used to support loads during construction.

short-lived item. A building component with an expected remaining economic life that is shorter than the remaining economic life of the structure as a whole.

short-term mortgage trust. A trust primarily engaged in making construction and development loans; its revenue is derived from interest and fees. [11]

shoulder. The land along the outer edge of a paved highway that is used to accommodate stopped vehicles; may or may not be paved.

side. A longitudinal wall of a structure.

side ditch. An open watercourse for the control and removal of storm water from the paved surface of an adjacent highway; may be paved.

side jamb. A piece of finish material that is laid vertically on the interior sides of a door or window to shape the opening.

siding
1. Finish lumber used on exterior walls; e.g., bevel siding, boards and battens, shingles.
2. An auxiliary railroad track used for meeting and passing trains, storing cars, loading and unloading, and other designated purposes; connects at both ends with the main track.

sight line. A line or area of unobstructed visibility; usually indicates the distance from which a business property or commercial site is visible to approaching vehicular traffic.

sight line easement. An easement granted to protect a sight line; usually prohibits construction or natural growth that might obstruct a property's visibility to approaching vehicular traffic.

silage. *See* ensilage.

sill
1. Framing lumber placed atop and around a foundation to serve as a level base for exterior wall studs and the ends of floor joists.
2. The lowest piece on which a window or exterior door rests; usually slanted downward slightly to provide for rainwater runoff.

silo. A structure of wood, concrete, or steel that is used to store fodder for conversion into silage; a storage bin for grain; a grain elevator. [7]

silt. Small mineral soil grains with particles that range in diameter from 0.050 to 0.020 millimeters.

silt clay loam. A soil composed of moderate amounts of fine grades of sand and of clay, but more than 50% silt and clay, with more clay than silt loam; cloddy when dry; tends to ribbon when wet soil is squeezed between finger and thumb.

silt loam. A soil made up of moderate amounts of fine grades of sand, small amounts of clay, and at least 50% silt; appears cloddy when dry; is smooth when wet and will not ribbon when squeezed.

simple interest. Interest that is paid only on the original principal, not on any interest accrued.

simulation. The use of an experimental model that is designed to approximate actual conditions.

single-family house. A dwelling that is designed for occupancy by one family.

single-pitch roof. A single-plane roof with a pitch of more than 20 degrees.

sinking fund. A fund in which periodic deposits of equal amounts of money are accumulated to pay a debt or replace assets; usually designed to receive equal annual or monthly deposits that will accumulate, with compound interest, to a predetermined sum at the end of a stated period of time.

sinking fund factor $(1/S_{\overline{n}|})$**.** The compound interest factor that indicates the amount per period that will grow, with compound interest, to $1.

sinking fund table. A tabulation of amounts that will accumulate to a desired sum at a specified date in the future if invested annually in a compound interest-bearing account at a stated rate.

siphon. A bent tube that carries water from an irrigation ditch to a field.

SIR®. *See* Society of Industrial REALTORS®.

site. Land that is improved so that it is ready to be used for a specific purpose.

site development costs. Direct and indirect costs incurred in preparing a site for use; e.g., costs for clearing, grading, installing public utilities.

site orientation. The relationship between a structure and its surroundings.

situs. In real estate, the physical location of a property; in personal property, the taxable location, because personal property may be moved from one place to another. [10]

six functions of $1. The six, related compound interest functions used in the mathematics of finance and shown in standard compound interest tables. They are: the amount of $1, the amount of $1 per period, the sinking fund factor, the present worth of $1, the present worth of $1 per period, and the partial payment factor.

skeleton steel construction. *See* steel construction.

skewness. In statistics, the degree of deviation from symmetry in a distribution.

skin. A covering, outer coating, or surface layer; in construction, the covering of a structure.

skin wall. External wall covering of aluminum, porcelain enamel, steel, or other material.

skylight. A glass opening in a roof.

slab. Any broad, flat, relatively thin piece of wood, stone, or other solid material; often used to describe a floor or foundation of concrete, either on the ground or supported above it.

slash. Debris left on the ground after logging; e.g., branches, bark, tops, chunks, cull logs, uprooted stumps, broken or uprooted trees; also, a large accumulation of debris left by wind or fire. *See also* slashing.

slashing. Forest area where logging has left tree limbs and tops; an area that is deep in debris from fire or wind.

sleeper. A timber that is laid horizontally, e.g., on the ground, to support something above it; a strip of wood that is anchored to a concrete floor or nailed to subflooring and to which the finished floor is nailed.

slip. Navigable water space between two piers; generally used for small boat storage.

slope. The degree of inclination or deviation of a surface from the horizontal; the grade, usually expressed as a percentage. In highway usage, the graded area beyond the shoulder that extends to natural and undistributed ground. Slopes are classified as 0%-2%, nearly level and/or gently undulating; 3%-8%, gently sloping and/or undulating; 9%-

15%, moderately sloping and/or rolling; 16%-30%, strongly sloping and/or hilly; 31%-45%, steep; and over 45%, very steep.

slope easement. An easement acquired to permit the cuts and fills of highway construction.

slow-burning construction. Mill construction in which structural members will char for some time under ordinary fire temperatures before they fail.

SMSA. *See* Standard Metropolitan Statistical Area.

snow fence. A portable, slat fence that is placed at strategic points along a highway or road to control drifting snow.

Society of Industrial REALTORS® (SIR®). A real estate organization that serves industrial property owners, users, and investors; confers the SIR® designation.

sod. Vegetation that grows to form a mat. *Also called* turf.

soffit. The underside of a building member, e.g., an arch, cornice, overhang, or stairway.

soft goods. Nondurable merchandise; e.g., wearing apparel.

software. A set of instructions that directs a computer to perform a function, e.g., a cost-analysis procedure. [16]

softwood. Wood from conifers; e.g., redwood, cedar, pine, fir; does not refer to the hardness of the wood.

soil. The natural medium for plant growth on the surface of the earth; a natural body in which plants grow; composed of organic and mineral materials.

soil aggregrate. A single mass or cluster of soil that consists of many soil particles held together; e.g., a clod, prism, crumb, granule. *See also* granular structure.

Soil Bank. A program administered by the Commodity Stabilization Service of the Department of Agriculture in which farmers contract to divert land from the production of unneeded crops to conservation uses, for which they receive an annual rent payment.

Soil Bank Act. A federal statute designed to help farmers divert a portion of their cropland from production, thereby avoiding the accumulation of excessive agricultural commodities, and to promote soil conservation by paying farmers to put cropland in the Soil Bank, i.e., take it out of production entirely or out of the production of certain crops. [7]

soil capability. The relative suitability of soils for crops, grazing, and other purposes. All of the soils in each of the eight capability classes have limitations and present management problems of the same relative degree, but of different kinds. Productivity may vary widely among the soils in each capability class. *See also* Land Capability Classification System.

soil conservation. Methods and techniques used to prevent soil depletion and to restore soil productivity; includes the use of chemical or organic fertilizers to replace elements lost through usage or leaching, the adoption of proper tillage methods and crop rotation to prevent the breakdown of soil structure, and the use of terracing or contour cultivation to reduce the erosion of topsoil.

Soil Conservation Service. A division of the Department of Agriculture concerned with obtaining a better balance of agriculture through physical adjustments in the use of land, conserving natural resources, and reducing flood hazards; provides technical assistance for local soil conservation districts.

soil erosion. The wearing or carrying away of topsoil by running water or wind. *See also* erosion.

soil fertility. The quality that enables a soil to provide the proper quantity and balance of compounds for the growth of specific plants when other factors, e.g., light, temperature, the physical condition of soil, are favorable; reflects the relative quantities of available soil nutrients.

soil fumigation. The practice of chemically treating the soil, usually before planting, to destroy diseases, fungus, nematodes, or noxious grasses and weeds. Chemicals may be sprayed or drilled into the soil; if chemical gas is used, retention is usually accomplished by covering the ground with plastic sheets.

soil genesis. The origin of the soil, particularly the processes responsible for developing the solum from unconsolidated parent material.

soil horizons. Layers or three-dimensional areas with characteristics produced by soil-forming processes; approximately parallel to the soil surface, but of varying thickness and irregular boundaries. In agricultural appraisal, the top six feet of soil, containing the surface soil, subsoil, and substratum horizons, are most significant.

soil map. A map that illustrates the distribution and location of soil types, phases, and complexes, as well as other cultural and physical features.

soil phase. A subdivision of soil type that denotes atypical characteristics; e.g., deep phase, shallow phase, poorly drained phase.

soil porosity. The degree to which the soil mass is permeated with pores or cavities; expressed as the percentage of the total soil volume that is unoccupied by solid particles.

soil profile. A vertical cross section of a soil showing its horizons and extending into the parent material.

soil profile group. A grouping of soils based on their profile characteristics. Alluvial soil profile groups are characterized by progressive increases in compaction and fine clay accumulations in the subsoils. Primary soil profile groups are differentiated based on the nature and composition of the underlying parent material.

soil sample. A vertical cross section of the soil profile that is usually taken from the top 6 to 18 inches of the soil.

soil series. A group of soils with the same type of profile; the same general range of color, structure, consistency, and sequence of horizons; the same conditions of relief and drainage; and common or similar origin, or parent material, and mode of formation.

soil structure. The arrangement of individual particles in a soil and the size and shape of soil aggregates; principal types are columnar, adobe, granular, buckshot, crumb, lumpy, cloddy, puddled, nut-like, and massive.

soil survey report. A written report that is accompanied by a soil map and describes the areas surveyed, the characteristics and use capabilities of the soil types and phases shown on the map, and the principal factors responsible for soil development.

soil texture. The relative proportion of the various size groups of individual soil grains.

soil type. A soil that has a relatively uniform texture throughout, in addition to the soil series characteristics.

solar design. A building design that makes use of the sun's energy; either active, using solar collectors outside the building envelope to gather energy for space or water heating, or passive, allowing the position and intensity of the sun to provide interior heating.

solar easement. A limitation on the use of property that prohibits any construction or activity that might obstruct or interfere with the reception of sunlight by an adjacent property of solar design. [3]

solar orientation. The position of a structure in relation to the sun.

sole. A piece of wood, usually a two-by-four, on which wall and partition studs rest. *Also called* sole plate. [2]

solid set. A sprinkler irrigation system with permanently installed laterals and sprinklers.

solum. The upper part of the soil profile, above the parent material, where soil-forming processes are taking place. In mature soil, this includes the A and B horizons where the character of the material may be, and usually is, very different from the parent material beneath. Living roots and life processes are mostly confined to the solum.

sonic. Pertaining to sound; also, denotes the approximate speed at which sound waves travel.

sound value. For fire insurance purposes, synonymous with depreciated cost.

Southern Colonial architecture. A style of architecture similar to Georgian and Modern Colonial, but distinguished by the use of two-story columns that form a porch across a long facade or on a side.

span. The horizontal, clear distance betweeen supports, e.g., of a bridge, or between columns in a structure.

spandrel. A triangular space formed by an arch, with a horizontal construction member above it and a vertical member or arch beside it; also, any horizontal space between two structural features of a building, e.g., between the top of first-floor windows and the windows on the second floor.

spandrel beam. A beam that lies in the same vertical plane as the exterior wall.

Spanish architecture. A residential, architectural style designed for outdoor living and characterized by a heavy tile roof, adobe or stucco walls, and an enclosed patio.

Spaulding rule. The statute rule of log measurement in California; employs a table to measure logs from 12 to 24 feet long, with longer logs scaled by doubling the values shown in the table; ignores the taper in logs and gives an overrun for large logs; produces considerable overrun when the modern band saw is used because it assumes a large saw kerf; used throughout the redwood region in its original form or as the Humboldt rule. *Also called* Spaulding scale.

special assessment. A legal assessment against real estate levied by a public authority to pay for public improvements, e.g., sidewalks, street improvements, sewers. [1]

special benefits. Specific, i.e., not general, benefits that accrue to the property remaining after a partial taking. *See also* benefits; general benefits; set-off rule.

special districts. Special service governments created to provide a particular service; e.g., economic development districts, water resource management districts. [13]

special exceptions. Uses that do not conform to the zoning code, but may be permitted under specific, tightly controlled circumstances.

special-purpose property. A property that is appropriate for one use or a limited number of uses; e.g., a clubhouse, a church property, a public museum, a public school; also, a building that cannot be converted to another use without a large capital investment; e.g., a hospital, a theater, a brewery. In some jurisdictions, courts have specifically defined this term.

special warranty deed. A warranty clause inserted in a deed of lands in which the grantor covenants that he and his heirs will defend title to the lands against legal claims created by the actions or omissions of the grantor or his heirs. If the warranty is against the claims of all persons, it is a general warranty. [2] *See also* quitclaim deed.

specifications. Written instructions to the builder that contain all necessary information pertaining to dimensions, materials, workmanship, style, fabrication, colors, and finishes; supplement the details shown on the working drawings.

specific heat. The quantity of heat required to raise the temperature of one pound of any substance by 1° Fahrenheit; expressed in Btus.

specific performance. An action that compels the performance of an agreement for the sale of land.

speculation. The purchase or sale of property motivated by the expectation of profiting from a rise or fall in its price.

speculative building. A structure that is built in the expectation that it will be sold or rented when completed. [11]

speculative land. Land that is held primarily for future sale.

speculator. One who speculates, i.e., one who buys a commodity, e.g., real estate, expecting to sell it at a higher price.

speed-change lane. An auxiliary travel lane designed and constructed to permit the acceleration and deceleration of vehicles entering and leaving the road.

spendable income. *See* after-tax cash flow (*ATCF*).

split-level house. A house with living areas on two or more levels of less than single-story height.

split rate capitalization. A capitalization procedure in which different discount rates are applied to different portions of the income flows earned by real property; e.g., one rate is applied to annual equity dividends and another is applied to the equity reversion. *Also called* fractional rate capitalization.

spot clearance. Demolition activities in which single structures or comparatively small groups of structures are removed from areas, but a substantial number of existing structures are retained.

spot zoning. An exception to the general zoning regulations; permits specific, usually small, parcels of land to be zoned for a use that is not permitted in the surrounding area. *See also* zoning variance.

spreader dam. A dam built across a gully so that accumulated runoff is diverted onto the flats on either side.

spreadsheet. A tabular representation of market data organized into useful, measurable categories.

sprinkler system. A fire protection system installed in buildings that consists of an overhead system of pipes that contain pressurized water and are fitted with valves, or sprinkler heads, that open automatically at certain temperatures.

spur track. A segment of track that serves an industrial site or plant with no regular train service; generally connected to the main track at only one end; may be applied to trackage of the railroad company used for siding purposes.

square. In roofing, a finished roof area of 100 square feet.

square foot cost. The cost of one square foot of an improvement; obtained by dividing the actual, or estimated, cost of a building by its gross floor area, or the actual, or estimated, cost of a land improvement by its square foot area; can also be multiplied by the number of square feet in a building or land improvement to produce the actual or estimated cost.

square foot method. *See* comparative-unit method; quantity survey method; unit-in-place method.

squatter's rights. Rights to the occupancy of land that are created by long, undisturbed use, but held without legal title or arrangement; in the nature of a right at common law.

SRS. Specialist in Real Estate Securities. *See also* Real Estate Securities and Syndication Institute (RESSI).

stabilized expense. A projected expense that is subject to change but has been adjusted to reflect an equivalent, stable annual expense.

stabilized income. Projected income that is subject to change but has been adjusted to reflect an equivalent, stable annual income.

stack. A vertical waste or vent pipe.

staging. A temporary scaffolding used to support workers and materials during construction.

stainless steel. An alloy of steel that contains a large percentage of chromium combined with nickel, copper, or other alloys; a hard, corrosion-resistant steel that retains a polish.

stairway. The flights of stairs and landings in a building that form a continuous passage from one floor to another.

Standard Consolidated Area (SCA). Two groupings of standard metropolitan statistical areas (SMSAs), as designated by the Office of Management and Budget.

standard cubic content. *See* cubic content.

standard deviation. In statistics, a measure of the extent of absolute dispersion, variability, or scatter in a frequency distribution; obtained by extracting the square root of the arithmetic mean of the squares of the deviations from the arithmetic mean of the frequency distribution.

standard error. In statistics, a measure of the distribution of an estimate of a parameter.

standard error of the estimate. In statistics, an estimate of the variation likely to be encountered when making predictions based on a regression equation.

standard fixed-rate mortgage. A mortgage that is fully amortizing, with a fixed interest rate and constant monthly payments; usually for a 30-year term.

Standard Metropolitan Statistical Area (SMSA). A single city with a population of at least 50,000; a city of at least 25,000 that is combined with contiguous areas with densities of at least 1,000 people per square mile to produce a population of at least 50,000; the city and contiguous areas must be located in a county or counties with a population of at least 75,000; not applicable after 1980, when it was replaced by Metropolitan Statistical Area (MSA). *See also* Consolidated Metropolitan Statistical Area (CMSA); Primary Metropolitan Statistical Area (PMSA).

standard of suitability. A description of the investor's background that an agency feels is required for a real estate offering to be fair, just, and equitable; may be expressed in terms of educational background, business experience and sophistication, profession, place of residence, annual income, net worth, or a combination of these factors. [1]

standard parallels. In the government survey system, the east and west lines that establish the north and south boundary lines of townships; run parallel to a baseline at 24-mile intervals.

standby commitment. A lender's promise to make a temporary loan to the borrower if he or she is unable to get other financing; requires payment, usually based on a percentage of the desired loan. A standby commitment usually serves as a basis for securing a construction loan because the construction lender must be sure that the loan will be paid off when construction is completed. [1]

stand cruise. An estimate of the lumber in a standing forest based on a particular log rule or volume table; no deduction is made for breakage or other waste.

standing timber. Timber that is still on the stump, i.e., in the tree.

starter course. The base on which and from which wall or roof shingles are laid; used to provide watertight joints at the first, or lowest, shingle course.

starting income. The level of income on the date of valuation; as distinguished from stabilized or projected income, which may or may not equal starting income.

starts. Units on which construction has begun; used as a statistical factor in evaluating the real estate market; e.g. housing starts. [1]

statistical inference. The process of reasoning from the specific to the general.

statistical table. A systematic arrangement of numerical data, presented in columns or rows for comparison.

statistics. The art or science concerned with the collection, classification, and use of numerical data relating to a particular subject; the data themselves.

statutory law. Law created by legislative enactment.

steel construction. A rigidly connected frame of steel or reinforced concrete that carries all external and internal loads and stresses to the foundations; enclosing walls are supported by this frame, usually at floor levels. If the steel frame has no fireproofing, it is known as unprotected metal construction.

steep land. Describes land with slopes ranging from 30% to 45%.

step-down annuity. A type of decreasing annuity, usually created by a lease contract, that calls for a succession of level annuities at different levels over different portions of the lease term.

step-up annuity. A type of increasing annuity, usually created by a lease contract, that calls for a succession of level annuities at different levels over different portions of the lease term.

step-up lease. A lease that provides for a certain rent for an initial period, followed by an increase or decrease in rent over stated periods. [1]

stile
1. A structural member of a parallel or glazed door.
2. An exterior or perimeter member of a window, other than the meeting, or check, rail in a double-hung window.

stock
1. All goods kept on hand by a commercial firm or merchant.
2. Livestock, e.g., cattle, sheep, horses; animals kept or raised on a farm or ranch.
3. An ownership share in a company or corporation.

stock corporation. A common, legal entity in which investors provide organizational capital by subscribing to shares that represent ownership and a right to all proprietary benefits, but are subject to the prior claims of operating expenses and debt service on capital raised by selling bonds, debentures, and other money market instruments.

stock driveway. A corridor of government-owned land that is used by local stock raisers to move herds between seasonal pastures or from the range to a shipping point.

stocking rate. The actual number of animals on a certain area at a specific time; expressed in animal units or cows.

stock trail. A trail through grazing land that permits greater use of the range in rough, steep, or heavily wooded areas.

stool. The wooden base or support at the bottom of a window; e.g., the shelf-like interior piece that extends across the bottom of a window opening.

stores. Raw materials held for use in manufacture, as distinguished from manufactured stock; various supplies for repairs, maintenance, etc., that are required in operations; the contents of a storeroom that is stocked to provide for current consumption; as distinguished from merchandise stock.

Storie Index. A rating system in which a soil's relative suitability for general, intensive agriculture is expressed numerically by assigning factors for the characteristics of the soil profile; the depth of soil, the texture of the surface, the dominant slope of the map unit, and other factors that are subject to management or modification, e.g., drainage, flooding, nutrient level.

storm sewer. A sewer that carries rainwater and sometimes industrial waters.

story. A horizontal division of a building; the portion between one floor and the floor above or below it.

straight-line depreciation. A depreciation method in which the cost, or another basis, of depreciable assets is written off in equal, annual amounts over the estimated useful life of the assets. [1]

straight-line method. A method in which the periodic amount of capital recapture or depreciation is estimated by dividing the total capital to be recovered by the number of periods over which it is to be recaptured; assumes an equal amount of capital is recaptured in each period.

straight-line recapture. The recovery of capital in equal, periodic increments over the remaining economic life of an asset.

stratification. The division of the urban real estate market into many submarkets.

stratified. Composed of, or arranged in, strata or layers; e.g., stratified alluvium; layers in soils that are inherited from the parent material, as distinguished from horizons, layers that are produced by the process of soil formation.

stratified random sample. A statistical sample in which the population is divided into fairly uniform groups, or strata, and a random sample is drawn from each selected stratum.

straw man. An individual who buys property in another's behalf to conceal the identity of the real buyer; one who holds title for another and appears as the owner of record. [3]

stream
1. A body of water that flows in a channel or bed; a river or brook; any flow of water, e.g., from a faucet.
2. The flow of income from a property, i.e., the income stream.

street improvements. Facilities that are provided and usually maintained by local government; e.g., paving, curbs, sidewalks, sewers.

strength in compression. The ability of a construction item to withstand an external force that tends to shorten it to the point of deformation.

stress. The action in a structural member caused by an outside force acting against it; any or all forces that act on a structural member at the same time.

stressed skin. A building design in which the frame and skin, or sheathing, are joined so that the skin helps resist strain.

stretcher. A brick or other masonry unit that is laid lengthwise in a wall.

stringer. A long, heavy, horizontal timber that supports a floor; an inclined member that supports the treads and risers of a stairway.

strip development. Commercial development in which the main thorough-fares of a city are bordered by an almost continuous row, or strip, of retail stores and allied service establishments; also, any shopping area that consists of a row of stores.

strip lumber. Yard lumber that is less than two inches thick and less than eight inches wide.

strip map. A map that shows the location of existing buildings, the land uses, the ownership of surrounding properties, the proposed tower locations, and various physical features of the land, e.g., roads, waterways, fences, pavements; covers a limited geographic area.

structural lumber. Lumber that is at least two inches thick and at least four inches wide.

structure. An edifice or building; an improvement.

structure limit line. A line in navigable waters, established by the federal government through the Army Corps of Engineers, that marks the boundary beyond which no structure is permitted.

strut. A piece of wood fixed between two other pieces or members; designed to receive pressure or weight along its length.

stubble. The basal portion of herbaceous plants that remains after the top portion has been harvested artificially or by grazing animals.

stucco. A cement plaster that is used as a finish for exterior wall surfaces; usually applied over a metal or wood lath base.

stud. A wooden or metal, vertical framing member to which horizontal boards or laths are nailed; e.g., the supporting elements in walls and partitions.

studio. A room that serves as an eating, sleeping, and living area. *Also called* efficiency apartment. [10]

stumpage. Standing timber; usually applied with reference to its value. *See also* stumpage value.

stumpage value. In timber cruising, the contributory value of economically merchantable timber as it stands in the forest; the contribution of timber to the total property value of the real estate.

subbase
1. The lower part of a structural base that consists of two or more horizontal members, e.g., the base of a column; a baseboard.
2. A bed of crushed rock or gravel that is used as a stable base under a slab or roadway.

subcontractor. A person or company that performs contractual work for a developer or general contractor; one who performs some phase of the work on a project, e.g., plumbing, electrical work; may or may not have a contract with the ultimate buyer. [1]

subdivision. A tract of land that has been divided into blocks or plots with streets, roadways, open areas, and other facilities appropriate to its development as residential, commercial, or industrial sites.

subdivision regulations. Laws that regulate the design and engineering standards for public improvements, e.g., streets, drainage, sewage, water, electricity, telephone, street landscaping in a subdivision; establish an application and review process that the prospective subdivider or developer must follow. [9]

subfloor. A floor that is laid on top of the floor joists and underneath the finish floor.

subjective probability. A decision maker's evaluation of the relative likelihood of unknown events.

sublease. An agreement in which the lessee in a prior lease conveys the right of use and occupancy of a property to another, the sublessee. *Also called* sandwich lease, except when the sublease involves only part of the premises included in the primary lease.

sublessee. One who enjoys the benefits, rights, and obligations of a sublease.

submarginal land. Land that does not have enough income to cover the cost of production, even if the land were free; may refer to the average, physical quality of the land, with reference to the area's average quality.

submarket. A division of a total market that is based on the preferences of buyers and sellers.

subordination. A contractual arrangement in which a party with a claim to certain assets agrees to make his or her claim junior, or subordinate, to the claims of another party. [5]

subscription agreement. A contract or other agreement that binds the subscriber to purchase an interest in a syndicate security. [1]

subsidence. The sinking of the upper part of the ground due to a number of causes, e.g., the lowering of the water table during a long period of drought, the removal of a mineral such as coal; when severe, can cause structural damage to buildings.

subsidy. A government grant that enables the sponsor to reduce the cost of one or more housing components, e.g., land, labor, material, financing, to lower the cost to the occupant. [1]

subsoil. Usually the B horizon of soils, but its identification depends on the type of soil profile; commonly, the part of the soil that lies below plow depth or below the solum.

substantial destruction. An effective destruction of a building that is so complete that the structure is untenantable and cannot be restored without constructing a new building; relieves a tenant of liability for rent.

substituted partner. The transferee of an initial partner, who purchased after the close of the original syndication. [1]

substitution. The appraisal principle that states that when several similar or commensurate commodities, goods, or services are available, the one with the lowest price will attract the greatest demand and widest distribution.

substructure. A building's entire foundational structure; located below grade, or ground, and provides the support base on which the superstructure rests.

subsurface easement. The right to use land at a designated distance below its surface, e.g., for pipelines, electric and telephone circuits and cables, storage facilities.

subsurface rights
1. The right to the use and profits of the underground portion of a designated property; usually, refers to the right to extract coal, minerals, oil, gas, or other hydrocarbon substances as designated in the grant; may include a right-of-way over designated portions of the surface.
2. The right to construct and maintain tunnels, subways, subcellars, pipelines, sewers, etc.

subsurface water sources. Sources of water below the earth's surface; e.g., underground streams running in defined underground channels, underground percolating waters channeling into surface or underground streams, diffused underground percolating waters, underground basins, wells, and springs drawing from underground percolating waters.

succession. The legal act or right of acquiring property by descent; obtaining an asset by will or inheritance. [2]

sum-of-the-years' digits. A variation of the declining-balance depreciation method in which successive numbers representing the life of the asset in years are added together. The first year's depreciation fraction is calculated using the asset's life in years as the numerator, and the sum of the digits as the denominator. In the second year, the process is repeated, using the second highest digit as the numerator, and so on. At the end of the last year, there is no remaining cost after writing off that year's depreciation. [1]

summation approach. *See* cost approach.

sump pump. An automatic, electric pump that is installed in a basement or other low area to empty the sump, or cesspool, a pit that serves as a drain.

superadequacy. An excess in the capacity or quality of a structure or structural component; determined by market standards.

superhighway. Any type of limited-access highway that is designed for high-speed through traffic; e.g., an expressway, freeway, toll road.

supermarket. A large, retail store built on one level and stocked with goods that are conveniently and conspicuously displayed so that customers may make their selections without the help of a clerk; usually sells food products and household supplies that are paid for at a checkout counter.

super-regional shopping center. A shopping center that provides an extensive variety of general merchandise, apparel, furniture, and home furnishings, as well as a variety of services and recreational facilities; usually built around at least three major department stores of at least 100,000 square feet each; theoretically contains about 750,000 square feet of gross leasable area, but in practice, its size may exceed 1,000,000 square feet.

superstructure. The portion of a building that is above grade.

supplemental feeding. Supplying concentrates or harvested feed to livestock to correct deficiencies in the range diet.

supplemental pasture. An artificial pasture used quantitatively or qualitatively to augment range forage, particularly in emergency situations; may be provided by annual grasses and legumes, or by the aftermath of meadows, grainfields, etc.

supplemental recreational use. A recreational use, e.g., hunting, fishing, that is incidential to the primary use of the land, e.g., for farm or ranch purposes; may provide additional income to the property owner or lessee.

supply. The schedule of the various amounts of types of real estate that are available for sale at different prices.

supply and demand. The appraisal principle that states that the price of real property varies directly, but not necessarily proportionately, with demand, and inversely, but not necessarily proportionately, with supply.

surety. One who accepts liability for any future debt, default, absence, or miscarriage of another, under the presumption that no loss is anticipated. Surety bonds are commonly required by municipal and county ordinances regarding licensing and contracting.

surface easement. The right to use the surface of the land only, e.g., for access, flowage, right-of-way.

surface soil. An area of soil about five to eight inches thick that is disturbed by plowing; an equivalent area in uncultivated land.

surface stream. A surface watercourse that flows, more or less permanently, in a well-defined, natural channel. [7]

surface water. Water that spreads over the surface of the ground, stands in swamps, or percolates through the soil.

surface well. A hole or shaft that is dug or drilled into the earth to obtain underground water, which is pumped or raised to the surface. [7]

surplus income. *See* excess income.

surplus productivity. The net income that remains after the costs of labor, capital, and coordination have been paid.

survey
1. The process in which the quantity and/or location of a piece of land is scientifically ascertained; may reflect the physical features affecting land, e.g., grades, contours, structures.
2. A map or plot that describes the courses, distances, and quantity of land and shows the lines of possession.

survey plat. *See* survey.

suspended ceiling. A ceiling system that is supported by overhead, structural framing. [8]

swamplands. Lands that require drainage to dispose of needless water or moisture before they are fit for successful cultivation. [7]

sweat equity. The entrepreneurial contribution in an investment.

switching. *See* free switching.

syndicate. *See* syndication.

syndication. A private or public partnership that pools funds for the acquisition or development of real estate projects. *See also* partnership.

synergism. A situation that results when a total effect is greater than the sum of the independent actions combined to create the effect; in real estate, usually applied to multiuse properties in which the value of the total development is greater than the sum of the individual parts.

T

takeout commitment. A lender's commitment to provide long-term financing when a building or other improvement on real estate is completed. [3]

talus. A slope; a sloping mass of rocky fragments at the foot of a cliff.

tangible property. Property that can be perceived by the senses; includes land, fixed improvements, furnishings, merchandise, cash, and other items of working capital used in an enterprise.

tax. A compulsory contribution exacted from persons, corporations, and other organizations by a government, according to law, for the support of government and the maintenance of public services.

tax abatement. An exemption or reduction of local taxes on a project for a specific period of time. [1]

taxable income
1. Income subject to income tax.
2. For income-producing property, net operating income minus depreciation and interest on debt.

taxable value. *See* assessed value.

taxation. The right of government to raise revenue through assessments on valuable goods, products, and rights.

tax base. The unit of value to which the tax rate is applied to determine the tax due; for property taxes, the assessed valuation; for income taxes, the net taxable income.

tax book. *See* tax roll.

tax deed. A deed that conveys title to a property purchased at a tax sale; may or may not convey absolute title, free of all prior claims and liens, depending on state law.

tax district. A political subdivision of one or more assessment districts where a governmental unit has the authority to levy tax.

tax exemption. Total exemption or freedom from tax; granted to educational, charitable, religious, and other nonprofit organizations. Partial exemptions from ad valorem tax are granted on homesteads in some states.

tax-free cash. A specific property's annual depreciation charges minus its annual mortgage amortization, or principal repayment.

tax-free exchange. The exchange, but not sale, of a real property held for investment or used in a trade or business for a similar property; allows the property holders to defer capital gains. [1]

tax-free income. Income that is free from taxation due to provisions in the federal income tax laws. Net spendable income that is sheltered by excess losses is not tax free. [1]

tax levy. In property taxation, the total revenue that will be realized by the tax.

tax lien. A lien that is automatically attached to property in the amount of property taxes unpaid.

tax map. A map, drawn to scale, that shows the boundaries and location of individual lots and parcels in an assessment jurisdiction. *Also called* assessment map or cadastral map.

tax participation. A provision in a lease that obligates the lessee to assume all or a part of the property taxes.

taxpayer. Describes an interim improvement that allegedly does not represent the ultimate, most profitable use of the land; usually a one-story, commercial building.

tax preference items. Certain types of income on which both individuals and corporations must pay some tax under the minimum tax schedule.

tax rate. The ratio between the tax and the tax base; applied to the assessed value to determine the amount of tax; obtained by dividing the amount of the tax levy by the total assessed value of all properties in the tax district; usually expressed in dollars per one hundred dollars of assessed value.

tax roll. The official list of all taxpayers subject to property tax, the amounts of their assessments, and the amounts of taxes due.

tax sale. The sale of a taxpayer's property to collect delinquent taxes from the proceeds of sale; conducted when the taxpayer has failed to redeem the property within the statutory period.

tax shelter. Various features of an investment that provide relief from income taxes or an opportunity to claim allowable deductions from taxable income; also, money saved by a taxpayer due to deductions in taxable income without reductions in actual income.

tax stop. A clause in a lease that limits the landlord's tax obligation because the lessee assumes any taxes above an established level.

tax title. *See* tax deed.

Taylor permit. A permit that allows a private party to use the public domain for grazing purposes; issued to a stock raiser under the terms of the federal Taylor Grazing Act.

t-distribution. In statistics, a symmetric, but abnormal, distribution; used in small samples, with fewer than 30 degrees of freedom, when the standard deviation may produce an inaccurate estimate; flatter than the normal curve and, thus, associates a lower probability to any given interval.

TDN. Total digestible nutrients; the portion of livestock feed that is digested and used by the animal for maintenance, growth, and production.

TDR. *See* transferable development right.

team track. A track on which a railroad spots cars for loading and unloading by shippers; open to public use, as distinguished from private, industrial siding. In a team yard, tracks are spaced to permit driveways in between to accommodate vehicles.

tempera. The process of painting transparent colors on plastered walls or panels using powdered pigment and parchment size mixed with water and gum arabic or egg white or yolk; applied to a hard surface of fine, thin plaster called *gesso*.

temporary easement. An easement granted for a specific purpose and a specific time period, e.g., a construction easement is terminated after the construction of the improvement and the unencumbered fee interest in the land reverts to the owner.

tenancy
1. The holding of property by any form of title.
2. The right to occupy and use property as conveyed in a lease.

tenancy at sufferance. An estate in real estate in which a person, who formerly had an estate in land, wrongfully continues in possession of the real estate after the estate is terminated.

tenancy at will. An estate in real estate that has no fixed term and may be cancelled at will by the landlord or the tenant.

tenancy by the entirety. An estate in real estate held by a husband and wife in which neither has a disposable interest in the property during the lifetime of the other, except through joint action. When one dies, the property passes to the survivor.

tenancy in common. An estate in real estate held by two or more persons, each of whom has an undivided interest; on the death of one, the estate passes to the heirs, not the survivor(s).

tenancy in severalty. An estate in real estate held by one owner.

tenant. One who holds or possesses real property; commonly, a person who occupies and uses the property of another under a lease, although such a person is technically a lessee, not a tenant.

tenant changes. *See* tenant improvements.

tenant contributions. All costs that are the responsibility of the tenant(s), over and above the contract rent specified in the lease. [1]

tenant farmer. A lessee of a farm, whose rental is usually in crops, cash, or a combination of the two.

tenant improvements
1. Fixed improvements to the land or structures installed and paid for by a tenant or lessee.
2. The original installation of finished, tenant space in a construction project; subject to periodic change for succeeding tenants.

tendon. The wires and cables used to reinforce prestressed and poststressed concrete.

tenement
1. Real property and the rights of ownership to real property; real property rights of a permanent nature that relate to, and pass with, the land; includes both corporeal and incorporeal rights. [3]
2. A type of dwelling house or unit.

tenement house. A multistory dwelling that consists of occupancy units that do not have private baths and/or private kitchens.

tenure. The holding or possession of anything; the right to possess and use property; the period of possession and use.

terminal. In transportation, the point at which people and goods can enter or leave the system.

terminal value. *See* reversion.

termite shield. A metal sheet that is placed in the exterior walls of a house near ground level, usually under the sill, to prevent termites from entering the house. [8]

terneplate. A plate of inferior quality in which tin is alloyed with a large percentage of lead; used as a roofing material.

terrace
1. A broad surface channel or embankment constructed across sloping lands on or near contour lines at specific intervals; used to control runoff or soil erosion.
2. A flat or undulating plain, usually rather narrow and with a steep front, that borders a river, lake, or sea. Many streams are bordered by a series of terraces at different levels, indicating floodplains in successive periods. Older terraces may be dissected by streams and become more or less hilly, but they are still considered terraces.
3. An elevated, level surface of earth with a vertical or sloping front and/or sides faced by masonry or turf; a series of such surfaces rising one above the other.
4. A finished, but unroofed, outdoor area adjacent to, and accessible from, a house or other structure; usually at grade or slightly elevated.

terra-cotta. Hard, usually unglazed, earthenware of fine quality that has been hard-burned and molded; used for architectural decoration, e.g., facing material.

terrazzo. A floor material made of small fragments of colored stone or marble that are embedded in cement and polished to a high glaze.

tertiary trade area. An outlying segment of the trade area that contributes a recognizable share of a shopping center's sales volume; designated when a tributary area appears to extend beyond the normal limits of the secondary trade area, usually in a specific direction. [17]

testate. One who dies leaving a valid will; the condition of dying with a valid will.

theory. A statement that sets forth an apparent relationship among observed facts and has been substantiated to a degree.

therm. A measure of heat equal to 100,000 Btus. *See also* Btu.

thermal. Of or pertaining to heat or temperature.

thermal conduction. The transmission of heat through or within a solid object.

thermal insulation. Material that has a high resistance to the passage of heat; used to block the passage of heat from a warm building to the exterior when outdoor temperatures are low, and the entrance of heat into a cooled interior when outside temperatures are high. [3]

thermostat. A device that is electrically operated and actuated by thermal conduction or convection and automatically acts to establish and maintain a desired temperature.

thoroughfare. A street or path that is open at both ends and free from any obstruction; a highway. [7]

thread of the stream. The center line between the banks of a stream.

threshold. A strip of wood, stone, or metal that is placed beneath a door.

tidal basin. A dock or basin, without water gates, in which the water level changes.

tidal waters. Waters in which the tide ebbs and flows. [7]

tide. The alternate rise and fall of the surface of a body of water. The inflow of the water is called the *flood tide*, or *high tide*; the reflux is called the *ebb tide*. Slack tide is the period between changes in the tide movement.

tie. A device that joins two or more structural members; e.g., timber, rod, chain, clip, wire.

tie beam. A structural member used to hold two, separated members together.

tier. A row of townships, running east and west, that lies between any two consecutive township lines; comprises an area six miles wide.

tile. Originally, a molded and burned clay or cement used for flooring, facing walls, and trim; commonly, includes tiles made of many different materials, e.g., asphalt, plastic, vinyl, fiberglass, and used for a number of purposes, e.g., field tile, sewer tile, ceiling tile, acoustical tile.

till. An unstratified deposit of earth, sand, gravel, and boulders that have been transported by glaciers.

tillable land. Land suitable for growing annual crops that require plowing, harrowing, planting, cultivating, and harvesting; as distinguished from farmland that is not so suited, e.g., marshland, swampland, woodlots.

till plain. A level or undulating land surface that is covered by glacial till.

tilth. The physical condition of a soil with respect to its fitness for the growing of a specific plant.

tilt-up construction. A method of construction in which concrete wall sections are cast horizontally and lifted or tilted into position.

timber. Forest stands and their products; wood in forms that are suitable for heavy construction; specifically, sawed lumber four by four inches or more in breadth and thickness.

timber cruising. *See* cruise.

timberland. Agricultural property from which merchantable timber is harvested periodically, usually every 20, 50, or 80 years depending on the species and growing conditions.

time period zero. The starting date of an investment.

time series. A statistical device for presenting data graphically. The analysis of a time series consists of describing and measuring the various changes or movements in the series over a period of time. These changes or movements are cyclical movements, random variations, seasonal variations, and secular trends.

time-series chart. In statistics, graphic representation of data in which the independent variable, plotted along the horizontal axis, is time, and the values of the dependent variable, plotted along the vertical axis, are shown at various time intervals. These values are connected by straight lines to form a continuous curve that extends over the entire period covered by the chart.

timesharing
1. The sale of limited ownership interests in residential apartments or hotel rooms; a timeshare purchaser receives a deed conveying title to the unit for a specific part of a year.
2. In computer usage, the utilization of central computer facilities at the same time. The computer moves quickly from one user to another, executing a portion of each user's job before moving on. The computer appears to be responding directly to each individual's commands.

title. The combination of all elements that constitute proof of ownership. *See also* abstract of title.

Title I. The portion of the Housing Act of 1949, as amended, that contains most of the basic legislative provisions pertaining to the urban renewal program; authorizes most of the federal financial and technical aids for communities participating in the program. Through the amending Housing Act of 1954, Title I sets out the workable program prerequisites and adds rehabilitating blighted areas as well as redeveloping slum areas.

title company. A corporation that issues or insures title to real property.

title defect. Legal right to claim property or make demands on the owner that is held by others. [1]

title insurance. Insurance against financial loss resulting from claims that arise out of defects in the title to real property that were undisclosed at the time the policy was issued. *See also* Torrens system.

title opinion. An analysis and interpretation of a title search that concerns present ownership, encumbrances, clouds on the title, and other infirmities.

title search. An investigation of public records to abstract the nature of instruments that relate to the status of the title to a specific piece of real estate; may include the study of liens, encumbrances, easements, and other conditions that affect the quality of the title of ownership.

tobacco barn. A farm building for the curing of tobacco; usually of simple frame construction and design with hinged side panels that open to provide ventilation; may also be used for grading and packing the tobacco for market.

toll road. A highway for which users must pay a toll charge.

tombstone ad. A simple notice announcing that a security issue is being offered for sale or has been sold; states the name of the underwriter, the issue, and the date sold; may also indicate whether the security issue is original or secondary. [1]

tongue and groove. A method of joining two pieces of board in which a tongue is cut in the edge of one board and a groove is cut in the other board to receive the tongue; describes any material prepared for joining in this fashion, e.g., tongue and groove lumber.

topographic map. A map that shows the topography of an area of the earth's surface, using contour lines, tinting, or shading.

topography. The relief features or surface configurations of an area; e.g., hills, valleys, slopes, lakes, rivers. Surface gradations are classified as compound slope, gently sloping land, hilly land, hog-wallows, hummocks, rolling land, steep land, undulating land, and very steep land.

top rail. The horizontal member that forms the top of a panelled door or a window. *Also called* top stile.

topsoil. The surface portion of the soil; includes the average plow depth of the A horizon when the horizon is deeper than plow depth. *See also* horizon.

Torrens system. A system of land registration used in some jurisdictions in which the sovereign governmental authority issues title certificates covering the ownership of land, which often serve as title insurance.

total load. Dead load plus live load; the total weight that must be compensated for in design.

total personal income. Monetary income plus noncash income, e.g., food stamps, imputed income.

town. Technically, a territorial quasi-corporation, e.g., a New England town, or a political subdivision of the state or county, e.g., townships; commonly, an urban community; sometimes applied to any form of municipal corporation. [7]

townhouse. A single-family, attached dwelling unit with party walls; usually an individual unit in a series of five to ten houses, with common walls between the units and side yards on the end units only; may have one to three stories and all necessary facilities and amenities.

township. In the government survey system, the area between two township lines and two range lines; normally contains 36 sections of approximately 640 acres each.

township lines. In the government survey system, survey lines that run east and west at six-mile intervals north and south of a baseline and form the north and south boundaries of townships.

township road. A rural road that is outside the primary state highway system and the county road system; under the jurisdiction of a township.

TPL. *See* Trust for Public Land.

tract. A parcel of land; an area of real estate that is frequently subdivided into smaller parcels. [7]

tract house. A house in a large, residential development where the houses are mass-produced and very similar in style, material, and price.

trade area. The geographic area from which the steady, sustaining patronage for a shopping center is obtained; its extent is governed by many factors, e.g., the shopping center itself, its accessibility, the extent of physical barriers, the location of competing facilities, the limitations of driving time and distance. [17]

trade fixture. An article that is owned and attached to a rented space or building by a tenant and used in conducting a business.

trading on equity. The use of borrowed funds in an effort to increase the rate of return on the equity investment. *See also* leverage.

traffic. The movement of people and vehicles along a path or past a specific point; the people and vehicles that move along a path or past a point.

traffic count. A count of the number of people and/or vehicles that move past a location over a period of time.

traffic density. The number of vehicles that occupy a particular length of a roadway's moving lanes at a given time; usually expressed in vehicles per mile.

traffic survey. A survey conducted to obtain traffic information, e.g., data on traffic quantity and composition, travelers' origins and destinations, the purpose of trips, means of transportation; usually related to a specific time on a certain day of the week.

trailer. A mobile home; a house trailer.

trailer park. Any site with facilities suitable for parking two or more mobile homes somewhat permanently.

transferable development right (TDR). A right to develop land that cannot be used by the landowner but can be sold to landowners in another district; generally used to preserve agricultural land; may also be used to preserve historic sites and open space or to protect scenic features.

transition. Changes in district or neighborhood use, e.g., agricultural to residential, residential to commercial.

transported soil. Secondary soils; soils that have been moved and redeposited by water or wind.

traveled way. The portion of a roadway that is designed for the movement of vehicles; excludes shoulders, acceleration and deceleration lanes, and other auxiliary lanes.

tread. The horizontal width of a step; the area between risers in a stairway.

Treasury bill. A short-term, direct debt obligation of the U.S. government; usually has a maturity of three months, six months, or one year.

trellising. A support system for grape or other vine crops; usually consists of wires or thin ropes that extend above the vine between anchor posts.

trend. A series of related changes brought about by a chain of causes and effects.

trim. The visible finishing work on the interior of a building; includes all wood, metal, or plastic ornamental parts used to cover joints between jambs and plaster around windows and doors; may also include hardware.

trimmer. A beam or floor joist that supports the end of a header in floor framing.

trip. In zoning and planning, refers to the use of an automobile, i.e. automobile trips to and from a particular property.

triplex. A three-unit apartment dwelling designed for occupancy by three separate households. [3]

truss. One of various structural frames based on the geometric rigidity of a triangle and composed of members that are subject to longitudinal compression and tension only; rigid under anticipated loads and able to span a large area without interior support. *See also* bowstring truss; camber; flat roof; sawtooth roof.

trust. A temporary, conditional, or permanent fiduciary relationship in which the legal title to, and control of, property is placed in the hands of a trustee for the benefit of another person; the instrument of such a relationship.

trust agreement. A written agreement between a grantor and a trustee that establishes the terms of a trust.

trust deed. A deed that establishes a trust; an instrument that conveys the legal title to property to a trustee, stating the trustee's authority and the conditions that bind the trustee in dealing with the property.

trustee. A person who controls legal title to property under a trust agreement.

Trust for Public Land (TPL). A nonprofit, charitable organization established in 1973 and interested in the open space needs of urban people as well as the preservation of wilderness; almost completely self-supporting, with 80% of its yearly income obtained from land transactions and the remainder from foundations and contracts. [9]

trust instrument. Any written instrument under which a trust is created; e.g., will, trust agreement, declaration of trust, deed of trust, or order of court.

tuck-pointing. Finishing joints along their center lines with a narrow, parallel ridge of fine putty or fine lime mortar; in existing brick or masonry work, raking out deteriorated mortar joints and refilling them with new mortar.

turnkey project. A construction project in which the builder is responsible for all aspects of construction and must deliver a completed facility, including all items necessary for occupancy; the occupant or user of the property need only "turn the key" and commence operation. [3]

turnpike. A controlled-access highway for which users pay a toll.

type soils. A group of soils, developed from a particular type of parent material, that have similar genetic horizons, including similar texture and arrangement in soil profile.

typical operator concept. Measuring the productive capacity of a farm or ranch based on a typical local operator using standard management.

U

unbalanced improvement. An improvement that does not represent the highest and best use for the site on which it is placed; may be an overimprovement or an underimprovement.

underfloor wiring system. A system in which ducts or raceways are built into a floor to house electrical wiring.

underground stream. Water that flows underground in a defined channel. [7]

underground waters. Waters that include underground streams, basins, or lakes; reservoirs; artesian waters; percolations contributing to underground and surface streams or watercourses; diffuse percolations; the underflow of watercourses. [7]

underimprovement. An improvement that is inadequate to develop the highest and best use of its site; usually, a structure that is of lesser cost, quality, and size than typical neighborhood properties.

underlying loan. The loan or loans that are covered by a wraparound mortgage, all-inclusive deed of trust, or contract of sale. [1]

underpass. A passageway under a street, highway, or railroad right-of-way; in rural areas, a passageway under a highway for the passage of animals and farm equipment; also, a grade separation where one traveled way passes underneath an intersecting traveled way or a railroad right-of-way.

underpinning. Timbers, steel beams, or other temporary props used to support a foundation during construction; also, permanent supports installed to increase the load-bearing capacity of a foundation or wall.

understocking. Placing a number of animals on a given area so that the area is underused at the end of the planned grazing period.

understory
1. The portion of a forest that is under, or below, the overstory, or top canopy.
2. The plants growing beneath the canopy of another plant; e.g., grasses, forbs, and low shrubs growing under a tree or brush canopy.

underwriter
1. An individual or organization that assumes a risk for a fee.
2. In investment, a party who agrees to guarantee payment for a securities issue.
3. In real estate, a party who evaluates the risk involved in making a mortgage.

undivided fee rule. In condemnation appraisal, a rule that states that property is to be valued as if the title were held by a single entity even if the real estate is divided into more than one estate owned by more than one individual or entity. *See also* unit rule.

undivided interest. Fractional ownership without physical division into shares. [2]

undivided partial interest. An interest in a specific property that cannot be dealt with freely by the separate owners.

undulating land. Land on compound slopes of 3% to 8%.

uniformity. In assessment, denotes assessed values that bear the same relationship to market value, or another value standard, as all other assessments in the tax district; implies equalization of the tax burden.

unimproved land. Vacant land or land that lacks the essential, appurtenant improvements required to make it useful.

unit. A single thing; any standard by which quantities of the same type may be measured.

unit cost. The price or cost of one of a number of similar items or units of property, which, when multiplied by the total number, will determine the price or cost of the whole; usually expressed as cost per square foot or cubic foot. *Also called* unit price.

United States Public Land Descriptions. *See* government survey system.

unit-in-place method. The cost-estimating method in which total building cost is established using unit costs for the various building components as installed. *Also called* segregated cost method.

unit rule. The rule that determines what constitutes the larger parcel, the complete unit affected by a partial taking; used to estimate severance damages and/or special benefits to the remainder. The test of unity involves three factors: physical location, use, and ownership. *See also* unity of title; unity of use.

units of comparison. The components into which a property may be divided for comparison purposes; e.g., square foot, front foot, cubic foot, room, bed, seat, apartment.

unit value. The market value of the whole reduced to a value per unit of measurement.

unity of title. The rule that states that, to be considered part of the remainder property, a parcel must be held by the condemnee under the same quality of ownership as the parcel from which the taking occurs; applied in both federal and state courts.

unity of use. The rule that states that, to be considered part of the remainder, a parcel must be devoted to the same use as the parcel from which the taking occurs.

universe. In statistics, the entire body of possible data; used to distinguish between all the data and a sample obtained from the data.

upland
1. A parcel that abuts a parcel with riparian rights; describes an owner once removed from a water right by a riparian owner.
2. Land above the surface of a body of water or above a mean high water line.

upland soil. Soil developed from the disintegration and decomposition of rocks in place and the weathering of the resulting debris; a primary soil; usually found on hilly to mountainous terrain.

upset price. In law, an amount representing the minimum bid at which a property may be sold.

urban land economics. The study of the allocation of urban space among alternative uses.

urban renewal. The controlled process of redevelopment in urban areas; often used to refer to public projects, but also includes private redevelopment efforts.

urban renewal area. A blighted, deteriorated, or deteriorating area, or an open land area, that is approved by the Department of Housing and Urban Development as appropriate for an urban renewal project.

urban renewal plan. A plan, developed by a locality and approved by its governing body, that guides and controls a special urban renewal project area.

urban renewal project. Specific activities conducted by a local public agency in an urban renewal area to prevent or eliminate slums and blight; may involve slum clearance, redevelopment, rehabilitation, conservation, or a combination of these activities.

use classification. Groups into which real estate is divided by its use: residential, commercial, industrial, agricultural, and special purpose.

use density. The number of buildings of a particular use classification per unit of area; sometimes expressed as a percentage of land coverage or density of coverage.

use factor. An index of the grazing use made of a particular forage species; based on a system of range management that will maintain more economically important forage species for an indefinite time; expressed as a percentage of the current year's weight production, located within reach of stock, that is consumed. *See also* weighted use factor.

useful life. The period of time over which a structure may reasonably be expected to perform the function for which it was designed.

use of an appraisal. The manner in which a client employs the information contained in an appraisal report.

use value. The value of a particular property for a specific use.

use value assessment. An assessment based on the value of property as it is currently used, not on its market value considering alternative uses; may be used where legislation has been enacted to preserve farmland, timberland, or other open space land on urban fringes.

use variance. A privilege that allows a property owner to develop or use his or her property in a manner that violates the strict terms of the applicable zoning authority or board of adjustment; made on a property-by-property basis. [3]

utilities. Services rendered by public utility companies; e.g., telephone, electricity, gas, water.

utility-probability analysis. The assessment of risk using quantitative methods.

utility room. A room that is designed or used for laundry, heating equipment, or related purposes.

V

VA. *See* Veterans Administration.

vacancy. Unrented space.

vacancy rate
1. The relationship between the amount of vacant space and total space in a building.
2. The relationship between the rent estimated for vacant building space and the total rent estimated for all the space in the building.

vacant land. *See* unimproved land.

valley
1. The line where two sloping roofs intersect.
2. The lowland that lies between two hills.

valley flashing. Pieces of lead, tin, or sheet metal that are placed along the valley of a roof to make the roof intersection waterproof.

valuation. The process of estimating the market value, investment value, insurable value, or other properly defined value of an identified interest or interests in a specific parcel or parcels of real estate as of a given date.

valuation accounts. In accounting, reserves for depreciation or amortization. To the appraiser, they represent a reduction in the cost of the assets to which they apply. [12]

valuation process. A systematic procedure employed to provide the answer to a client's question about real property value.

valuator. *See* appraiser.

value
1. The monetary worth of property, goods, services, etc.
2. The present worth of future benefits that accrue to real property ownership.

3. The quantity of one thing that can be obtained in exchange for another.
4. The act or process of estimating the monetary worth of real property. *See also* valuation.

value after the taking. In condemnation, the market value of the remainder parcel in a partial taking.

value before the taking. In condemnation, the market value of the whole property affected by the taking.

value for other use. A means of valuing a corridor of real estate; used particularly in valuing railroad corridors. *See also* across the fence method.

value in exchange. *See* exchange value.

value in place. The amount a prudent purchaser would pay for an item, e.g., equipment, fixtures, in place; determined by the use it contributes to the whole.

value in use. *See* use value.

valve. A device that regulates the flow of liquids or gases in a pipe.

vapor barrier. Material that is used to retard the passage of vapor or moisture into walls and floors and prevent condensation; e.g., foil-surfaced insulation placed in walls, paints applied to exterior foundation walls.

variability. In statistical analysis, the scattering of the values of a frequency distribution from the measure of central tendency. The three most common measures of dispersion or data variability encountered in assessment are the range, the average absolute deviation, and the standard deviation. [10]

variable. A quantity that may take any one of a specified set of values.

variable-amortization loan. A mortgage loan in which amortization payments may not be required for an initial period, i.e., a standing loan, or may be increased or decreased during the loan term. The rate of interest on the outstanding principal remains the same, but the amount of interest paid differs because the outstanding principal varies as the loan is amortized. *See also* variable-payment mortgage (VPM).

variable annuity. A determinable income stream in which the amounts vary per period.

variable expenses. Operating expenses that usually vary with the level of occupancy or the intensity of property operation.

variable-payment mortgage (VPM). A mortgage that calls for installment payments of varying amounts during its term; may or may not be fully amortized, or liquidated, at maturity. *See also* constant-payment mortgage; variable-amortization loan; variable-rate mortgage (VRM). [3]

variable-rate mortgage (VRM). A mortgage with an interest rate that may move up or down following a specified schedule or the movements of a standard to which the interest rate is tied. *See also* variable-payment mortgage (VPM). [3]

variance
1. In statistics, a measure of the degree of spread among a set of values; a measure of the tendency of individual values to vary from the mean value.
2. In real estate, *see* zoning variance.

variate. The specific value of a variable; generally called a *variable*.

vault
1. A continuous length of arched ceiling.
2. A room specially designed for secure storage.

vegetation. Plants collectively; the community of plants in a region, as distinguished from the kinds of plants that comprise the plant community.

vegetative density. The estimated percentage of the ground covered in rangeland; the area that would be represented by projecting all herbaceous plants and all the current year's growth of shrubby plants onto the ground surface and viewing it from directly above. *See also* forage density.

veneer. An ornamental or protective layer of material that covers a base of another substance; e.g., walnut veneer on less valuable wood, a brick exterior finish over less expensive construction or cheaper material.

veneered construction. A method of construction in which a layer of facing material is applied to the external surface of steel, reinforced concrete, or frame walls; e.g., face brick veneer over frame construction.

vent. A small opening that allows the passage of air through any space in a building, e.g., an attic, an unexcavated area under a first-floor construction, the soffits of an overhang.

ventilation. The circulation of air in a room or building; a process of changing the air in a room by natural or artificial means.

vent pipe. A small pipe that extends from plumbing fixtures to a vent stack in the roof, allowing sewer gases to escape to the outside air.

vertical division. The division of real property into air, ground, and subterranean rights.

vestibule. A small entrance hall to a building or room.

vest-pocket park. A park or playground that is built on a small plot; often located in built-up areas or on vacant or abandoned lots.

Veterans Administration (VA). An independent organization of the U.S. government entrusted with the execution of all laws that benefit war veterans; administers special compensation and allowances, pensions, vocational rehabilitation, education, insurance, loans, hospitalization, and medical care.

view
1. A drawing that represents a particular viewpoint, e.g., front view, side view.
2. The scene or prospect viewed from a site or property.

virgin forest. A mature or overmature forest.

visual rights. The right to clear vegetation and restrict structures at intersections; where enabling legislation has been enacted, the right to prohibit advertising media along the highway rights-of-way.

vital statistics. Statistics pertaining to births, marriages, deaths, health, diseases, and other human factors.

vitrified tile. Pipe made of clay that is hard-baked and glazed to make it impervious to water; used particularly for underground drainage.

volt. A unit of electromotive force. Residences are usually wired with 110-volt or 110- and 220-volt circuits. Factories and large commercial properties may have 440-volt power circuits in addition to 110 and 220 circuits.

VPM. *See* variable-payment mortgage.

VRM. *See* variable-rate mortgage.

W

wainscot
1. A facing or panel that is applied to the walls of a room.
2. The lower part of an interior wall that is finished with a material different from the upper part.

wall. A vertical structure of stone, brick, wood, or other similar material that encloses, divides, supports, and protects; e.g., one of the vertical, enclosing sides of a building or room; also, a solid masonry fence or retaining wall.

wall-bearing. Describes a wall that supports a vertical load in addition to its own weight; e.g., a wall-bearing partition.

wall-bearing construction. Construction in which the roof and floors are carried directly by exterior walls of plain brick, pilastered brick, or other masonry; posts and columns are used only when the length of the interior span requires intermediate support for a roof or floor.

wallboard. Any artificially prepared sheet materials or panels that are used to cover walls or ceilings as a substitute or base for plaster.

wall furnace. A small, gas-fired, hot air furnace that fits between the studs of a wall; has no ducts; uses a small fan to circulate room air through the furnace and to distribute heated air.

wall panel. A nonbearing or curtain wall between the columns or piers in a structure; supported by the girders or beams of the structural frame at each story height.

wall tile. Ceramic or plastic tile that is used as a finish material for interior walls or wainscot.

warehouse. A structure that is designed and used for the storage of wares, goods, and merchandise; usually classified as industrial.

warehousing of mortgages. An arrangement in which an originator-mortgagee obtains short-term, interim credit secured by mortgages to bridge the gap between the completion of construction and the eventual sale of the mortgage on the property to an investor-mortgagee; characterized by the lender/borrower relationship, an outright lending of funds, and an agreement in which the lender collects interest on the amount of the loan.

warm air system. A heating system in which air is heated in a furnace and moves to living space through a single register or a series of ducts; the air is circulated by natural convection in the gravity system or by a fan or blower in the ductwork in the forced system.

warranty deed. A deed that conveys to the grantee title to the property free and clear of all encumbrances, except those specifically set forth in the document.

wash fountain. *See* Bradley fountain.

waste. A type of range vegetation that includes all vegetated areas that have insufficient value because they cannot be used economically due to inaccessibility, dense timber, or sparse forage growth. Large areas of sparse forage are classified as waste for grazing unless they are near a better type; it is impracticable to run stock over large areas to get to a small amount of feed.

waste line. A pipe that carries waste from a bathtub, shower, lavatory, or any other fixture or appliance, except a toilet. [8]

waste pipe. *See* waste line.

wasting assets. *See* diminishing assets.

water. *See* ground water; irrigation; surface water.

waterfront property. Land abutting a body of water; a part of a community abutting a body of water.

water-holding capacity. The amount of water that soil with free drainage will hold against the pull of gravity; expressed as a percent of the dry weight of the soil.

water level. The level of the surface of any body of water. *See also* water table.

water line easement. Similar to a sewer line easement, except that water is to be supplied through the line.

water measures. *See* acre-foot; acre-inch; cubic foot per second; hour-inch; miner's inch; second foot.

water power. Power created by a quantity of water passing from a higher to a lower level; adaptable to commercial and industrial use.

water power plant. A plant or mill that uses water power to operate its equipment. *See also* hydroelectric plant; power plant.

waterproofing
1. To make impervious to water or dampness.

2.   Any material used to waterproof; e.g., pitch or other bituminous materials.

water rights. A right to a definite or conditional flow or quantity of water, usually for use at stated times and in stated quantities, e.g., for irrigation or for hydroelectric power development; may be a right acquired by prescription, e.g, arising from the open, notorious, and undisputed use of water for the statutory term of years; a right acquired by appropriation, e.g., a grant from an agency of government with the right to distribute the unappropriated surplus waters of the state; or a riparian right under the common law doctrine of riparian ownership of waters that wash land. *See also* riparian rights.

watershed. The drainage area that contributes water to a bordering stream. *Also called* drainage basin.

water table
1.   The upper limit of the part of the soil, or underlying material, that is wholly saturated with water; the depth below the surface at which free water is found.
2.   A projection at the bottom line of a building superstructure, outside the vertical plane of the foundation, that provides for the runoff of rainwater.

watt. A measure of electricity equal to the power created by a current of one ampere flowing at one volt pressure.

watt-hour. The standard measure of electrical energy; the power in watts times the number of hours that the power is maintained.

WCR. *See* Women's Council of REALTORS®.

wealth. All things that are owned; material objects themselves or the evidences of possession, e.g., securities; commonly, includes money or anything of monetary value; technically, money is not wealth, but a medium of exchange for acquiring wealth.

weathering. The chemical and physical disintegration and decomposition of rocks, minerals, and other organic materials or surfaces.

weatherstrip. A thin strip of metal, felt, wood, etc., that is used to cover the joint between a door or window sash and the jamb, casing, or sill; keeps out air, dust, rain, etc.

weep holes. A series of small holes in a retaining wall or similar structure that permits the drainage of water through the wall, reducing the pressure against the wall.

weighted average. An average in which each component is adjusted by a factor that reflects its relative importance to the whole; obtained by multiplying each component by its assigned weight, adding the products, and dividing the sum of the products by the sum of the weights. *See also* band of investment.

weighted rate. A rate that has been adjusted to reflect its relative influence on a total result. *See also* band of investment; weighted average.

weighted use factor. The factor obtained by multiplying the use factor of each vegetative species on the range by its respective percentage in the composition and totalling these products.

weir. A device installed in an irrigation ditch or stream to measure the quantity of water passing a particular point.

well. A hole drilled into the earth, usually by boring, to obtain water, petroleum, natural gas, etc.

Western framing. Framing in which the studding of each story rests on a sill; as distinguished from balloon framing.

wetlands. Areas that are frequently inundated or saturated by surface or ground water and support vegetation typically adapted for life in saturated soil conditions; generally include swamps, marshes, bogs, and similar areas, but classification may differ in various jurisdictions.

wharf. A structure along which vessels can be held or docked for loading and unloading; usually constructed parallel to the shoreline; if the long side extends into the water from the shore, it is called a *pier*.

wheel leveler. A small elevator that raises the floor of a truck or trailer to a loading dock by lifting the truck's rear wheels.

whole property. *See* larger parcel.

wild land. Land that has been left natural, uninhabited, unoccupied, and uncultured, and is not used by the owner, an agent, or a lessee for any artificial purpose.

will-cut cruise. The estimated amount of lumber that can be sawed from the timber in a given area; calculated by deducting an allowance for breakage or other waste from the stand cruise.

windbreak. A physical feature that shelters a house from the wind, especially a tall hedge of trees or shrubs planted for this purpose.

windfall. *See* blowdown.

wind load. The amount of pressure that the wind exerts on the exposed surface of a wall or roof; usually expressed in pounds per square foot of surface area.

window. A glassed opening in a wall or ceiling that provides natural light and ventilation; types include awning, casement, circlehead or fan, clerestory, double hung, fixed, and traverse or sliding.

window jamb trim. A thin, vertical strip of molding that covers the junction of the vertical members of the window frame and the jamb. [8]

window sash. A movable frame that holds the window glass. Sash windows move vertically and may be single, in which only the lower half of the window opens, or double, in which both portions are movable. [8]

window sill. The lower, or base, framing of a window opening.

window well. *See* light well.

wing. A building section or addition that projects from the main structure.

winter fat. A type of range vegetation that includes areas where winter fat (*eurotia*) constitutes the predominant vegetation.

wire glass. Window glass in which fine, wire mesh is embedded to prevent shattering or breaking when exposed to extreme heat.

witness corner. In the metes and bounds system, a monument that identifies a point on the land surface that corresponds to a point in the legal description of a site.

Women's Council of REALTORS® (WCR). The professional real estate organization that prepares women members for leadership roles in business and community service.

wood frame construction. Construction in which walls and partitions are formed by the wood framing of studs, or posts and girts, supporting a wooden roof and floor decks; may be covered with wood, metal, stucco, composition siding, or shingles, or veneered with brick or stone facing.

woodland. Any land with trees; usually the wooded land of a farm as distinguished from cropland; wooded land with trees that are usable for timber or will grow to become timber.

working assets. Assets that are consumed in business activities, but not themselves integral parts of the product, e.g., supplies used in an operation.

working capital. The readily convertible capital that a business uses to conduct operations free from financial embarrassment; in accounting, current assets minus current liabilities as of a certain date.

working drawing. A drawing, usually a blueprint, of all or part of a structure, drawn to scale; contains detailed dimensions and instructions to guide workers on a construction job.

workinghouse. A penthouse structure above the storage section of a grain elevator that houses the mechanical equipment necessary to the elevator's operation. *Also called* headhouse.

work letter. An agreement, usually part of a lease, that specifies the level of interior finish and equipment that the landlord is to provide the tenant, including lighting, partitioning, door allowance, and electrical capacity.

wraparound mortgage. A mortgage that is subordinate to, but inclusive of, any existing mortgage(s) on a property. Usually, a third-party lender refinances the property, assuming the existing mortgage and its debt service and wrapping around a new, junior mortgage. The wraparound lender gives the borrower the difference between the outstanding balance of the existing mortgage(s) and the face amount of the new mortgage.

writ of certiorari. *See* certiorari.

writ of execution. A legal order that directs a proper agent of the court, often a sheriff, to carry out an order of the court.

wrought iron
1. A comparatively pure form of iron with practically no carbon, that is easily forged, welded, etc.
2. Steel that has been molded and worked into ornamental shapes and patterns; used for railings, gates, furniture, etc.

wye. A railroad juncture track, with one track joining the main track from one direction and another joining the main track from another direction.

wythe. A masonry partition wall between flues in the same chimney stack.

X

x-bracing. The cross-bracing of a partition or floor joist. [2]

Y

yard lumber. Lumber of all sizes and patterns that is intended for general building purposes. The grading of yard lumber is based on the intended use of the particular grade; it is applied to each piece with reference to its size and length when graded, without considering its further manufacture.

yearling. An animal approximately one year of age. A short yearling is from 9 to 12 months old; a long yearling is from 12 to 18 months old.

year-long grazing. Continuous grazing for a 12-month period, or a calendar year.

yield. *See* current yield; yield to maturity.

yield capitalization. A capitalization method used to convert future benefits to present value by discounting each future benefit at an appropriate yield rate or by developing an overall rate that reflects the investment's income pattern, value change, and yield rate.

yield rate (Y). In appraising, a measure of investment return that is applied to a series of incomes, including reversion, to discount each to present value; e.g., interest rate, discount rate, internal rate of return, equity yield rate. *See also* current yield; yield to maturity.

yield to maturity. In finance, interest return on investment.

Z

zero-interest mortgage. A debt secured by real estate with no interest; under some circumstances, a rate of interest may be imputed, e.g., income taxation.

zero lot line. In zoning, the location of a structure on a lot so that one or more sides rest directly on the boundary line of the lot, i.e., there is no setback of the building. [3]

zonal soil. Any of the great groups of soils that has well-developed soil characteristics reflecting the influence of the active factors in soil genesis, e.g., climate and living organisms, chiefly vegetation.

zoning. The public regulation of the character and intensity of real estate use through police power; accomplished by establishing districts or areas with uniform restrictions relating to improvements, structure heights, areas, bulk, density of population, and other limitations on the use and development of private property.

zoning exception. *See* special exceptions.

zoning map. A map that depicts the various sections of a community and divides the sections into zones of land uses permitted under the zoning ordinance.

zoning ordinance. A statute enacted by a legislative body, under the police powers of the sovereign, to regulate and control the use of real estate for the health, morals, safety, and general welfare of the public.

zoning variance. A legally authorized modification in the use of property at a particular location that does not conform to the regulated use set forth in the zoning ordinance for the surrounding area; not an exception or change in the legally applicable zoning.

z-value. The standard normal deviate; represents the number of standard deviation units that the random variable, or observation, in a data set is above or below the mean. Tables for the area under a normal curve are constructed in terms of z values for a given z; the tables provide the basis for determining the probability of an outcome between two values or the probability of an outcome being greater or less than a specific value.

Sources

[1] From *Real Estate Accounting and Reporting Manual* by Benedetto Bongiorno and Robert R. Garland. Copyright © 1983 by Warren, Gorham & Lamont, Inc. Reprinted by permission.

[2] From *Guide to the New York Real Estate Salespersons Course, 1983* by Norman Weinberg, Paul J. Colletti, William A. Colavito, and Frank A. Melchior. Copyright © 1983 by John Wiley & Sons, Inc. Reprinted by permission of John Wiley & Sons, Inc.

[3] From *The Arnold Encyclopedia of Real Estate* by Alvin L. Arnold and Jack Kusnet. Copyright © 1978 by Warren, Gorham & Lamont, Inc. Reprinted by permission.

[4] From *Dictionary of Banking and Finance* by Jerry M. Rosenberg. Copyright © 1982 by John Wiley & Sons, Inc. Reprinted by permission of John Wiley & Sons, Inc.

[5] From *Real Estate Accounting and Reporting: A Guide for Developers, Investors and Lenders* by James J. Klink. Copyright © 1980 by John Wiley & Sons, Inc. Reprinted by permission of John Wiley & Sons, Inc.

[6] From *The Language of Cities: A Glossary of Terms* by Charles Abrams. Copyright © 1971 by the Estate of Charles Abrams. Reprinted by permission of Viking Penguin, Inc.

[7] From *Glossary of Real Estate Law* by John M. Cartwright. Copyright © 1972 by The Lawyers Co-operative Publishing Co. Reprinted by permission.

[8] From *Fundamentals of Real Estate Appraisal*, 3d ed. by William L. Ventolo, Jr., and Martha R. Williams. Chicago: Real Estate Educa-

tion Company. Copyright © 1983, by Longman Group, USA Inc. Reprinted with permission.

[9]   From *Land in America* by Peter Wolf. Copyright © 1981 by Peter Wolf. Reprinted by permission of Pantheon Books, a division of Random House, Inc.

[10]   From *Property Assesment Valuation* by the International Association of Assessing Officers. Copyright © 1977 by the International Association of Assessing Officers. Reprinted by permission.

[11]   From *Industrial Real Estate* by William N. Kinnard, Jr., Stephen D. Messner, and Byrl N. Boyce. Copyright © 1967, 1971, 1979 SIR® Educational Fund. Reprinted by permission of the Society of Industrial REALTORS®.

[12]   From *Business Valuation Handbook* by Glenn M. Desmond and Richard E. Kelly. Copyright © 1980 Valuation Press. Reprinted by permission.

[13]   From *Residential Development Handbook* by Paul W. O'Mara. Copyright © 1978 by ULI—the Urban Land Institute. Reprinted by permission.

[14]   From *Dollars & Cents of Shopping Centers: 1984*. Copyright © 1984 by ULI—the Urban Land Institute. Reprinted by permission.

[15]   From *Real Estate* by George F. Bloom, Arthur M. Weimer, and Jeffery D. Fisher. Copyright © 1982 by John Wiley & Sons, Inc. Reprinted by permission of John Wiley & Sons, Inc.

[16]   From *Small Business Computers*, January/February 1984. Copyright © 1983 Arck Publications, Inc. Reprinted by permission.

[17]   From *Market Research for Shopping Centers* by Ruben A. Roca. Copyright © 1980 by the International Council of Shopping Centers. Reprinted by permission.

[18]   From *A Guide to Real Estate Information Sources*. Copyright © 1980 by Therese E. Byrne. Reprinted by permission.

Appendix A

Symbols

a	Annualizer
$a_{\overline{n}}$	Present worth of $1 per period
$1/a_{\overline{n}}$	Partial payment factor
AIRR	Adjusted internal rate of return
app	Appreciation
ATCF	After-tax cash flow
B	Balance outstanding
BTCF	Before-tax cash flow
C	Mortgage coefficient
DCR	Debt coverage ratio
Δ	Delta; denotes relative change, usually relative change in value or income of overall property or components, e.g., land, buildings, mortgage, equity, leased fee estate, leasehold estate
dep	Depreciation
EGI	Effective gross income
EGIM	Effective gross income multiplier
FMRR	Financial management rate of return
GIM	Gross income multiplier
GRM	Gross rent multiplier
I	Nominal interest rate; also used to denote income
i	Effective interest rate
IRR	Internal rate of return
J	Income adjustment factor
K	Income stabilization factor
MIRR	Modified internal rate of return
n	Number of compounding periods in compound interest formulas; in mortgage-equity formulas n represents the projection period in years
NOI	Net operating income
NPV	Net present value
NRV	Net realizable value

OER	Operating expense ratio
PGI	Potential gross income
PGIM	Potential gross income multiplier
PTCF	Pre-tax cash flow
PV	Present value
PW	Present worth
R	A capitalization rate
r	Basic rate
R_B	Building capitalization rate
R_E	Equity capitalization rate
R_L	Land capitalization rate
R_M	Mortgage constant
R_{Mp}	Mortgage capitalization rate for the projection period
R_O	Overall capitalization rate
S	The base; one plus the periodic rate
S^n	Amount of \$1 per period
$S_{\overline{n}}$	Amount of \$1
$1/S_{\overline{n}}$	Sinking fund factor
$1/S^n$	Present worth of \$1
V	Value
Y	Yield rate
Y_E	Equity yield rate

Appendix B
Sources of Information

Bibliographies and Reference Guides

Abrams, Charles. *The Language of Cities: A Glossary of Terms*. New York: Viking, 1971.

Akerson, Charles B. *Capitalization Theory and Techniques: Study Guide*. Rev. ed. Chicago: American Institute of Real Estate Appraisers, 1984.

Almy, Richard R. *Improving Real Property Assessment: A Reference Manual*. Chicago: International Association of Assessing Officers, 1978.

American Institute of Real Estate Appraisers. *The Appraisal Journal Bibliography: 1932-1969*. Chicago: American Institute of Real Estate Appraisers, 1970.

————. *The Appraisal of Real Estate*. 8th ed. Chicago: American Institute of Real Estate Appraisers, 1983.

————. *Readers' Guide to The Appraisal Journal, 1970-1980*. Chicago: American Institute of Real Estate Appraisers, 1981.

————. *Real Estate Appraisal Bibliography*. 2d ed. Chicago: American Institute of Real Estate Appraisers, 1973.

————. *Real Estate Appraisal Bibliography: 1973-1980*. Chicago: American Institute of Real Estate Appraisers, 1981.

American Society of Appraisers. *Appraisal and Valuation Manual*. Vols. I-IX. Washington, D.C.: American Society of Appraisers, 1956-1972.

Anderson, Kenneth R., and Stacey L. Ruiz, eds. *Income-Expense Analysis: Apartments,* 1983 edition. Chicago: Institute of Real Estate Management, 1983.

Arnold, Alvin L., and Jack Kusnet. *The Arnold Encyclopedia of Real Estate.* Boston: Warren, Gorham & Lamont, 1978.

Barash, Samuel T. *Complete Guide to Appraising Condominiums and Cooperatives.* Englewood Cliffs, N.J.: Prentice-Hall, 1981.

————. *Encyclopedia of Real Estate Appraising Forms and Model Reports.* Englewood Cliffs, N.J.: Prentice-Hall, 1983.

————. *Standard Real Estate Appraising Manual.* Englewood Cliffs, N.J.: Prentice-Hall, 1979.

Bogen, Jules J., ed. *Financial Handbook.* 4th ed. New York: Ronald, 1968.

Bongiorno, Benedetto, and Robert R. Garland. *Real Estate Accounting and Reporting Manual.* Boston: Warren, Gorham & Lamont, 1983.

Brownstone, David M., and Irene M. Franck. *The VNR Real Estate Dictionary.* New York: Van Nostrand Reinhold, 1981.

Burchell, Robert W. *The Fiscal Impact Handbook.* New Brunswick, N.J.: Center for Urban Policy Research, 1978.

Burchell, Robert W., and David Listokin. *Practitioner's Guide to Fiscal Impact Analysis.* New Brunswick, N.J.: Center for Urban Policy Research, 1980.

Canestaro, James C. *Real Estate Financial Feasibility Analysis Handbook.* Blacksburg, Va., 1982.

————. *Real Estate Financial Feasibility Analysis Workbook.* Blacksburg, Va., 1982.

Cartwright, John M. *Glossary of Real Estate Law.* Rochester, N.Y.: Lawyers Co-operative, 1972.

Collison, Koder M. *The Developers' Dictionary and Handbook*. Lexington, Mass.: D.C. Heath, 1974.

Cummings, Jack. *Complete Guide to Real Estate Financing*. Englewood Cliffs, N.J.: Prentice-Hall, 1978.

Daniells, Lorna M. *Business Information Sources*. Berkeley: University of California Press, 1976.

Denne, Robert C. *Bibliographic Series: Computer-Assisted Appraisal and Assessment Systems*. Chicago: International Association of Assessing Officers, 1977.

Dumouchel, J. Robert, ed. *Dictionary of Development Terminology*. New York: McGraw-Hill, 1975.

Ellwood, L. W. *Ellwood Tables for Real Estate Appraising and Financing*. 4th ed. Chicago: American Institute of Real Estate Appraisers, 1977.

Everett, E. Roger, and William N. Kinnard, Jr. *A Guide to Appraising Apartments*. Chicago: Society of Real Estate Appraisers, 1979.

Financial Publishing. *Capitalization Rate Tables*. AIREA ed. Boston: Financial Publishing, 1974.

————. *Financial Compound Interest and Annuity Tables*. 4th ed. Boston: Financial Publishing, 1966.

Friedman, Edith J., ed. *Encyclopedia of Real Estate Appraising*. 3d ed. Englewood Cliffs, N.J.: Prentice-Hall, 1978.

Guedes, Pedro. *Encyclopedia of Architectural Technology*. New York: McGraw-Hill, 1979.

Harrison, Harold S. *Harrison on Eminent Domain: A Guide for Appraisers and Others*. Chicago: Society of Real Estate Appraisers, 1980.

Harrison, Henry S. *Houses—The Illustrated Guide to Construction Design and Systems*. Rev. ed. Chicago: REALTORS NATIONAL MARKETING INSTITUTE®, 1976.

————. *Illustrated Dictionary of Real Estate and Appraisal.* Reston, Va.: Reston, 1981.

Hoel, Arline Alchian, Kenneth W. Clarkson, and Roger LeRoy Miller. *Economics Sourcebook of Governmental Statistics.* Lexington, Mass.: Lexington Books, 1983.

Institute of Planning, Zoning, and Eminent Domain. *Proceedings.* Albany, N.Y.: Matthew Bender. Annual.

Johnsich, John R. *Modern Real Estate Dictionary.* San Francisco: Canfield, 1975.

————. *Real Estate Books and Periodicals in Print.* Sacramento: Real Estate Publishing, 1982.

Johnson, Irvin E. *The Instant Mortgage-Equity Technique.* Lexington, Mass.: Lexington Books, 1972.

————. *Instant Mortgage-Equity.* Lexington, Mass.: Lexington Books, 1980.

Kent, Frederick C., and Maude E. Kent. *Compound Interest and Annuity Tables.* New York: McGraw-Hill, 1963.

Kinnard, William N., Jr., and Byrl N. Boyce. *Appraising Real Property.* Rev. ed. Chicago: Society of Real Estate Appraisers, 1984.

Kleeman, Leonard. *Handbook of Real Estate Mathematics.* Englewood Cliffs, N.J.: Prentice-Hall, 1978.

MacBride, Dexter D., ed. *The Bibliography of Appraisal Literature.* Washington, D.C.: American Society of Appraisers, 1974.

Manis, Michael S. *Real Estate Investment Analysis: A Practical Guide.* New York: John Wiley & Sons, 1983.

Mason, James J., ed. and comp. *American Institute of Real Estate Appraisers Financial Tables.* Rev. ed. Chicago: American Institute of Real Estate Appraisers, 1982.

Miles, Martin J. *Encyclopedia of Real Estate Formulas and Tables*. Englewood Cliffs, N.J.: Prentice-Hall, 1978.

Moskowitz, Harvey S., and Carl G. Lindbloom. *Illustrated Book of Development Definitions*. New Brunswick, N.J.: Center for Urban Policy, 1981.

National Association of Home Builders. *Homes and Homebuilding: 1983*. Washington, D.C.: National Association of Home Builders, 1983.

NATIONAL ASSOCIATION OF REALTORS®. *Bibliography Series*. Chicago: Herbert U. Nelson Memorial Library, NATIONAL ASSOCIATION OF REALTORS®. Revised periodically.

———. *Guide to Real Estate Services*. Chicago: NATIONAL ASSOCIATION OF REALTORS®, 1983.

National Industrial Zoning Committee. *A Brief Bibliography on Planning and Zoning*. Washington, D.C.: Society of Industrial REALTORS®, 1969.

O'Mara, W. Paul. *Residential Development Handbook*. Washington, D.C.: Urban Land Institute, 1978.

Paulus, Virginia, ed. *Housing: A Bibliography, 1960-1972*. New York: AMS, 1974.

Range Term Glossary Committee, ed. and comp. *A Glossary of Terms Used in Range Management*. 2d ed. Denver: Society for Range Management, 1974.

Reilly, John W. *The Language of Real Estate*. Chicago: Real Estate Education Company, 1982.

Robinson, Peter C. *Complete Guide to Appraising Commercial and Industrial Properties*. Englewood Cliffs, N.J.: Prentice-Hall, 1977.

Rosenberg, Jerry M. *Dictionary of Banking and Finance*. New York: John Wiley & Sons, 1982.

Sackman, Julius L., and Patrick J. Rohan. *Nichols' Law of Eminent Domain.* 3d ed. rev. Albany, N.Y.: Matthew Bender. Looseleaf service.

Sirmans, C. F., and Austin J. Jaffe. *The Complete Real Estate Investment Handbook.* Englewood Cliffs, N.J.: Prentice-Hall, 1981.

Society of Industrial REALTORS®. *Industrial Real Estate: An Annotated Bibliography.* Washington, D.C.: Society of Industrial REALTORS®, 1982.

Society of Real Estate Appraisers. *Appraisal Information Sources.* Vols. I and II. Chicago: Society of Real Estate Appraisers, 1971 and 1979.

————. *A Compendium: A Guide to Appraising Specific Property Types.* Chicago: Society of Real Estate Appraisers, 1973.

————. *A Guide to Appraising for Federal Agencies.* Chicago: Society of Real Estate Appraisers, 1979.

Spink, Frank H., Jr., ed. *Shopping Center Development Handbook.* Washington, D.C.: Urban Land Institute, 1976.

Stebbins, Grady, Jr. *A Guide to Appraising Residences.* Chicago: Society of Real Estate Appraisers, 1976.

Stiebritz, H. R. *Mathematics for Real Estate Appraisers.* Winnipeg: Appraisal Institute of Canada, 1975.

Talamo, John. *The Real Estate Dictionary.* 2d ed. Boston: Financial Publishing, 1979.

Tandy, Janet K., and Mickey T. C. Wu. *Computer Applications in Real Estate: A Selected Bibliography with Annotations.* Rev. ed. Lexington: Center for Real Estate and Land Use Analysis, University of Kentucky, 1978.

Troy, Leo. *Almanac of Business and Industrial Financial Ratios.* Englewood Cliffs, N.J.: Prentice-Hall, 1976.

Urban Land Institute. *Dollars & Cents of Shopping Centers: 1984.* Washington, D.C.: Urban Land Institute, 1984.

———. *Industrial Bibliography.* Washington, D.C.: Urban Land Institute, 1974.

Urban Land Institute and Touche Ross & Co. *Standard Manual of Accounting for Shopping Centers.* Washington, D.C.: Urban Land Institute, 1971.

U.S. Department of Housing and Urban Development. *Statistical Yearbook.* Washington, D.C.: U.S. Department of Housing and Urban Development, 1980.

U.S. Small Business Administration. *Real Estate Business.* Washington, D.C.: U.S. Small Business Administration, 1969.

Weinberg, Norman, et al. *Guide to the New York Real Estate Salesperson's Course.* 2d ed. New York: John Wiley & Sons, 1983.

Whittick, Arnold. *Encyclopedia of Urban Planning.* New York: McGraw-Hill, 1974.

Books

Akerson, Charles B. *The Internal Rate of Return in Real Estate Investments.* Chicago: American Institute of Real Estate Appraisers and American Society of Real Estate Counselors, 1976.

———. *An Introduction to Mortgage-Equity Capitalization.* Chicago: American Institute of Real Estate Appraisers, 1975.

Albritton, Harold D. *Controversies in Real Property Valuation: A Commentary.* Chicago: American Institute of Real Estate Appraisers, 1982.

American Association of State Highway Officials. *Acquisition for Right of Way.* Washington, D.C.: American Association of State Highway Officials, 1962.

American Institute of Real Estate Appraisers. *The Appraisal of Real Estate.* 8th ed. Chicago: American Institute of Real Estate Appraisers, 1983.

———. *The Appraisal of Rural Property.* Chicago: American Institute of Real Estate Appraisers, 1983.

———. *Condemnation Appraisal Practice.* Vol. II. Chicago: American Institute of Real Estate Appraisers, 1973.

———. *Readings in the Appraisal of Special Purpose Properties.* Chicago: American Institute of Real Estate Appraisers, 1981.

———. *Readings in Highest and Best Use.* Chicago: American Institute of Real Estate Appraisers, 1981.

———. *Readings in the Income Approach to Real Property Valuation.* Vol. I. Chicago: American Institute of Real Estate Appraisers, 1977.

———. *Readings in Real Estate Investment Analysis.* Vol. I. Chicago: American Institute of Real Estate Appraisers, 1977.

———. *Readings in Real Property Valuation Principles.* Vol. I. Chicago: American Institute of Real Estate Appraisers, 1977.

American Society of Real Estate Counselors. *Real Estate Counseling.* Englewood Cliffs, N.J.: Prentice-Hall, 1984.

Andrews, Richard B. *Real Estate Investment: Its Meaning and Role in Urban Development.* Madison, Wis.: Center for Urban Land Economics Research, 1978.

Andrews, Richard N. L. *Land in America.* Lexington, Mass.: D.C. Heath, 1979.

Appraisal Institute of Canada. *Real Estate Appraising in Canada.* Winnipeg: Appraisal Institute of Canada, 1970.

Arthur Young & Company. *Federal Income Taxation of Real Estate.* San Francisco: Arthur Young & Company, 1982.

Atteberry, William, et al. *Real Estate Law.* 2d ed. Columbus, Ohio: Grid, 1978.

Babcock, Frederick M. *The Valuation of Real Estate.* New York: McGraw-Hill, 1932.

Babcock, Henry A. *Appraisal Principles and Procedures.* Homewood, Ill.: Richard D. Irwin, 1968.

Barlowe, Raleigh. *Land Resource Economics.* 3d ed. Englewood Cliffs, N.J.: Prentice-Hall, 1978.

Beckett, John A. *Management Dynamics: The New Synthesis.* New York: McGraw-Hill, 1971.

Betts, Richard M., and Silas J. Ely. *Basic Real Estate Appraisal.* New York: John Wiley & Sons, 1982.

Bierman, Harold, Jr., and Seymour Smidt. *The Capital Budgeting Decision.* 5th ed. New York: Macmillan, 1980.

Bish, Robert L., and Hugh O. Nourse. *Urban Economics and Policy Analysis.* New York: McGraw-Hill, 1975.

Black, Thomas, and Michael Morina. *Downtown Office Growth & the Role of Public Transit.* Washington, D.C.: Urban Land Institute, 1982.

Bloom, George F., and Henry S. Harrison. *Appraising the Single Family Residence.* Chicago: American Institute of Real Estate Appraisers, 1978.

Bloom, George F., Arthur M. Weimer, and Jeffery D. Fisher. *Real Estate.* 8th ed. New York: John Wiley & Sons, 1982.

Bonright, James C. *The Valuation of Property.* New York: McGraw-Hill, 1932.

Boykin, James H. *Financing Real Estate.* Lexington, Mass. Lexington Books, 1979.

Britton, James A., Jr., and Lewis O. Kerwood, eds. *Financing Income-Producing Real Estate*. New York: McGraw-Hill, 1977.

Brueggeman, William. *Real Estate Finance*. 7th ed. Homewood, Ill.: Richard D. Irwin, 1981.

Burchell, Robert W., and David Listokin. *Fiscal Impact Handbook*. New Brunswick, N.J.: Center for Urban Policy Research, 1978.

Burton, James H. *Evolution of the Income Approach*. Chicago: American Institute of Real Estate Appraisers, 1982.

Center for Urban Land Economics Research. *The Nature of Urban Land Economics and Its Relation to Urban Land Use*. Madison, Wis.: Center for Urban Land Economics Research, 1978.

Chapin, F. Stuart, Jr., and Edward J. Kaiser. *Urban Land Use Planning*. Urbana: University of Illinois Press, 1979.

Church, Albert M., and Robert H. Gustafson. *Statistics and Computers in the Appraisal Process*. Chicago: International Association of Assessing Officers, 1976.

Clark, Louis E., Jr., and F. H. Treadway, Jr. *Impact of Electric Power Transmission Line Easements on Real Estate Values*. Chicago: American Institute of Real Estate Appraisers, 1977.

Conroy, Kathleen. *Valuing the Timeshare Property*. Chicago: American Institute of Real Estate Appraisers, 1981.

Conway. *Industrial Park Growth*. Atlanta: Conway, 1979.

————. *Pitfalls in Development*. Atlanta: Conway, 1978.

Cook, Charles C., ed. *Proceedings of Colloquium on Computer Assisted Mass Appraisal Potential for Commercial and Industrial Real Property*. Cambridge, Mass.: Lincoln Institute of Land Policy, 1978.

Costonis, John J. *Space Adrift*. Urbana: University of Illinois Press, 1974.

Dasso, Jerome. *Computerized Assessment Administration.* Chicago: International Association of Assessing Officers, 1974.

Desmond, Glenn M., and Richard E. Kelley. *Business Valuation Handbook.* Marina del Rey, Calif.: Valuation Press, 1980.

Dilmore, Gene. *The New Approach to Real Estate Appraising.* Englewood Cliffs, N.J.: Prentice-Hall, 1971.

————. *Quantitative Techniques in Real Estate Counseling.* Lexington, Mass.: Lexington Books, 1981.

Dombal, Robert W. *Residential Condominiums: A Guide to Analysis and Appraisal.* Chicago: American Institute of Real Estate Appraisers, 1973.

Downs, Anthony. *Neighborhoods and Urban Development.* Washington, D.C.: The Brookings Institution, 1981.

————. *Rental Housing in the 1980s.* Washington, D.C.: The Brookings Institution, 1983.

Eaton, J. D. *Real Estate Valuation in Litigation.* Chicago: American Institute of Real Estate Appraisers, 1982.

Ellsworth, John D. *Real Estate Syndicate Offering Handbook.* San Francisco: Questor Information Services, 1983.

Elzey, Freeman F. *A First Reader in Statistics.* Belmont, Calif.: Wadsworth, 1974.

Findlay, M. Chapman, III, Stephen D. Messner, and Rocky A. Tarantello. *Real-Estate Portfolio Analysis.* Lexington, Mass.: Lexington Books, 1983.

Foreman, Robert L. *Communicating the Appraisal: A Guide to Report Writing.* Chicago: American Institute of Real Estate Appraisers, 1982.

French, William B., and Harold F. Lusk. *Law of the Real Estate Business.* Homewood, Ill.: Richard D. Irwin, 1979.

Garrett, Robert L., et al. *The Valuation of Shopping Centers.* Chicago: American Institute of Real Estate Appraisers, 1976.

Gibbons, James E. *Appraising in a Changing Economy: Collected Writings.* Chicago: American Institute of Real Estate Appraisers, 1982.

Gibson, Frank, James Karp, and Elliot Klayman. *Real Estate Law.* Chicago: Real Estate Education Company, 1983.

Gimmy, Arthur E. *Tennis Clubs and Racquet Sport Projects: A Guide to Appraisal, Market Analysis, Development and Financing.* Chicago: American Institute of Real Estate Appraisers, 1978.

Gipe, George W. *Mass Appraisal of Apartments with Comparable Sales.* Cambridge, Mass.: Lincoln Institute of Land Policy, 1977.

Graaskamp, James A. *A Guide to Feasibility Analysis.* Chicago: Society of Real Estate Appraisers, 1980.

Greer, Gaylon E. *The Real Estate Investor and the Federal Income Tax.* Rev. ed. New York: Wiley Interscience, 1978.

————. *The Real Estate Investment Decision.* Lexington, Mass.: Lexington Books, 1979.

Greer, Gaylon E., and Michael D. Farrell. *Investment Analysis for Real Estate Decisions.* Chicago: Dryden, 1984.

Greynolds, Elbert B., Jr., and Julius S. Aronofsky. *Practical Real Estate Financial Analysis: Using the HP-12C Calculator.* Chicago: Real Estate Education Company, 1983.

Gruen, Nina, Claude Gruen, and Wallace F. Smith. *Demographic Changes and Their Effects on Real Estate Markets in the '80's.* Washington, D.C.: Urban Land Institute, 1982.

Hadjimichalakis, Michael G. *Monetary Policy and Modern Money Markets.* Lexington, Mass.: Lexington Books, 1982.

Hanford, Lloyd D. *Feasibility Study Guidelines.* Chicago: Institute of Real Estate Management, 1972.

Harwood, Bruce. *Real Estate: An Introduction to the Profession.* 3d ed. Reston, Va.: Reston Publishing, 1983.

Heuer, Karla L., and Cecil McKay, Jr. *Golf Courses: A Guide to Analysis and Valuation.* Chicago: American Institute of Real Estate Appraisers, 1980.

Higgins, J. Warren. *Impact of Federal Taxation on Real Estate Decisions.* 3d ed. Storrs: Center for Real Estate and Urban Economic Studies, University of Connecticut, 1980.

Hochlery, Irwin. *Financial Feasibility in Real Estate.* New York: New York University Real Estate Institute, 1979.

Hoover, Edgar M. *An Introduction to Regional Economics.* New York: Knopf, 1971.

Horowitz, Carl F. *The New Garden Apartment.* New Brunswick, N.J.: Center for Urban Policy Research, 1983.

Hughes, James W. *Methods of Housing Analysis.* New Brunswick, N.J.: Center for Urban Policy Research, 1977.

Hunt, William Dudley, Jr. *Comprehensive Architectural Services—General Principles and Practice.* New York: McGraw-Hill, 1965.

Institute of Real Estate Management. *Lease Escalators and Other Pass-Through Clauses.* Chicago: Institute of Real Estate Management, 1979.

————. *Managing the Shopping Center.* Chicago: Institute of Real Estate Management, 1983.

International Association of Assessing Officers. *Property Assessment Valuation.* Chicago: International Association of Assessing Officers, 1977.

————. *Use-Value Farmland Assessments: Theory, Practice, and Impact.* Chicago: International Association of Assessing Officers, 1974.

Jacobus, Charles J., and Donald R. Levi. *Real Estate Law*. Reston, Va: Reston Publishing, 1980.

Jaffe, Austin J. *Property Management in Real Estate Investment Decision-Making*. Lexington, Mass.: Lexington Books, 1979.

Jaffe, Austin J., and C. F. Sirmans. *Real Estate Investment Decision Making*. Englewood Cliffs, N.J.: Prentice-Hall, 1982.

Jensen, David L. *The Role of Cluster Analysis in Computer Assisted Mass Appraisals*. Cambridge, Mass.: Lincoln Institute of Land Policy, 1977.

Johnson, Irvin E. *The Instant Mortgage-Equity Technique*. Lexington, Mass.: Lexington Books, 1972.

————. *Mini-Math for Appraisers*. Chicago: International Association of Assessing Officers, 1972.

Kahn, Sanders A., and Frederick E. Case. *Real Estate Appraisal & Investment*. 2d ed. New York: Ronald Press, 1977.

Kain, John F., and John M. Quigley. *Housing Markets and Racial Discrimination*. New York: Columbia University Press, 1975.

Kinnard, William N., Jr. *An Appraisal Report Primer for Residential Lenders and Underwriters*. Storrs: Center for Real Estate and Urban Economic Studies, University of Connecticut, 1978.

————. *Income Property Valuation*. Lexington, Mass.: Lexington Books, 1971.

Kinnard, William N., Jr., et al. *Special Application of Appraisal Analysis*. Rev. ed. Chicago: Society of Real Estate Appraisers, 1980.

Kinnard, William N., Jr., and E. Roger Everett. *A Guide to Appraising Apartments*. Rev. ed. Chicago: Society of Real Estate Appraisers, 1979.

Kinnard, William N., Jr., Stephen D. Messner, and Byrl N. Boyce. *Industrial Real Estate*. 3d ed. Washington, D.C.: Society of Industrial REALTORS®, 1979.

Klaasen, Romain L. *Practising Real Estate Appraisal.* Winnipeg: Appraisal Institute of Canada, 1977.

Klink, James J. *Real Estate Accounting and Reporting: A Guide for Developers, Investors and Lenders.* New York: John Wiley & Sons, 1980.

Kratovil, Robert. *Real Estate Law.* 7th ed. Englewood Cliffs, N.J.: Prentice-Hall, 1979.

Kratovil, Robert, and Raymond J. Werner. *Real Estate Law.* 8th ed. Englewood Cliffs, N.J.: Prentice-Hall, 1983.

Lukens, Reaves C., Jr. *The Appraiser and Real Estate Feasibility Studies.* Chicago: American Institute of Real Estate Appraisers, 1972.

Lusht, Kenneth M. *The Behavior of Appraisers in Valuing Income Property: A Status Report.* University Park: Pennsylvania State University Press, 1979.

Lynn, Theodore S., and Harry F. Goldberg. *Real Estate Limited Partnerships.* 2d ed. New York: John Wiley & Sons, 1983.

MacBride, Dexter D. *Power and Process: A Commentary on Eminent Domain and Condemnation.* Washington, D.C.: American Society of Appraisers, 1969.

McClave, James T., and P. George Benson. *Statistics for Business and Economics.* Rev. ed. San Francisco: Dellen, 1982.

McKenzie, Dennis J., and Richard M. Betts. *The Essentials of Real Estate Economics.* 2d ed. New York: John Wiley & Sons, 1980.

McMahan, John. *The McGraw-Hill Real Estate Pocket Guide.* New York: McGraw-Hill, 1979.

McMichael, Stanley L. *McMichael's Appraising Manual.* 4th ed. Englewood Cliffs, N.J.: Prentice-Hall, 1951.

McMichael, Stanley L., and Paul T. O'Keefe. *Leases: Percentage, Short and Long Term.* 6th ed. Englewood Cliffs, N.J.: Prentice-Hall, 1974.

Maisel, Sherman J., and Stephen E. Roulac. *Real Estate Investment and Finance.* New York: McGraw-Hill, 1976.

Messina, John P. *Real Estate Appraisers and the Problems of Malpractice.* Chicago: Society of Real Estate Appraisers, 1977.

Messner, Stephen D., et al. *Marketing Investment Real Estate: Finance, Taxation, Techniques.* 2d ed. Chicago: REALTORS NATIONAL MARKETING INSTITUTE®, 1982.

————. *Analyzing Real Estate Opportunities: Market and Feasibility Studies.* Chicago: REALTORS NATIONAL MARKETING INSTITUTE®, 1977.

Miller, George H., and Kenneth W. Gilbeau. *Residential Real Estate Appraisal: An Introduction to Real Estate Appraising.* Englewood Cliffs, N.J.: Prentice-Hall, 1980.

Murray, William G., et al. *Farm Appraisal and Valuation.* 6th ed. Ames: Iowa State University Press, 1983.

National Association of Home Builders. *Cost Effective Site Planning: Single Family Development.* Washington, D.C.: National Association of Home Builders, 1976.

North, Lincoln W. *Real Estate Investment Analysis and Valuation.* 2d ed. Winnipeg: Saults & Pollard, 1976.

O'Connell, Daniel J. *Apartment Building Valuation, Finance & Investment Analysis.* New York: John Wiley & Sons, 1982.

Olin, Harold B., John L. Schmidt, and Walter H. Lewis. *Construction—Principles, Materials, and Methods.* 4th ed. Chicago: Institute of Financial Education and Interstate Printers and Publishers, 1980.

O'Mara, W. Paul, et al. *Residential Development Handbook.* Washington, D.C.: Urban Land Institute, 1978.

Orgel, Lewis. *Valuation Under the Law of Eminent Domain.* 2d ed. Vols. I-II. Charlottesville, Va.: Michie, 1953.

Parisse, Alan J., and Jack Kusnet. *Financial Analysis of a Real Estate Investment.* Boston: Warren, Gorham & Lamont, 1981

Phyrr, Stephen A., and James R. Cooper. *Real Estate Investment.* Boston: Warren, Gorham & Lamont, 1982.

Rams, Edwin M. *Analysis and Valuation of Retail Locations.* Reston, Va: Reston Publishing, 1976.

―――. *Rams' Real Estate Appraisal Handbook.* Englewood Cliffs, N.J.: Prentice-Hall, 1975.

―――. *Valuation for Eminent Domain.* Englewood Cliffs, N.J.: Prentice-Hall, 1973.

Ratcliff, Richard U. *Modern Real Estate Valuation: Theory and Application.* Madison, Wis.: Democrat, 1965.

―――. *Urban Land Economics.* New York: McGraw-Hill, 1949.

―――. *Valuation for Real Estate Decisions.* Santa Cruz, Calif.: Democrat, 1972.

REALTORS NATIONAL MARKETING INSTITUTE®. *Guide to Commercial Property Leasing.* Chicago: REALTORS NATIONAL MARKETING INSTITUTE®, 1974.

Reynolds, Judith. *Historic Properties: Preservation and the Valuation Process.* Chicago: American Institute of Real Estate Appraisers, 1982.

Ring, Alfred A. *The Valuation of Real Estate.* 2d ed. Englewood Cliffs, N.J.: Prentice-Hall, 1970.

Roca, Ruben A. *Market Research for Shopping Centers.* New York: International Council of Shopping Centers, 1980.

Rockham, J. B., and T. F. Smith, eds. *Automated Mass Appraisal of Real Property.* Chicago: International Association of Assessing Officers, 1974.

Rose, Jerome G., ed. *Transfer of Development Rights*. New Brunswick, N.J.: Center for Urban Policy Research, 1975.

Roulac, Stephen E. *Modern Real Estate Investment*. San Francisco: Property, 1976.

————. *Tax Shelter Sale-Leaseback Financing*. Cambridge, Mass.: Ballinger, 1976.

Rushmore, Stephen. *Hotels, Motels, and Restaurants: Valuations and Market Studies*. Chicago: American Institute of Real Estate Appraisers, 1983.

Schmutz, George L. *The Appraisal Process*. 3d ed. rev. Manhattan Beach, Calif: George L. Schmutz, 1959.

Selden, Maury, ed. *The Real Estate Handbook*. Homewood, Ill.: Dow Jones-Irwin, 1980.

Selden, Maury and Richard H. Swesnik. *Real Estate Investment Strategy*. 2d ed. New York: Wiley Interscience, 1979.

Shenkel, William M. *A Guide to Appraising Industrial Property*. Chicago: Society of Real Estate Appraisers, 1967.

————. *Modern Real Estate Appraisal*. New York: McGraw-Hill, 1978.

Sherwood, Gerald E. *How to Select and Renovate an Older Home*. New York: Dover, 1976.

Sirota, David. *Essentials of Real Estate Finance*. 3d ed. Chicago: Real Estate Education Company, 1983.

————. *Essentials of Real Estate Investment*. 2d ed. Chicago: Real Estate Education Company, 1984.

Smith, Halbert C. *Real Estate Appraisal*. Columbus, Ohio: Grid, 1976.

Smith, Halbert C., et al. *Real Estate and Urban Development*. Rev. ed. Homewood, Ill.: Richard D. Irwin, 1977.

Society of Industrial REALTORS® and National Association of Industrial and Office Parks. *Guide to Industrial Site Selection.* Washington, D.C.: Society of Industrial REALTORS®, 1979.

Spurr, William S., and Charles P. Bonini. *Statistical Analysis for Business Decisions.* Rev. ed. Homewood, Ill.: Richard D. Irwin, 1973.

Stafford, Howard A. *Principles of Industrial Facility Location.* Atlanta: Conway, 1979.

Sternlieb, George, and James W. Hughes. *The Future of Rental Housing.* New Brunswick, N.J.: Center for Urban Policy Research, 1981.

Sternlieb, George, James W. Hughes, and Connie O. Hughes. *Demographic Trends and Economic Reality.* New Brunswick, N.J.: Center for Urban Policy Research, 1982.

Stone, David. *New Home Sales.* Chicago: Real Estate Education Company, 1982.

Suter, Robert C. *The Appraisal of Farm Real Estate.* 2d ed. Danville, Ill.: Interstate, 1980.

Sutte, Donald T., Jr. *Appraisal of Roadside Advertising Signs.* Chicago: American Institute of Real Estate Appraisers, 1972.

ULI Research Division. *Effects of Regulations on Housing Costs: Two Case Studies.* Washington, D.C.: Urban Land Institute, 1977.

Urban Land Institute. *Dollars & Cents of Shopping Centers: 1984.* Washington, D.C.: Urban Land Institute, 1984.

————. *Industrial Development Handbook.* Washington, D.C.: Urban Land Institute, 1975.

————. *Shopping Center Development Handbook.* Rev. ed. Washington, D.C.: Urban Land Institute, 1977.

Ventolo, William L., Jr., and Martha R. Williams. *Fundamentals of Real Estate Appraisal.* Chicago: Real Estate Education, 1980.

Vernor, James D. *Introduction to Risk Management in Property Development*. Washington, D.C.: Urban Land Institute, 1981.

Von Furstenburg, George M., ed. *Patterns of Racial Discrimination: Housing*. Lexington, Mass.: Lexington Books, 1974.

Walsh, Albert A. *Real Estate Investment After the Tax Acts of 1981 and 1982*. Washington, D.C.: Urban Land Institute, 1982.

Walters, David W. *Real Estate Computerization*. Berkeley: Center for Real Estate and Urban Economics, University of California, 1971.

Wendt, Paul F. *Real Estate Appraisal Review and Outlook*. Athens: University of Georgia Press, 1974.

Wendt, Paul F., and Alan R. Cerf. *Real Estate Investment Analysis and Taxation*. 2d ed. New York: McGraw-Hill, 1979.

Wiley, Robert J. *Real Estate Accounting and Mathematics Handbook*. New York: John Wiley & Sons, 1980.

Wolf, Peter. *Land in America*. New York: Random House, 1981.

Zerbst, Robert H. *Principles of Real Estate Valuation with Energy Applications*. Washington, D.C.: Urban Land Institute, 1981.

Building Cost Services and Data

Boeckh Building Cost Guides (Residential, Commercial, Light Industrial, Institutional, Agricultural, and Mobile Home). Milwaukee: Boeckh. Annual.

Boeckh Building Cost Index Numbers. Milwaukee: Boeckh. Looseleaf; Bimonthly.

Boeckh Building Valuation Manual. Milwaukee: Boeckh. Looseleaf; Bimonthly.

Boeckh General Estimate Manual. Milwaukee: Boeckh. Looseleaf; Semiannual.

Building Cost File (regional editions). New York: Construction. Annual.

Building Cost Manual. 8th ed. Carlsbad, Calif.: Craftsman, 1984.

Building Construction Cost Data. Kingston, Mass.: Robert Snow Means. Annual.

Design, Cost & Data. Glendora, Calif.: Allan Thompson Publishers. Bimonthly.

Dodge Building Cost Calculator & Valuation Guide. New York: McGraw-Hill Information Systems. Looseleaf; Quarterly.

Dodge Manual for Building Construction Pricing and Scheduling. New York: McGraw-Hill Information Systems. Annual.

Marshall Valuation Service. Los Angeles: Marshall and Swift. Looseleaf; Monthly.

Means Construction Cost Indexes. Kingston, Mass.: Robert Snow Means. Quarterly.

National Construction Estimator. 32d ed. Carlsbad, Calif.: Craftsman. 1984.

Real Estate Evaluation Guide. Milwaukee: Boeckh. Monthly.

Residential Cost Handbook. Los Angeles: Marshall and Swift. Looseleaf; Quarterly.

Operating Expense Standards and Business Operating Ratios

Building Owners and Managers Association International. *Downtown and Suburban Office Building Experience Exchange Report.* Washington, D.C. Annual.

Dun & Bradstreet, Inc. *Key Business Ratios in 125 Lines.* New York. Annual.

Harris, Kerr, Forster & Company. *Clubs in Town and Country.* New York. Annual.

————. *Trends in Hotel-Motel Business.* New York. Annual.

Horwath & Horwath International and Laventhol & Horwath. *Worldwide Lodging Industry.* Philadelphia: Laventhal & Horwath. Annual.

Institute of Real Estate Management. *Income/Expense Analysis: Apartments.* Chicago. Annual.

————. *Income/Expense Analysis: Condominiums, Cooperatives and Planned Unit Development.* Chicago. Annual.

————. *Income/Expense Analysis: Downtown and Suburban Office Buildings.* Chicago. Annual.

Laventhol & Horwath. *Restaurant Operations.* Philadelphia. Annual.

————. *U.S. Lodging Industry.* Philadelphia. Annual.

National Retail Merchants Association. Controllers' Congress. *Department Store and Specialty Store Merchandising and Operating Results.* New York. Annual.

————. *Financial and Operating Results of Department and Specialty Stores.* New York. Annual.

Periodicals

AIA Journal. American Institute of Architects. Washington, D.C. Monthly.

AIM. Appraisal Institute of Canada. Winnipeg. Quarterly.

American Planning Association Journal. American Planning Association. Chicago. Quarterly.

Apartment Management Newsletter. Mattco Equities. New York. Monthly.

Apartment Management Report. Apartment Owners and Managers Association of America. Watertown, Conn. Monthly.

Apartment Owner. Apartment Association of San Fernando Valley. Van Nuys, Calif. Monthly.

Apartment Owner-Builder. Apartment News. Long Beach, Calif. Monthly.

Appraisal Briefs. Society of Real Estate Appraisers. Chicago. Semimonthly.

Appraisal Digest. New York State Society of Real Estate Appraisers. Albany. Quarterly.

Appraisal Institute Digest. Appraisal Institute of Canada. Winnipeg. Semiannual.

The Appraisal Journal. American Institute of Real Estate Appraisers. Chicago. Quarterly.

The Appraiser. American Institute of Real Estate Appraisers. Chicago. Monthly, except July and August.

Area Development Magazine. Halcyon Business. New York. Monthly.

AREUEA Journal. American Real Estate and Urban Economics Association. Dallas. Quarterly.

Assessment and Valuation Legal Reporter. International Association of Assessing Officers. Chicago. Looseleaf; Monthly.

Assessment Digest. International Association of Assessing Officers. Chicago. Bimonthly.

Assessor's Data Exchange. International Association of Assessing Officers. Chicago. Quarterly.

Assessors Review. Institute of Municipal Assessors of Ontario. Ontario. Quarterly.

Boston College Environmental Affairs Law Review. Environmental Law Center, Boston College School of Law. Newton Centre, Mass. Quarterly.

Builder. National Housing Center. Washington, D.C. Monthly.

Building Operating Management. Trade Press. Milwaukee. Monthly.

Buildings. Stamats. Cedar Rapids, Iowa. Monthly.

Chartered Surveyor Weekly. Royal Institution of Chartered Surveyors. London. Monthly.

Cornell Hotel and Restaurant Administrations Quarterly. Cornell University. Ithaca, N.Y. Quarterly.

Crittenden Bulletin. Crittenden Research. Novato, Calif. Weekly.

Crittenden Report. Crittenden Research. Novato, Calif. Weekly.

Developments for Real Estate Executives. Peat, Marwick, Mitchell. Chicago. Periodically.

Downtown Idea Exchange. Alexander Reports. New York. Biweekly.

Economic Geography. Clark University. Worcester, Mass. Quarterly.

Environmental Comment. Urban Land Institute. Washington, D.C. Monthly.

Existing Home Sales. NATIONAL ASSOCIATION OF REALTORS®. Chicago. Monthly.

Farm and Land Realtor®. Farm and Land Institute. Chicago. Monthly.

Federal Reserve Bulletin. Board of Governors of the Federal Reserve System. Washington, D.C. Monthly.

Housing. McGraw-Hill. New York. Monthly.

Housing and Urban Development References. U.S. Department of Housing and Urban Development. Washington, D.C. Bimonthly.

Housing Market Report. Community Development. Silver Spring, Md. Biweekly.

HUD Newsletter. U.S. Department of Housing and Urban Development. Washington, D.C. Weekly.

Industrial Development. Conway Research. Atlanta. Bimonthly.

Investing in Real Estate. Harcourt Brace Jovanovich. New York. Monthly.

Journal of Housing. National Association of Housing and Redevelopment Officials. Washington, D.C. Monthly.

Journal of Property Management. Institute of Real Estate Management. Chicago. Bimonthly.

Journal of Real Estate Taxation. Warren, Gorham & Lamont. Boston. Quarterly.

Journal of the American Society of Farm Managers and Rural Appraisers. American Society of Farm Managers and Rural Appraisers. Denver. Semiannual.

Journal of Valuation. Henry Stewart. London. Quarterly.

Just Compensation. Just Compensation. Sherman Oaks, Calif. Monthly.

Land Economics. University of Wisconsin Press. Madison. Quarterly.

Land Use Law and Zoning Digest. American Planning Association. Chicago. Monthly.

Landauer Library Letter. Landauer Associates. New York. Biweekly.

Lawyers Title News. Lawyers Title Insurance. Richmond, Va. Bimonthly.

Legal Bulletin. U.S. League of Savings Associations. Chicago. Bimonthly.

Library Periodical Index. Advisory Commission on Intergovernmental Relations. Washington, D.C. Monthly.

Mortgage Banking. Mortgage Bankers Association of America. Washington, D.C. Monthly.

Mortgage and Real Estate Executives Report. Warren, Gorham & Lamont. Boston. Biweekly.

Multi Housing News. Gralla. New York. Monthly.

National Property Law Digests. National Property Law Digests. Chevy Chase, Md. Monthly.

National Real Estate Investor. Communication Channels. New York. Monthly.

National Savings & Loan League Journal. National Savings & Loan League. Washington, D.C. Monthly.

National Tax Journal. National Tax Association, Tax Institute of America. Columbus, Ohio. Quarterly.

New Zealand Valuer. New Zealand Institute of Valuers. Wellington. Quarterly.

Operating Techniques and Products Bulletin. Institute of Real Estate Management. Chicago. Monthly.

The Partnership Strategist. Newsletter Management. Boca Raton, Fla. Monthly.

Proceedings of the Annual National Seminar. American Right of Way Association. Los Angeles. Annual.

Professional Builder and Apartment Business. Cahners. Denver. Monthly.

Property Tax Journal. International Association of Assessing Officers. Chicago. Quarterly.

Property Tax Report. Institute of Property Taxation. Washington, D.C. Monthly.

The Real Estate Appraiser and Analyst. Society of Real Estate Appraisers. Chicago. Bimonthly.

The Real Estate Briefing. Real Estate Services Group. San Francisco. Quarterly.

Real Estate "Insider" Newsletter. New York. Weekly.

Real Estate Insight. Laventhol & Horwath. New York. Monthly.

Real Estate Investing Letter. Harcourt Brace Jovanovich. New York. Monthly.

Real Estate Investment Digest. Newsletter Management. Boca Raton, Fla. Monthly.

Real Estate Investment Ideas. Institute for Business Planning. Englewood Cliffs, N.J. Semimonthly.

Real Estate Issues. American Society of Real Estate Counselors. Chicago. Seminannual.

Real Estate Law Journal. Warren, Gorham & Lamont. Boston. Quarterly.

Real Estate Law Report. Warren, Gorham & Lamont. Boston. Monthly.

Real Estate Newsletter. Coopers & Lybrand. Boston. Quarterly.

Real Estate Newsletter. Laventhol & Horwath. New York. Quarterly.

Real Estate Report. Alster International. New York. Semiannual.

Real Estate Report. Real Estate Research. Chicago. Quarterly.

Real Estate Review. Warren, Gorham & Lamont. Boston. Quarterly.

Real Estate Review. Touche Ross. San Francisco. Bimonthly.

THE REAL ESTATE SECURITIES JOURNAL®. REAL ESTATE SECURITIES AND SYNDICATION INSTITUTE®. Chicago. Quarterly.

Real Estate Tax Ideas. Warren, Gorham & Lamont. Boston. Monthly.

real estate today®. NATIONAL ASSOCIATION OF REALTORS®. Chicago. Monthly.

Real Estate Update. Price Waterhouse. New York. Quarterly.

Real Property, Probate and Trust Journal. American Bar Association. Chicago. Quarterly.

REALTOR NEWS®. NATIONAL ASSOCIATION OF REALTORS®. Chicago. Weekly.

REIT Fact Book. National Association of Real Estate Investment Trusts. Washington, D.C. Annual.

The REIT Report. National Association of Real Estate Investment Trusts. Washington, D.C. Six times per year.

Rental House & Condo Investor. Harcourt Brace Jovanovich. New York. Semimonthly.

Reports. National Cooperative Highway Research Program. Washington, D.C. Irregular series.

RESSI REVIEW®. REAL ESTATE SECURITIES AND SYNDICATION INSTITUTE®. Chicago. Monthly.

Retail Technology. Lebhar-Friedman. New York. Monthly.

The Ricks Report. Portola Valley, Calif. Six times per year.

Right of Way. American Right of Way Association. Culver City, Calif. Bimonthly.

Savings Bank Journal. National Association of Mutual Savings Banks. New York. Monthly.

Savings Institutions. U.S. League of Savings Associations. Chicago. Monthly.

Shopping Center World. Communication Channels. Atlanta. Monthly.

S.I.R.® Industrial Real Estate Market Survey. Society of Industrial REALTORS®. Washington, D.C. Semiannual.

Site Selection Handbook. Conway Research. Atlanta. Quarterly.

Skylines. Building Owners & Managers Association. Washington, D.C. Monthly.

Strategic Real Estate. Kenneth Leventhal. San Francisco. Monthly.

The South African Journal of Property. Juta. Kenwyn, Republic of South Africa. Bimonthly.

Syndication Advisor. Long & Fisher. San Diego. Quarterly.

Taxation of Foreign Investment in United States Real Property. Arthur Young. San Francisco. Periodically.

Title News. American Land Title Association. Washington, D.C. Monthly.

Transportation Quarterly. Eno Foundation. Westport, Conn. Quarterly.

Urban Land. Urban Land Institute. Washington, D.C. Monthly.

Valuation Magazine. American Society of Appraisers. Washington, D.C. Semiannual.

Valuer. Australian Institute of Valuers. New South Wales. Semiannual.

Valuer. Incorporated Society of Valuers and Auctioneers. London. Eleven issues a year.

WG&L Real Estate Outlook. Warren, Gorham & Lamont. Boston. Quarterly.

Zoning and Planning Law Report. Clark Boardman. New York. Monthly.

Real Estate Market Data

Annual Housing Survey. Washington, D.C.: U.S. Department of Commerce, Bureau of the Census. Annual.

Bureau of the Census Catalog. Washington, D.C.: U.S. Department of Commerce. Quarterly; monthly supplements.

Business Conditions Digest. Washington, D.C.: U.S. Department of Labor, Bureau of Economic Analysis. Monthly.

1982 Census of Construction Industries. Washington, D.C.: U.S. Department of Commerce, Bureau of the Census. 1983-85.

1982 Census of Manufacturers (Geographic Area and Industry Series). Washington, D.C.: U.S. Department of Commerce, Bureau of the Census. 1983-85.

1982 Census of Retail Trade (Geographic Area Series). Washington, D.C.: U.S. Department of Commerce, Bureau of the Census. 1983-85.

1982 Census of Wholesale Trade (Geographic Area Series). Washington, D.C.: U.S. Department of Commerce, Bureau of the Census. 1983-85.

County and City Data Book. Washington, D.C.: U.S. Department of Commerce, Bureau of the Census. 1983.

County Business Patterns. Washington, D.C.: U.S. Department of Commerce, Bureau of the Census. Annual.

Current Construction Reports. Washington, D.C.: U.S. Department of Commerce, Bureau of the Census. Monthly.

Current Housing Reports. Washington, D.C.: U.S. Department of Commerce, Bureau of the Census. Quarterly; annual summary.

Current Population Reports. Washington, D.C.: U.S. Department of Commerce, Bureau of the Census. Monthly and quarterly.

Current Retail Trade. Washington, D.C.: U.S. Department of Commerce, Bureau of the Census. Monthly.

Current Wholesale Trade. Washington, D.C.: U.S. Department of Commerce, Bureau of the Census. Monthly.

Economic Indicators. Washington, D.C.: Council of Economic Advisers. Monthly.

Economic News Notes. Washington, D.C.: National Association of Home Builders. Monthly and quarterly.

Employment and Earnings. Washington, D.C.: U.S. Bureau of Labor Statistics. Monthly.

Existing Home Sales. Washington, D.C.: NATIONAL ASSOCIATION OF REALTORS®, Economics and Research Division. Monthly.

Federal Home Loan Bank Board Journal. Washington, D.C.: Federal Home Loan Bank Board. Monthly.

Federal Home Loan Bank Board News. Washington, D.C.: Federal Home Loan Bank Board. Biweekly.

Federal Reserve Bulletin. Washington, D.C.: Board of Governors of the Federal Reserve System. Monthly.

Housing and Urban Development Trends. Washington, D.C.: U.S. Department of Housing and Urban Development. Quarterly.

Housing Industry Outlook Report. Housing Industry Dynamics. Crofton, Md. Semiannual.

Monthly Catalog of U.S. Government Publications. Washington, D.C.: U.S. Government Printing Office. Monthly.

Mortgage Banking. Mortgage Bankers Association of America. Washington, D.C. Monthly.

National Real Estate Investor. Communication Channels. Atlanta. Monthly.

Questor Real Estate Syndication Yearbook. Questor Information Services. San Francisco. Annual.

Real Estate Forum. Real Estate Forum. New York. Monthly.

Real Estate Investment Journal. Century 21 Real Estate Corporation. Irvine, Calif. Bimonthly.

Real Estate Quarterly. NATIONAL ASSOCIATION OF REALTORS®. Washington, D.C. Quarterly.

Real Estate Tax Digest. Matthew Bender. Albany, N.Y. Monthly.

Realty. Woodhaven, N.Y. Biweekly.

Southeast Real Estate News. Communication Channels. Atlanta. Monthly.

Southwest Real Estate News. Communication Channels. Atlanta. Monthly.

Statistical Abstract of the United States. Washington, D.C.: U.S. Department of Commerce, Bureau of the Census. Annual.

Survey of Current Business. Washington, D.C.: U.S. Department of Commerce. Monthly.

Computer Timesharing Information Services [18]

Applied Logic. Princeton, N.J.

Computer Sciences. Los Angeles.

Comshare. Ann Arbor, Mich.

Control Data. Minneapolis.

Cyphernetics. Ann Arbor, Mich.

Data Resources. Lexington, Mass.